Praise for *Finding Memories, Tracing Rout*

also published by the Chinese Canadian Historical Society of BC

"*Finding Memories, Tracing Routes* gives us the voices of Chinese Canadians so often silenced or missing from our understanding of the past. It is a wonderful reminder of the multiplicity of historical experience, of the challenges and triumphs of Canadians who struggled, often in the face of relentless racism, to build a better future for themselves and their families."
~Dr. Mona Gleason, Associate Professor, History of Education, Children and Youth, Department of Educational Studies, University of British Columbia

"This book is a must-read for anyone interested in Chinese Canadian history and family history. Each piece is just as much about the process of recalling and rediscovering the past as about the families themselves. The eight authors have given us profoundly moving stories of struggle, tragedy, wisdom, and perseverance."
~Dr. Christopher Lee, Assistant Professor, English, University of British Columbia

"In these always poignant and sometimes humourous vignettes, the contributors draw on memories, mainly of childhood and youth, to explore their sense of belonging. Collectively, their stories provide a remarkable insight into the family lives, across the generations, of Chinese Canadians."
~Dr. Patricia Roy, Professor Emeritus of History, University of Victoria

"*Finding Memories, Tracing Routes* is an important contribution to our understanding of the Chinese immigrant experience in British Columbia. We are presented with eight distinctive and moving perspectives on the challenges faced by new arrivals. These stories linger in the memory."
~Paul Whitney, City Librarian, Vancouver Public Library

"Reading this little gem of a book is like being comfortably settled in someone's kitchen and being entertained by a variety of wonderful storytellers. These family histories provide a rich understanding of life in Canada for people of Chinese origin and of their enormous contribution to this country."
~Jean Wilson, Associate Director and Editor, British Columbia and Western Canadian History, UBC Press

"These stories are compelling, funny, and fascinating. Perfect for teaching or as a gift, this book presents stories that rediscover the lost voices of Chinese in B.C. and Canadian history."
~Larry Wong, Past President, Chinese Canadian Historical Society of British Columbia

About the Chinese Canadian Historical Society of British Columbia

Registered under the Society Act of B.C. on May 18, 2004, the Chinese Canadian Historical Society of British Columbia (CCHSBC) is a broadly based membership society with educational goals. Our main objective is to bring out the untold history of ethnic Chinese within the history of British Columbia. We achieve this through sustained efforts at document preservation, research, family and oral history promotion, public education programmes, an active website, and many other initiatives.

One such initiative is the establishment of the Edgar Wickberg Scholarship for Chinese Canadian History. In honour of Edgar Wickberg's vision in creating the CCHSBC, his continued commitment and dedication to its goals, and his many years of teaching students at the University of British Columbia, proceeds of this book will help grow a scholarship fund for encouraging education and research on Chinese Canadian history.

For inquiries about supporting this scholarship fund and the overall goals of the CCHSBC, or to become a member, please email **info@cchsbc.ca** or visit **http://www.cchsbc.ca**. To order additional copies of this book or our first publication, *Finding Memories, Tracing Routes: Chinese Canadian Family Stories*, visit our website. Educational, institutional, and retail bulk discounts are available.

Eating Stories

a Chinese Canadian & Aboriginal Potluck

Chinese Canadian Historical Society
of British Columbia

加華歷史協會

Chinese Canadian Historical Society of British Columbia
Vancouver, British Columbia, Canada
http://www.cchsbc.ca

Book design by Brandy Liên Worrall.

All images and photographs herein used with permission by respective authors. Back cover image by Janice Wong.

ISBN 978-0-9783420-2-9

Table of Contents

Recipes

Recipes Cont'd

Foreword

Margaret Gallagher

Most of my family memories revolve around food. Especially on my mother's side. Which makes me a pretty typical Chinese Canadian, I figure.

All significant family occasions are marked by a meal, whether it be a dim sum feast to welcome a visiting relative, or your grief-stricken mother absentmindedly trying to feed you noodle soup at three in the morning when you've just found out that your grandmother has passed away.

Food is the answer to joy and to sorrow. It's woven into the routine of everyday lives, fueling our family histories. You may not realize it at the time, but the way your grandmother makes rice may be what you will remember most about her.

A friend once remarked that in many families, food is the language of love. It's how we show our feelings when the words just won't come. It can be an unspoken peace offering or a heartfelt hug. Food conquers the cultural divide that arises when families are constantly on the move in an evolving world. I know that in our family a plate of steaming *pisang goreng* (fried bananas) did much to bridge the generation gap between three roguish, Canadian-born hapa kids and our old-fashioned Chinese-Indonesian grandparents.

This collection of writing captures that connection between family and food. In reading some of the work, I was struck by how it was often a small moment, occurring years ago, that resonated with the writer. Each sensory detail so vividly evoked, and the people who shared the meal so lovingly recalled. These stories welcome you into the writers' homes—and into their lives. You're invited to sit around the table with people's mothers, fathers, siblings and lovers. You'll partake in the special occasions, but also in the everyday rituals that ultimately bind us to each other. Whether or not you are Chinese Canadian or Aboriginal, you may recognize your own family, your memories stirred by the words written here.

It's fitting that the word "stir" is attached to emotions, memory, and food—they are all connected. Food itself is perishable, fleeting—but the memories and emotions it evokes are indelible. My grandparents have long since passed away, but I am easily reminded of them through the smallest things—pouring a cup of tea, slicing a mango (their favourite fruit, because it reminded them of home), the smell of rice, which permeated their house.

There are also the family recipes, each one a story. And like a story, a recipe changes a bit each time someone new tells it—a detail added here, a spice omitted there. Some are written down, but many are preserved only in memory. They need to be dusted off and shared in order to thrive, or risk being lost forever, as with the one dish I associate most with my grandfather.

Grandpa wasn't very comfortable in the kitchen. He could make plain rice, thanks to the rice cooker. And he could make an Indonesian-style fried egg, topped with soy sauce made sweet with sugar and ginger. But he made the most amazing *nasi goreng* (fried rice) I have eaten. To this day, I'm not exactly sure what was in it—chilies, bacon, shrimp, egg, ginger and garlic, for starters. Yet I can vividly recall the first time he made it for my brothers and me.

We came into the kitchen, shocked to see our grandfather standing at the stove, stirring a fragrant pan of colourful rice. We had no idea that he could cook. I can still see him there, singing to himself, his glasses fogging up from the steam rising from the pan. I was nine years old, and at the time I didn't like rice and generally refused to eat it. (I much preferred potatoes, which my family attributed to the Irish in me.) But my grandfather was so proud of his creation, and it smelled so delicious. I took one bite and was hooked. It was spicy, salty, sweet and crunchy. And it filled me with warmth.

In the years that have passed, I've tried to recreate his dish, but I have never succeeded.

Luckily, the food that most reminds me of my grandfather isn't cooked at all. He had a lifelong love affair with fresh fruit. At 90 years old, Grandpa could recount the taste of a mango he picked as a boy with the enthusiasm of a kid climbing the tallest tree in the village. Every time he ate a banana, he told us of the countless varieties available back home in Indonesia, and lamented the sorry sameness of those available in North American grocery stores. But Grandpa grew to love the bounty of the Okanagan, where he spent the last two decades of his life. The peaches, the apples, and the cherries.

One of the last times I visited my grandfather, it was high summer. The morning I left for home, we

Photograph courtesy of author.

My grandfather, (Patrick) Kwee Djie Hoo, in the early 1990s, when he was about 90 years old.

went for a stroll, before it got too hot. Grandpa had grown quite creaky by then, but he insisted in taking a daily walk, lifting his feet with purpose each step of the way.

We slowly made our way to a neighbour who had a small cherry orchard. The cherries were unusually plump and abundant that year, and Grandpa wanted to make sure I didn't miss out. He was determined to choose the best cherries for me to take back to Vancouver with me. He surveyed the boxes of deep red fruit with a well-practiced eye, finally pronouncing one of them fit for his granddaughter. And he insisted on carrying it.

Today, every time I eat a cherry, I can see my grandfather proudly marching down the street, clutching the heaping box of shiny cherries with both hands. He looked as proud as he did when his fickle granddaughter declared his fried rice one of the best things she'd ever tasted.

Food is love. This book is a testament to many meals and lives shared. Capture your own family stories and recipes if you can. And if you can't get it exactly right, think of your loved ones each time you try.

Fried Egg Recipe with Improvised *Kechap Manis* (Sweet Soy Sauce)

This is our time-honoured family recipe. My mom made it for us all the time as kids, but I was surprised to find out my grandfather could make it too. Make it for breakfast, a quick lunch, or a midnight snack while you stay up chatting.

Kechap manis is Indonesian sweet soy sauce. It wasn't available in Canada when I was growing up, so my mom just made up her own. I think homemade tastes better anyway.

½ cup soy sauce

1 Tbsp brown sugar

2-3 slices of ginger (optional)

1 sliced small red or green chili (optional)

2 eggs

1 small shallot, diced (a couple tablespoons of onion will do as well)

A wee bit of oil or butter for frying

1.) In a small bowl, use a fork to whisk together the soy sauce, sugar, ginger and chili.

2.) In another bowl, lightly whisk the eggs together with a few drops of the soy sauce mixture, just enough for some colour (but not too much).

3.) In a small frying pan, over medium heat, sauté the diced shallot in a bit of oil or butter until just soft and translucent. Tip the egg into a pan.

4.) Once it begins to set, gently flip the egg. Cook briefly, until just golden on both sides.

5.) Serve with sweet soy sauce mixture spooned over top to taste.

6.) This is nice on a piece of white bread, wrapped in a roti, or with plain rice.

Margaret Gallagher *has cooked up some award-winning radio as part of CBC Radio's The Early Edition. She recently co-hosted Flavour of the Week, a national program all about the culture of cooking and eating. Her most prized possession is an ancient Buddhist vegetarian cookbook written by her great-grandmother in Kediri, Indonesia.*

For Starters

Brandy Liên Worrall

This is a weird book. It's a cornucopia—a bunch of stuff, odds and ends, meat and potatoes and rice and fish, Church's chicken, pizza, fruit salad and apple pie, here and there—much like a potluck. As the editor and facilitator of the workshop from which this book was created, I decided to call this hodgepodge of stories, essays, recipes, poems, and images *Eating Stories: A Chinese Canadian & Aboriginal Potluck*, as a way of clueing the reader in on the motley assortment that the authors and I have arranged on the table. In the title, "eating" serves as both an adjective to describe the type of stories contained herein, and also as an active verb that was very much a part of the writing process and re-creation of family food memories. We also consume stories all the time, and as you will see, in many ways they make us feel very full.

The "Food and Family" workshop was a follow-up to the first workshop I organized, out of which came *Finding Memories, Tracing Routes: Chinese Canadian Family Stories*. That pilot workshop catered to eight participants, who toiled away and enjoyed the process of writing vignettes about their families' histories. At the beginning of the workshop, we didn't know that we were going to publish a book for certain, much less a bilingual Chinese-English edition! Fortunately, the workshop, the books, and the new authors were all received with enthusiasm, so we decided to hold another workshop, this time with a specific theme on food and family memories.

In my own history I wasn't always a foodie. In fact, I hated eating when I was a kid. Chalk it up to a stubborn phase, or perhaps it was a side effect of the medication that I took everyday for a childhood illness, or both—whatever the case may be, I would sit for hours at the dinner table, staring at the cold pork and hardened rice with margarine until it was time for bed. But like most kids, I grew out of that, especially when I left home to attend university in Boston.

Maybe I was also stifled by the limited array of culinary choices in my rural hometown, even though my mother occasionally prepared Vietnamese food (her eggrolls were one of the few things that I could eat anytime). When I arrived in Boston, I discovered sushi, falafel, gyros, burritos, chicken korma, pita and hummus, pad thai, hot and sour soup, and other East coast ethnic specialties like crab rangoon (deep-fried wontons filled with fake crab and cream cheese). And now that I live in Vancouver, a city known for having some of the best restaurants in the world, I'm in food heaven!

After having gained some distance from my hometown and my family, I began to see how food was symbolic of family and neighbourhood dynamics, and how many of my most vivid memories involve food.

My mother and my half-sister were the first Asians in my hometown, arriving in rural Pennsylvania at the height of the Vietnam War, in 1971. Most of the townspeople saw them as the enemy, and even my father's family was not quick to accept them. In order to become part of the family, my mother had to learn how to cook Pennsylvania Dutch food. But she wasn't able to get rid of her Vietnamese palate. For four years—until 1975 when the war ended and Vietnamese refugees flocked to the States and established communities—she wrote to her mother in Vietnam, asking her to send her rice paper wrappers and fish sauce, so she could make her specialty—eggrolls. She had to substitute cabbage for the bean sprouts that would normally go into the eggrolls, but perhaps that was best suited for the Worrall family anyway. Who's to say if making eggrolls helped win her acceptance into the family, but looking back over the thirty-five years she's been in the States, my mother would say that it didn't hurt.

When I created this Food and Family workshop, I had my family's struggles and their tastes in mind. And I knew that this would be a popular topic, but I didn't really think that the number of participants would jump from eight to twenty-four, or that there would, in fact, be a waiting list to get into the workshop! It seemed that people had food stories—eating stories—to tell, and plenty of them!

For six weeks, we convened to talk about our cooking roots, clusters, and offshoots. The twenty-four participants were split up into two groups: Wednesday evening workshops—with Lilly Chow, George Jung, Roy Mah, Gordy Mark, Dan Seto, Bob Sung, Hayne Wai, Evelyn Wong, Larry Wong, Todd Wong, and May Yan-Mountain—were held at Rhizome Café. Saturday morning sessions—with Jacquie Adams, Jennifer Chan, Shirley Chan, Allan Cho, Grace Chow, Betty Ho, Jackie Lee-Son, Amy Perreault, Harley A. Wylie, Candace Yip, Gail Yip, and Ken Yip—were at St. John's College at the University of British Columbia. (I'd like to acknowledge the participation of Meena Wong, who unfortunately became ill during the workshop and therefore was unable to complete it.) When it comes to holding workshops, the most important and challenging thing to figure out is space—especially a space that can accommodate thirteen (boisterous, serious, silly) people for three hours at a time. Luckily, the owners of a new local café with a social conscience were willing to host us in their meeting room on Wednesday nights. Not only were we drooling from the stories being shared, but we were also able to satisfy our growling tummies with soups and sandwiches right in our workshop! Our other location, St. John's, has its own roots in China, as St. John's University in Shanghai was one of the most prestigious institutions in the world from 1879 until its closing in 1952. St. John's College UBC is an international graduate residential college with a mission for serving society. So as it turned out, the histories, missions, and vibes of both our locations matched with and enhanced what we wanted to accomplish in the workshop.

The energy during workshop was fierce—and it usually made us really hungry! I was introduced to the famous Hong Kong Café apple tarts—which sadly, only exist in memories and, now, in stories—and

Arborite countertops and the Marco Polo and other restaurants that thrived in Chinatown's heyday. We talked about Vancouver Chinatown, from the 1940s through the 1990s—and the poignant mixture of Chinese and Canadian cuisine of the *lo wah kiu*, the early generations of bachelors in Chinatown. Through the weekly exercises and discussions, the participants explored themes of food and community; fusion in the family; food as the sixth sense; food as characters in their stories; kitchen and restaurant scenes; and anything else that struck their minds, hearts, and stomachs. We had one ground rule that was occasionally broken: no "flat" adjectives like "delicious," "tasty," or "good" were allowed on paper or in discussion. I challenged them to make their food come off the page through their senses, and wow, did they deliver!

A few weeks into the workshop, we held a storytelling potluck at the Vancouver Museum. Each participant brought a dish that he or she made or bought. But the catch was that everyone had to tell a story about his or her dish. We sat in a circle, and each person placed a bite on everyone's plates. As we ate, we got to hear the meanings and significance of the culinary contributions. I hope that this book acts much in the same way that our little potluck did in that you are able to get a taste of the memories and the food through the stories and recipes!

Besides the dramatic increase in the number of participants, the other main difference between the first workshop and this one is that we broadened our cultural and ethnic range, as three Aboriginal participants joined the workshop. Two of the participants, Jacquie Adams and Harley A. Wylie, attended a one-day workshop we had in November 2006, as they were interested in learning about how to set up this type of collaboration for their communities. Because of that one day in November, their interest was piqued even further, and they signed up to take the six-week workshop. At the same time, another participant, Amy Perreault, a UBC student, was working on a film with another student, Karrmen Crey. Their film, *Why Do Indians Like Chinese Food?*, explores the shared history between Chinese Canadian and First Nations peoples. Amy took this workshop both to gain perspective for her film and also to explore her own personal history as a Métis woman in a relationship with a second-generation Korean Canadian. Jacquie, Harley, and Amy's participation demonstrated how food, memories, and histories can be shared across cultures, generations, communities and backgrounds.

The Chinese Cook Book: Covering the Entire Field of Chinese Cookery in the Chinese Order of Serving, from Nuts to Soup, ed. by Mr. M. Sing Au, Culinary Arts Press, 1936.

Madame Chiang's Chinese Cook Book (Translated in English): Prepare a Delicious Dinner in Your Own Home and Surprise Your Friends, by the Chinese Cook Book Company, 1941.

Throughout this book, you will notice images from cookbooks from the 1930s to the 1960s. These cookbooks are from my personal collection of North American Orientalia that I acquired on eBay. I became interested in these vintage cookbooks after taking a class on Asian American Foodways with Professor Valerie Matsumoto at UCLA. Professor Matsumoto passionately taught us how foodways (the study of how food is tied to culture, society, identity, history, and communities) can shed light on how our present societies were formed and how they've come to operate. The period in which these cookbooks were published saw a feverish enthusiasm for Chinese cooking. I feel that it is also important to note that when I searched for these cookbooks on eBay, some of the key words I used, in addition to "Chinese cookbooks," "vintage," and "kitsch," were "racist," "offensive," and "Oriental." So as you can see, while there was a genuine interest in Chinese cooking, the illustrations and language used in the cookbooks also reflect a darker period in Chinese North American history and prompt us to examine the way we perceive and talk about that period today—which were also other points of discussion that arose during our workshops.

A few items of housekeeping about this book:

1.) The unit of temperature used in the recipes is Fahrenheit.

2.) The publisher assumes no responsibility for the recipes contained herein. On a less serious note, some of the authors wrote the recipes by testing, researching, and interviewing family members and friends—and what you see in this book is the best that they've come up with. . .so far! A lot of heart and soul and frustration and second-tries and pride went into these recipes, as many of these recipes never existed before on paper—only in the heads of moms, aunties, and grandmas who used eyeballs and fingers as measuring tools. I'm sure that the authors would agree that the dishes are up for modification. With that in mind, prepare these dishes with an openness and a spirit for experimentation!

3.) In this book Chinese names of food are not standardized in the Romanized alphabet. Each author's individual and familial usage and dialect of terms have been maintained.

Without further ado, I welcome you to the table. Help yourself! We hope you get full. . .maybe take a nap. . .come back for seconds. . .heat up the leftovers. . .make a gravy sandwich. *Bon appétit*!

Fish Stories

Jacquie Adams

Food was the cement in my family—the glue that held us together through challenges and adversity. It was also plentiful for celebrations. We had shared breakfasts, hodgepodge grab-what-you-can lunches during playtime—British bulldogs or *cheekii*[1]—fresh bread with homemade jam, a coupla pieces of *uptskwii*[2] and a cuppa tea, and sit-down dinners where whoever was home sat at the table and ate. I think Nan[3] and Mom tried to compensate for us starving during the ten long months of residential school by ensuring that food was always abundant. Those winter nights with not enough in the stomach were doctored at home in the summer time and during the two brief weeks of Christmas break. We were never allowed to go to bed hungry in our home, and tea and toast are still a bedtime ritual at my mom's house.

My favourite comfort foods have always been *simt-chuu, muuxhtsuu* and *khwhuk-mis*. My old Nan, my favourite guy in the whole world, made the best *simt-chuu*. *Simt-chuu* begins with *awkhwasht*—dog salmon or chum—fully smoked and cured. After the process of curing was completed, we'd enjoy the *awkhwasht* by roasting it over an open fire, transforming it into *simt-chuu*. *Muuxhtsuu* is rendered dog salmon roe, fondly called stink eggs. Nan Esther made the best *muuxhtsuu*. And then there's *khwhuk-mis*—a delicacy that is nourishment for my very soul; I would challenge anybody or barter my most important valuables just to get some.

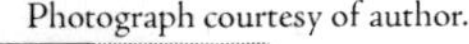
Photograph courtesy of author.

My old Nan, Mr. Adams.

Nan's *Awkwasht* and *Simt-chuu*

He lived the values of old. He experienced the banning of the potlatches and feasting. And he participated in the revival, once we were "allowed" to gather and feast again.

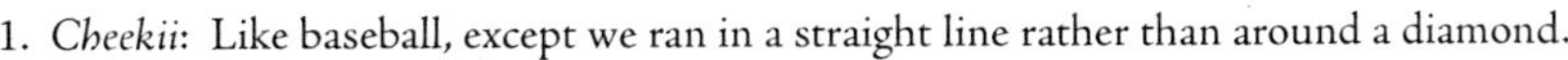
1. *Cheekii*: Like baseball, except we ran in a straight line rather than around a diamond.

2. *Uptskwii*: Dried fish or "jerky."

3. Nan is short for *naniiksuu*, which means grandparent. The Nuu-chah-nulth language also uses this term for great-aunts and great-uncles.

Mr. Adams, who was known to us as Nan, adopted my father and his brother when their mother died in childbirth. He left his home in Ahousaht to raise my father in Ehattesaht country, near Zeballos and Tahsis, after the Queen Huh-nahkit requested that my father—a young child—take on the responsibilities of the house of Whahiinuuxh-takuumlthaht.

Mr. Adams was a tough old bugger. When he was seventy-two years old, he'd still pack a hundred-pound sack of potatoes up the wharf, thrown over his back as he stooped over to balance out the weight. Yet he was soft and gentle. When he really enjoyed something, his mouth would be hanging open, tears streaming down his cheek, and his shoulders would be shaking up and down, but no sound would be coming out.

In the fall, when the leaves were turning colours and the sun shone, or rather, before the long soaking winter rains began, our family would be ready to begin the process of making *awkhwasht* and *simt-chuu*. Nan used to say that the dog salmon (doggies) were the most important food source of sustenance for the Ahousaht.[4] It was even more important than sockeye, mostly because of the abundance of it in the rivers surrounding Ahousaht, but also because it cured better than sockeye or other fish.

The fishers brought the dog salmon into the dock. Brailers laden with the fish hoisted them onto the dock if the fish were in abundance, or in a slimmer year the fishers threw the fish manually from the hatch of the fishing boat. Doggies were covered with a gelatinous, opaque slime—lots of it. Seagulls screamed overhead, knowing that their bellies would be full soon.

The work began assembly line-style with our family. Nan's job was to sharpen the knives and chop the cedar cross pieces for hanging. One of the stronger guys would chop off the heads, another would fin the fish.We would always offer the guts and gills back to the ocean. My mother, one of my brothers, or I began filleting and thinning. Sometimes the work went well into the night, with gas or propane shedding light on our labour.

A slice down the headless doggie's back, a bit above the fin, through and over the spine to the belly. The click-click of the knife along the spine lets you know you're not being wasteful. A quick flip, and another slice down the other side of the spine, a quick rip—and the spine is removed, and the meat is there for thinning. These fish skins are hung up in the smokehouses overnight with a low alder fire to cure them just a bit to make the thinning easier and to reduce the slime.

Ever so carefully and gently, the knife slices strips three to five inches in width, and roughly a quarter-inch deep and the length of the fish is cut. The strip is then taken and hung over the cedar sticks lengthwise in the smokehouse. During times of abundance, the walls of the smokehouse are full of these strips. The fully

4. Ahousaht is a community on Flores Island. In Nuu-chah-nulth language, it means the people of Ahous.

smoked thin meat results in *uptskwii*, dried fish jerky. Several strips are taken off of each side of the skin, leaving just enough meat for *awkhwasht*, about a quarter to half an inch. The skin part is laced with two thin cedar sticks, which keep the skin flat while hanging, and one thicker one is laced through the smaller tail end for hanging. Depending on the weather, the smokehouse could be smoking for up to a week to fully cure the *awkhwasht*.

Photograph courtesy of author.

Mom thinning the doggies.

Mr. Adams, with his scratchy beard and white-white hair, tooling around in his wool pants, fishermen's Romeos and plaid cotton shirt with the brightest of suspenders, would haul the bundle of *awkhwasht* down from the rack that was above the kitchen and select the biggest and best skin from the bunch to prepare the *simt-chuu*.

With gnarled fingers, scarred from years of fishing, logging, and digging out canoes, he would pump up the gas or propane stove, then strike a wooden match to light it. If the skin were a particularly tough one, long into the winter or spring, his fingers would twist and work the skin in an attempt to soften it. Gently and gingerly, he would hold the skin over the open flame, turning and searing and roasting, burning it just a little bit, 'cause the burnt stuff was good for the blood.

The mouth-watering aroma of burnt fish would waft through the air, waking up everyone's bellies. Once it was burnt just enough, he would take a grocery bag or an old newspaper and roll the fish up in it, and he would work it for just a bit more tenderness. He unrolled it onto a table set with only newspapers, salt, a small bowl of eulachon grease[5] if I was lucky—seal oil if I was not—and *muuxhtsuu*, setting it all out silently, with his mouth hanging open just so.

Nan Esther's *Muuxhtsuu*

Nan Esther was my white-haired granny who lived next door. She wore gold-rimmed glasses, the size of lenses that are in style now—tiny. They rested halfway down her nose while she peered out at us over the top. Her hair had a windblown look to it, and she loved her red cardigan. Nan was tiny but strong-willed. We never tested her patience. She wasn't mean—just firm, always respectful to us, thus earning our respect.

5. The process of rendering eulachon grease is another tribe's story. Eulachon grease came to the Ehattesaht through the grease trails between Zeballos and Woss and Nimpkish Lakes through intermarriage with the Kwakiutl.

Photograph courtesy of author.

The beginnings of *awkhwasht*.

Nan Esther's *muuxhtsuu* began with the arrival of the dog salmon. While the fish were being cleaned down the float for smoking, she would gently harvest the eggs. She carefully watched that no Coho eggs mixed in—the blend of the two eggs is highly toxic, and people have died when this caution had not been exercised.

She'd sift through the eggs with her fingers, painstakingly removing any and all of the membranes and slime that could ruin her batch. Nan Ester would place the eggs in a rice, cotton, sugar, or flour sack, and hang it up in the smokehouse while the skins for *awkhwasht* and the *uptskwii* were getting smoked. When it was ready, the outside of the *muuxhtsuu* was caked much like the texture of dried fruit jerky and was easily sliced. The inside was just the rotten slimy eggs.

Many of my old Nans preferred the slimy eggs from the inside. Their sliminess and gooiness wrinkled my nose, but I liked the dried part. The eggs—they stank. They stank to high heaven. No potpourri could chase away the smell, or even hide it. For aficionado of *muuxhtsuu*, the smell is only a part to cherish.

Khwhuk-mis Showdown

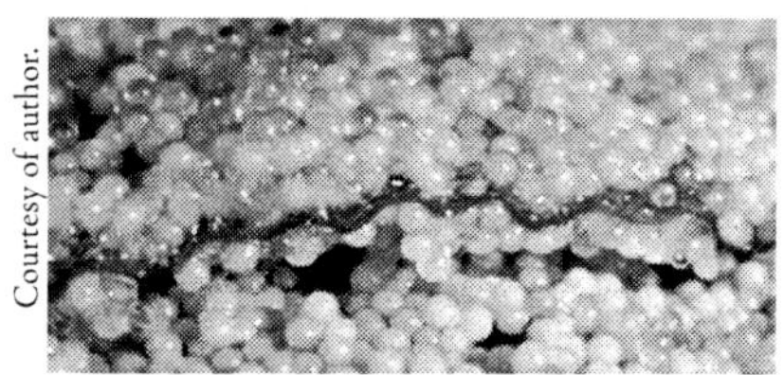

Courtesy of author.

Mmm. . .*khwhuk-mis!*

My favourite food as a child, a teenager, a mom, a student, a career woman, and as an adult today has been *khwhuk-mis* (herring roe), on kelp, on trees, raw, steamed, blanched, plain, with oil, *tlii-nuh* (eulachon grease), Mazola oil, butter, or even with soy sauce.

Khwhuk-mis, tiny golden raw or cream-coloured cooked eggs, no real flavour, just a whole lot of texture. They crunch a million times as you chew on them, and you have to eat a million to get full.

They're harvested in the spring when the herring return, after the first thunder. Their presence is notable by the thousands of *kwin-ii* (seagulls). The water around the spawning beds turns milky white. The men go out to put trees down, suspending the trees upside down in the water with an anchor to hold them and a buoy to keep them afloat. Sometimes you can just harvest the roe on kelp.

Mom said that when she was a kid, she and her siblings were taught to paddle into the spawning grounds in canoes with war paddles, the kind that had the pointed end that paddled quieter than the ones with the round or square ends. They used these quieter paddles so as not to disturb the spawning herring. This respect to the spawning herring has long been lost since we got motorized boats. Now people just bomb in and out of and around the spawning beds with their noisy Johnson's or Evinrude's with no thought at all to the herring giving birth. No wonder they are getting scarce.

◈ ◈ ◈

I was raised by my Nan in my dad's northern community, which hadn't been so tainted by Christianity and patriarchy. The women there had a different social standing and respect for their roles and responsibilities than my mom's family in the south had.

Nan had a great deal to do with my upbringing. I remember spending a lot of time with Nan at Mahtlulthnit, in his one-room cabin near Esperanza, or on his boat where he gave me coffee or tea half-and-halved with Pacific milk. The boat was about seventeen feet long, powered by a Brigg's and Stratton, and named Toot. He talked a lot to me, but more importantly, he taught me to question. He never responded to my why's with a simple and final *because* like other adults always had. Being raised by Nan was a wonderful adventure, but it was also one of the main reasons I had a difficult time when I visited my mom's mother, I think.

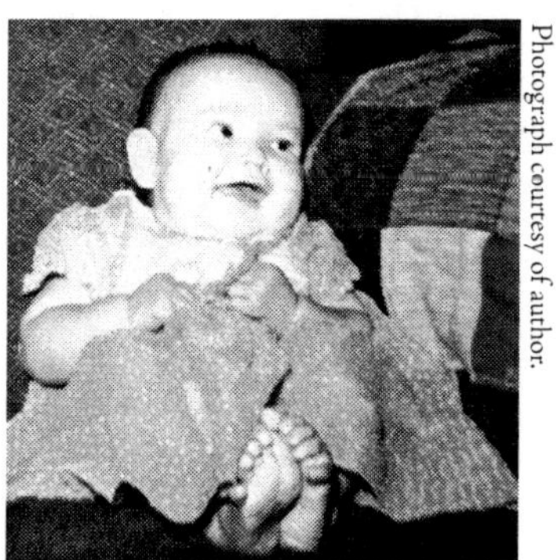

Photograph courtesy of author.

This cute little baby is me, who grew up to stand up to and challenge the grand matriarch, Jemima Frank.

In Ahousaht, Jemima Frank née Sam was the matriarch. She bore many children, mostly sons. Mom was her eldest daughter. She wore a cotton print dress and apron. She also wore stockings. She had a way of taking the top of the stocking, tightening it, and doing a flip, so that they stayed up without a garter. On special days, like Sunday mass, she wore a navy, cobalt, and purple print dress of some synthetic fabric, adorned with a brooch. She had huge dimples, and she shone when she smiled, especially when her grandsons were around.

She was voluptuous; today many of her female descendants jokingly yearn about inheriting some of her ampleness. I don't remember her being warm or cuddly—she just bossed us around. She kept us in line with her broom. Whenever we got in her way or weren't listening, she would jab at us with her broom.

One morning, on one of our few visits to that southern community, she asked, "What do you want for breakfast, Jacqueline?"

"Khwhuk-mis."

"You can't have khwhuk-mis for breakfast. What do you want?"

"Khwhuk-mis," I calmly asserted. I was only three and a half years old, and as I mentioned, had not been socialized like the rest of my maternal family. I was raised by my northern Nans to assert.

She put her hands on her hips. "You can't have khwhuk-mis for breakfast. Do you want cereal or eggs?"

"I want khwhuk-mis."

The room went silent while the locals slinked into the other rooms of the house or out the door. She said, ever more loudly, "I said you can't have khwhuk-mis for breakfast."

Mirroring her posture with my hands on my hips, I stated, "Well, then, I'll jolly well starve!"

Anyone who was brave enough to stick around while this little brat from the north stood up to the giant matriarch was starting to look for safety with shifting eyes, pretending not to notice the drama.

Finally, she lost her cool. "Well, you can jolly well take your jolly well and jolly well jolly well it!" Her broom dropped to the floor as she stalked off to the kitchen, and the locals stared in wonder at my survival.

Uptskwii Midnight Snacks

My children loved *uptskwii*, just as I used to as a child.

When my daughter Jeannine was just two and a half years old, I awoke in the middle of the night, around 2:30 A.M., from a dead sleep. The T.V. was on! And Jeannine was not in bed! I scrambled to the living room, panic-stricken. There on the floor, propped up against pillows, one leg crossed over the other, one arm crossed behind her neck, was my toddler. Her free hand reached into the paper bag by her side every once in a while and came out with a small chunk of *uptskwii*.

Blasphemy

If we added any condiments or spices to our fish, Nan would sternly yet teasingly say, "Why you wrecking good fish like that?" The wildest he ever got with seasoning was salt and once in a while, some salal leaves.

Since his passing in 1993, he still comes to visit my memory and tickle my conscience, as I foray out into the world of the Food Network—Rachel Ray, Kylie Kwong and Chef at Home/Large—and find all measures of sacrilegious acts to commit to my fish. My favourite canned salmon recipe, which my family has copied and made their own, was discovered on a Saturday morning hunting and gathering forage (read: free food samples) to Costco in Victoria.

Canned Salmon Salad

A couple of big handfuls of organic spring greens

2-3 cups cooked penne, depending on how many Indians are coming for supper

3 Tbsp sun dried tomatoes, soaked in olive oil

Roasted pumpkin or sesame Salad Crunchies (from Thrifty's)

1 English cucumber, diced

Caesar salad dressing

Parmesan cheese

1-2 pints of canned sockeye, again depends on how many Indians

Mix it all up. Blasphemous!

⬥ ⬥ ⬥

Hunt and Gather

tide's out—table's set.
ha-yishtuup
tuutsuup
uptsin
haiyxk
kluutchuum
deadhead's brigg's and stratton
put-putting out of the harbor, then

salivation and rumbling stomachs
magnetic pull of return put-puts
draws us toward the float
crudely carved clubs, hatchet handles.
giggling kids, rez dawgs barking
chop-chop-chop—hatchets meeting wood,
smoking snap crackle of fires starting
to cook the mussels

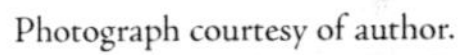
Photograph courtesy of author.

Smokin' chum.

Author's Note

Writing has always been a dream. Fighting for time to sit to let the words and sentences and paragraphs flow has been my challenge. Timelines at work and personal challenges like moving residences and jobs have gotten in my way. Thomas King autographed my copy of his novel, *Green Grass Running Water*, with the words "Well, don't just stand there—do it." That was back in 1993. Now I am doing it.

Working through this workshop with nine Chinese Canadians and two other Aboriginals was enlightening. Sharing our laughter, tears, common oppression, insights, experiences, and food over the last months banked some memories.

A long time ago, I dreamed about writing. I knew then that I had a gift, an ability to string words together in a way that made sense to others. I dream of being able to fulfill my dream. I put the dreams aside for kids, career, personal growth, and other priorities. I hope to be able to keep alive the flame that the CCHSBC workshop has rekindled for me.

Jacquie Adams

Tastes of Exile and Home

Jennifer Chan

EATING MEMORY AWAY

popo opened her
        eyes
gazing at her vagabond grandchild
for the first time
        for a few brief seconds
our spirits crossed before
she let go

i had finally come
        home
too late
cancer chipped popo
        away
she had waited, mom said
could not let go

life throbbed
        between deathbed and kitchen:
stewed pork, steamed chicken, boiled shrimps, fish balls,
yu a la vapeur, *san choi*, and *dong qwu*
        seven dishes
to remember
eighty-four years of a life

the whole village
        showed up
two hundred forty people in
tables of eight
        eating memory away
swallowing rice wine
and sorrow

a cacophony of
        sobs, wail, and howl
i looked at mom's
profile in white hat and gown
        i should have come earlier, i said
popo was happy, mom murmured
in memory

Always Food in My Bag

Every famine produces haunting memories.

When we were small, Dad used to sing a favourite refrain: "*ding dong, leung lup mai, yat woon shui.*" He said that was how he grew up. Survived on two grains of rice in a big bowl of water and little else. And so he would not allow us to leave even one grain of rice in our bowl.

Then there was another one: "*Mo zut zig. Mo fan sek.*" Chairman Mao means no food to eat.

Even to this day, Dad always likes to put lots of yam to boil together with rice in the rice cooker. "Eat lots of yam and you feel full," he says.

I did not know until well into my twenties that I was a Great Leap Forward baby. I would not have been born where I was born without the famine.

In a quiet spring evening on April 30, 1962, Dad and Mom tiptoed into a sampan with ten other people in a small fishing village called Shanmi in southern China. It was their third attempt to wrestle with fate. Destination: Fragrant Harbor. There, they were told, would be plenty of food, good work, and an impeccably run British administration.

The year my eldest sister, Mui Lin/Plum Lotus, was born, in 1958, Mao had ordered villagers to apply fertilizers to their fields. Each village wanted to please the Chairman and carried out the decree in earnest. Soon, the fields turned into grassland, and people began to die in each village. Mom tried to breastfeed little Plum Lotus, but only drops of milky water would flow from her breasts. By the time Plum Lotus made it to her first birthday, there was no rice harvest. Mom grew winter melons instead, but even the miniscule squash were stolen. For two years, the young family scouted yam roots and worms until the government finally sent some rations in 1961. Some villagers died of overeating. Mom said there were no coffins, because all wood was sent away to build a modern China.

One day, Grandpa came home with a fish the size of the pinkie. The whole family surrounded the boiling pot, putting their hopes in the pink creature lost in ten litres of water. Meticulously, Grandpa added some fish sauce until the soup tasted fishy enough. Everybody had a big bowl of hot fish soup. Dad's bowl overflowed because streams of tears kept adding to the salty liquid. That must have been when he made up his mind.

First attempt: April 3, 1962. Mom had gone to see Grandma, and Dad decided to go solo. He had left his watch and his rice ration card with a relative for Mom. Fate had it that a storm stirred up, and the hazardous crossing was cancelled. That would become the first of a long series of marital disappointments felt by Mom toward Dad. Why did he want to flee alone?

Second attempt: April 15, 1962. Mom went to buy some extra eggs, the only food they could carry for the journey. The shopkeeper asked her, "What are you doing with so many eggs?" She responded, "For hatching little chicks." The weather was fine, and everything seemed ready, except that there was not enough water in the river to launch the boat. Nothing could be done, and they had to run home for fear of being caught.

On April 30, Mom took Plum Lotus and baby Mui Ying/Plum Cherry to Grandma's place to leave them with her for the time being. At eleven o'clock in the evening, Mom and Dad boarded the sampan in the direction of the south. They had no water; bottles were not invented yet. Mom remembered waves ten feet high and vomiting all night long. The hard-boiled eggs were of no use. Just before 6:00 A.M., they arrived in the shore of Shatin in the New Territories of Hong Kong. Barefoot, they trekked up a hill and stayed with a Chan relative until they found a tin shack of their own.

A year later, in March 1963, Dad and Mom sent money to arrange for Plum Lotus to join them. Eldest Sister took a train and arrived at Lo Wu Station in a baggy black pants that belonged to my aunt. She looked emaciated but happy. Mom, pregnant with Yuk Kam/Jade Piano, finally felt that they could re-establish the family.

Then seven months later, a letter came from home. Plum Cherry, a sickly child, fell from Aunt Mei's back into a pond when she bent over to catch her laundry, and my sister drowned.

I did not even know of Plum Cherry's existence until sometime in high school. We had a little altar at home with the Goddess of Mercy. Mom would prepare offerings and mutter things I couldn't understand. I wonder whether they were for elder sister Plum Cherry.

If life was a distillery of happy as well as painful moments, no one escapes famines unmarked. Thanks to the great leap forward of my parents, I grew up with plenty of good food. There is always food in the house, and it is to be treasured, enjoyed, and shared.

I have carried this famine syndrome with me. There is always food in my bag, and I make sure my two children do not leave a grain of rice in their bowls.

◆ ◆ ◆

GET WELL SOON

dad makes
hot and sour ginger
chicken soup
again

he slices the root, flips the cleaver, then
like a gung-fu master, chop chop chopchopchopchopchopchop,
mashes the pungent herb hanging
in threads

mom lies
in bed, pale, recuperating
from we don't know what
encore

she's quiet
immobile
for a week, waking up
a different person

why do you like that soup so much
sister jade piano asks me
why don't you like that soup
i say

can't you see
that is mom's sickness soup?
it surely is
nutritious

ginger takes away
excess air in the body, chicken
fortifies the nerves,
the soul

can't you see
that is mom's abortion soup?
vinegar cleans
old wounds, heals broken spirits

dad throws
in two eggs to top it all
mom needs protein, he says
but nothing seems to heal that way

you are lucky
mom said to me once
your generation has
more control

i look into her eyes, trying
to understand
her, her life,
me, my life

i am not so sure, mom,
how many
children
did you have?

eight born, eight gone
destiny
for women of my
generation

mom makes
hot and sour ginger
chicken soup
again, for me, her child

Jennifer Chan

Hot and Sour Ginger Chicken Soup

half a root of ginger, finely mashed

1 lb skinless, boneless chicken breast, cut into 1-inch pieces

4-6 Tbsp rice vinegar

2 eggs, optional

¼ tsp salt

1.) Heat the oil in a wok over medium-high heat.
2.) Add the ginger and sauté 2 minutes.
3.) Add chicken and sauté 4 minutes.
4.) Add rice vinegar and then water to cover the chicken; bring to a boil.
5.) Lower heat and simmer 20 minutes.
6.) Optional: Add two eggs at the end, stirring as you drop in the egg. Sprinkle with salt.

Of Pigeons, Oysters, and Eels

Photograph courtesy of author.

My family, 1974: front row—sister Winky, my father with my brother Roy, Godmother, my mother, and me; back row—my brother Tak, my sister Plum Lotus, and my sister Jade Piano.

For almost two decades, I have been living far away from home, in a sort of self-imposed exile, for I don't know what reason. It wasn't until I left for graduate school in France that I realized how spoiled I was growing up in Hong Kong, the best food available 24/7.

One of the earliest memories of family gourmet expeditions is going out for grilled pigeon in Shatin. I must have been seven or eight years old. Back in the early 1970s, it took a whole day to go back and forth to Shatin from where we lived in Aberdeen. Dad had a Crown sedan. Seven of us children piled in the back of the car, bumping along the country roads of the New Territories until we reached the pigeon Shangri-la tucked in the thick of a bamboo forest.

Shatin yu garp. There was only one. The famed pigeons were raised on a special diet, grilled to perfection, with crunchy skin and tender meat. Served with fine salt or soy sauce. Whenever Dad made a good deal in his car business, he would indulge the whole family in a pigeon binge. There wasn't any worry about bird flu or mad pigeon back then. Now, I am not so sure I would enjoy it as much. The restaurant changed hands several times, and the legendary *Shatin yu garp* was gone.

Another fancy of my parents was oysters in Yuen Long. There was this place called Lau Fau San, Floating Mountain, right by the Chinese border. Oysters were cultivated there. Mom and Dad like to order oysters *sam mei*/three ways: steamed, sautéed, and deep-fried. The meat was so succulent that the milky juice would flow out of the corner of our mouths. It was also the best place to stock up on dried oysters, *ho si* (good fortune), used in Chinese New Year and other festival dishes. From the restaurant, one could have an expansive view of the undeveloped New Territories. The Floating Mountain still exists, and so do the oysters. But the water is so polluted that oyster tasting means taking chances with one's life. And Yuen Long is no longer just one green field. It has become the nexus to dragon next door.

When we were not making the day trips to Shatin or Yuen Long, we frequented Shanghai restaurants throughout town. Dad and Mom developed a liking for this Northern cuisine even though they were from the South. They enjoyed the hot and sour soup, stir-fried Shanghai fat noodle, and steamed pork bun (*siu long bao*). Their favourite was eel stew served with hot steamed buns (*man tao*). We must have tried almost all the Shanghai restaurants in Hong Kong, large and small. There was one in Yau Yat Tsuen that the family particularly liked. It was spacious and quiet. The children could play in the amusement center right under the restaurant. I still remember the bathroom with shiny marble. It must have been a pricey place because Dad always took out a stack of one hundred dollar bills after the meal. Yau Yat Tsuen is still around, developed into a full-blown upscale residential neighbourhood.

Dad's car business went bankrupt in the mid-1980s. I graduated from college and left Hong Kong. The pigeons, oysters, and eels became part of me. I carry them in exile and savour them when I feel hungry.

FUSION OR THE LACK OF

dim sum in paris:
har gao, *s'il vous plaît*
et le dessert
lychee au sirop ou gateau au noix de coco?
chinese food, french touch
auspicious beginning, wedding bells ringing

ramen in tokyo
work was too busy
dinner was sushi
i did wifely things
baking quiche lorraine
you went to karaoke, drank sake

no, no, there's got to be more
to life than being a salarywoman
dalai lama counseled universal responsibility
sayonara to japan inc
around the world in 455 days
sans domicile fixe

hot and sour soup in katmandu
potstickers in mandalay
ton yum gong in pattaya
pho in ho chi minh
fresh tuna in polynesia
i was in heaven, you were in fear

grad school was the way
peace and freedom we thought
theory instead we got
so much pain
in academia
in idyllic california

you never cooked, your mom
never cooked, your grandma
never cooked
french progress:
les soupes en cartons
le tout congelé

why did you pick on me, you asked
because you killed my palate, because
un mariage sans cuisine
comme prêt à consommer
i have lost taste
of all, of life

for eight years I have made
lunchboxes for the kids
now that we are parting
it's both relief and pain
you hire a chefchezvous
my palate, cleansed

Author's Note

Food, like family, like life itself, is one long adventure. The workshop gave me the pleasure to reminiscence about episodes of food memory, some fun, some painful. I had not pre-meditated on the appropriate form to put these memories in words. They gushed out in fragments that I could hardly contain.

One always begins with parents and grandparents when it comes to food. I have always considered myself immensely fortunate to have been raised in a culture, family, and city where food was so abundant and treasured. I treasure these memories even more now that I have been in "self-imposed exile" for the past two decades in France, Japan, and North America. Nothing can be taken for granted—especially not good food, pleasurable moments, and love shared over dishes.

In the string of prose and poems collected here, I remember the first and last time I saw my maternal grandma; the immigrant odyssey of my parents from Communist China to Fragrant Harbour; Mom recovering from childbirth and clandestine abortions; quintessential Hong Kong family outings to eat Shatin yu garp, Lau Fau Shan oysters, and eel Shanghai-style; and finally the tensions in food and cross-cultural marriage.

Food adventures never end. I am always ready to eat!

Jennifer Chan

Laying It All on the Table: A Family Affair

Shirley Chan

Kids lunching at the kitchen table. Left to right—Wally, Roxanne (with just her head peeking out from behind Wally), Nellie, Larry, Monty, Dick, and Chris.

Small Bites, a prelude

Noodle Soup[1]: Swimming in chicken broth, long white Farkay noodles, green *choi* providing a crunch, chicken/pork/beef bits, spicy ginger slivers, salted preserved vegetable. Comforting, warming, eaten at lunch or when not feeling well, made by my grandmother, Jo Po, who looked after us while Mom was at work.

Chicken Feet[2]: Easy to grip, browned, bathed in soy sauce, anise and garlic, simmered for hours, bits of bone to gnaw off, spit out, fun to eat and gross out non-Chinese friends!

---

1. Mom immersed the whole chicken—head, feet, and all—into a huge pot of boiling water, seasoned with ginger and salt. It cooked slowly without heat to ensure the skin would be firm when served. Mom chopped the bird into bite-sized pieces with the bone in and served it with a variety of sauces—ginger and green onion, soy, oyster, sinus-clearing Keen's yellow mustard and red chili. While I enjoyed the tender pieces of chicken, especially the bony pieces like the wing, I really craved the noodle soup served for lunch the next day. With ivory chopsticks and a ceramic spoon, I sipped a spoonful of rich broth and picked up a long noodle, carefully curling it into my spoon before eating. "Stop playing with your food!" Mom reprimanded. But my noodle soup deserved the ritual I observed in its eating.

2. Carefully stripped of their yellow covering after being blanched and de-clawed, the feet were braised with an assortment of spices like star anise, garlic, ginger and sweet dark soy sauce. My grandmother, Jo Po, then simmered the feet until they absorbed all the flavours and were tender enough to eat. When we heard Jo Po chopping off the claws, we knew we were in for a treat. I watched as the big chopping block became surrounded by a pile of clawed feet on newsprint. We asked impatiently, "How much longer before they're ready to eat?" Jo Po replied, "Take time, take time. You go play." When the chicken feet were ready, Jo Po extinguished the flame on the gas stove and fished some feet out of the pot. She put them into a bowl to cool before we came in and grabbed some feet. With a foot clutched tightly in each hand, we ran back out to play.

Ha Gow[3]: Plump, pleated packets of pleasure, juicy, slightly sticky rice noodle shell filled with sweet shrimp, crunchy water chestnuts, bamboo shoots, special treat seldom made at home. Eaten in restaurants or in a booth at back of the Chinatown gambling dens filled with mahjjong tables.

Yu[4]: Fresh fish, picked from a row of fish on ice, clear eyes, bought from Chinatown fish monger scraping off scales. Cleaned, steamed in a bamboo steamer, served with hot oil, soy, ginger, green onion poured on top. Smooth flaky flesh, moist tender cheeks. A regular guest at our dinner table.

◈ ◈ ◈

"Lunch time!"

My friends headed toward the Strathcona School cafeteria as I collected my little sister, Nellie, and brother, Larry, for our dash, heads down, through driving rain and across the street for home. Jo Po, in her favourite green and white checkered apron, opened the door. Immediately, the seductive aroma of hot oatmeal and beef spiked my hunger.

Hot oatmeal with minced beef that Jo Po prepared lovingly, filling and warming from the inside out. Thick, smooth, chewy bits of beef, tangy ginger, crunchy salted dried turnip slid easily down my throat.

Jo Po—with her bobbed, permed, salt and pepper hair; soft huggable body that had borne and nourished thirteen babies; a personality so sweet and patient that even Mom couldn't rattle—cared for us while Mom and Dad worked. Every day, Jo Po waited for us with a hot lunch of noodles, rice, wonton or oatmeal.

---

3. The *ha gow* of my earliest memories were made by the cooks in the back of Chinatown gambling dens where my godfather *Kai yeh* used to take my sister, brother, and me. He was one of the lonely old men stranded in Canada after coming here to seek their fortunes. He lived in a rooming house on Pender Street and often visited and helped Jo Po by taking us kids on an outing. We walked to Chinatown and entered one of the non-descript, windowless storefronts on the 100 block of East Pender. There were several mahjjong tables where old men were playing noisy games. We said hello to all the *Bak bak* and sang a song. Then we proceeded to the back of the building, where there was a restaurant with stools at the counter and booths along the wall. Kai yeh ordered *cha siu bow* and *ha gow*, bigger than the ones we get today.

4. Jo Po carefully cleaned the fish that Mom brought home. She cooked it on low so that the flesh was smooth and firm rather than rubbery. She had to work surreptitiously around her impatient daughter, who favoured high heat when she cooked. Mission accomplished, we sat down to eat the whole fish—eyes and all. There was always a small battle at the table about who would get an eye. "Me, me, me! It's my turn! I didn't get one last time!" We all shouted, each of us hoping that having the loudest voice meant success in scoring a black jelly-filled eye with the pearl in the middle. Jo Po sighed, "One fish, two eyes, three children. . .what to do?"

Jo Po would cut off a small piece of lean beef before returning the rest to its place in the fridge. She chopped and folded the beef over and over on the large chopping block. Then she scooped the meat into a bowl and splashed it with soy sauce for marinade.

While the meat marinated, she slivered salted turnip and a small piece of ginger root. Jo Po boiled three cups of water with a teaspoon of salt in a medium saucepan, stirring in two cups of whole rolled oats. She brought the oatmeal to a boil, then turned down the heat, letting it simmer for ten to twelve minutes while stirring frequently. Breaking the beef into small pieces, Jo Po blended it into the bubbling oatmeal and added the turnip. She covered the oatmeal, removed it from the heat and let it cool.

Hearing our feet pounding up the front steps, she ladled oatmeal into bowls and set them on the green and chrome table before opening the door. "What's for lunch, Jo Po?" we asked. "We're hungry!" Because Jo Po was Buddhist and did not eat meat, she set on the table ginger, pepper and soy, if we needed to enhance the taste of the already rich oatmeal. With our mouths full, we thanked Jo Po in muffled words, before hurrying back to school, leaving her behind to prepare our after-school snacks.

Photograph courtesy of author.

Jo Po in Chinatown in 1974.

◈ ◈ ◈

The evening meal was central to our family's daily life, with Jo Po and Mom doing virtually all the cooking. Oftentimes, they didn't agree on the ingredients or the method. "Who turned down the flame?" Mom shouted at Jo Po. "Stop interfering with my cooking!"

Jo Po shrugged her shoulders and murmured, "The oil was smoking while you were at the sink."

It was Mom's kitchen, even though she was working outside the home in garment factories from 8:00 A.M. until 4:00 P.M., sometimes longer. It was *her* home and *her* family that her mother was helping to look after and raise while she and Dad were hard at work.

Mom had the loudest voice—she was the one we feared as well as loved. Jo Po was soft-spoken but always stood her ground. She resisted Mom's bullying, her quiet interventions pushing Mom's buttons effectively.

Dinner preparation became a scary, noisy affair. The sounds of vegetables being washed, meat being sliced, diced or minced; garlic, ginger, and onions sizzling in the pan; and rice simmering in the pot became the accompaniments to Mom's directing and scolding Jo Po, her sous-chef. The rest of us silently assisted, did our homework, or just stayed out of the way.

"My family must eat good food everyday. It's important for the development of bones and brains," Mom often proclaimed. She kept a tight budget on many things, but it was a point of pride that the refrigerator was always well stocked with good-quality food. Dinners consisted of rice, soup, vegetables, meats and fish seasoned with soy, black bean, hoisin, fermented shrimp and bean paste. Mom also shopped at Woodward's on Fridays after work. There, she bought bread, juice, cold cereal and processed foods that we liked to eat but couldn't buy in Chinatown markets.

Photograph courtesy of author.

A family outing at Queen Elizabeth Park, 1961. Seated—my brother Larry, me, my sister Nellie and Jo Po. Standing—my mother and father.

Dad was home for dinner only on weekends. During the week, he ate at the store where he worked, heading straight after work to the Chan Wing Chun Family Association where as Secretary-Treasurer he was responsible for taking care of their finances, record-keeping and letter-writing. He came home when we were already in bed, and we saw him in the morning for Chinese lessons before going to school. I don't recall him ever doing any cooking, but apparently, he knew how to cook many things. He taught my sister, Nellie, how to cook when she became a teenage housewife living a block away with her husband and children.

"What do you mean? Dad taught you how to cook? He never cooked anything during all the years I lived at home!" I said. I couldn't believe what Nellie was telling me.

"Well, you were away in Toronto and Ottawa when Dad was sick at home," Nellie replied. "I visited him with Karen and then Sam. He explained how to make whatever I asked him about, like soup. He told me to soak the dried vegetables overnight, then blanch the soup bones. He taught me that soup should always be cooked at a low temperature to make sure it stayed clear. Then he told me to use red dates and salted vegetables for flavour."

Nellie learned how to cook from Dad or Jo Po, but I was always too busy with school or work. Even Suelina, my brother's wife, and Jenny, my cousin Wylen's wife, can make Mom's famous sticky rice, although they confess to using a rice cooker rather than a steamer.

"You've eaten it enough, you should be able to make it," Nellie said. "Even if you get the proportions wrong, it'll still turn out if you use enough sausage, mushrooms, dried shrimp, peas, onions and seasonings. Mom taught you how to stir-fry, so apply that basic principle to make it. Just go to Chinatown and buy all the ingredients."

But I'm paralyzed by fear of failure. Memories of being yelled at for burning the rice, slicing the meat wrong, or leaving sand in the vegetables spring to mind. Yet I have entertained friends with dinner parties and taught them how to cook Chinese meals before I got married and my husband, Steve, took over the kitchen.

Christmas Day at our house is a family potluck we look forward to after the kids open their presents. Steve rises early to prepare the roast beef, inserting slivers of garlic and sprinkling on generous quantities of Italian seasoning, salt and pepper before placing it in the oven to brown at a high temperature, and then lowering the temperature to cook it to a perfect medium rare. Then in go the spareribs that have been marinating in his special sauce of hoisin, honey, lemon juice, ketchup, soy and chili. Mom's favourite. I baked brownies the day before while Steve baked loaves of Swedish rye bread from a recipe handed down from his mom's great-aunt Sal. While the beef is roasting, we slice the rye bread and assemble the fresh fruit, cheese, and smoked salmon platters, with cream cheese and condiments.

When everyone begins to arrive shortly after noon, the rest of the meal arrives as well. Nellie tosses her Caesar salad with the anchovy, garlic and parmesan dressing she whipped up at home. She also brings along homemade butter tarts and shortbread. My brother Larry, his wife Suelina, and their daughters bring chicken chow mein and beef fried rice noodles. When Mom arrives with her sticky rice in the rice cooker, she plugs it in to keep it warm while Steve slices the roast beef. Steve then splits the ribs along the bone. My cousin Wylen, his wife Jenny, and their son Spencer bring BBQ duck with plum sauce from Chinatown, as well as a box of Chinese mandarins.

Every one digs into the meal as there is something for every taste—and even my vegan daughter, Emma, can have some salad, fruit and bread to eat. A true family potluck.

◈ ◈ ◈

Photograph courtesy of author.

The Chan clan in Strathcona, 1968. Front row—my brother Larry, Jo Po (Lim Hop Lee), and me. Back row—my mother Mary, my niece Karen in her dad's arms (my brother-in-law Nick Lum), and my father Walter.

My mother, Mary, was a natural-born organizer. I was only nine years old when Mom dragged me door-to-door to try and stop the City of Vancouver from demolishing our home and community. Although she made herself understood on every doorstep, she insisted, "I need you to translate." She was persuasive, and people responded positively to her pitch.

Not successful the first time, we repeated the canvassing twice more. Finally, in 1968, when I was twenty-one, Phase 3 for the freeway plans was announced, and Mom swung into action again. This time we changed tactics and used the documented failures of massive public housing projects, hardship to displaced residents, and food to organize. No more paid lawyers to make our case. We spoke for ourselves through the media, at meetings and banquets. Four members of our own family were actively involved: Mom, Dad, my brother Larry, and myself. And of course, the food.

Mom organized the neighbours. She invited people to our home to strategize, serving tea and apple tarts from Hong Kong Café, *cha siu bow* from BC Royal Cafe, moving tea and goodies to spread maps out on our green and chrome kitchen table.

My father penned articles for the *Chinese Times*, raising awareness in the Chinese community and rallying support for a united cause. He wrote, "Chinatown must work with Gastown and Strathcona to stop the government from destroying our communities. The survival of Chinatown depends on Strathcona where workers and shoppers live. From the new bridge the freeway will run along the waterfront, plowing through Gastown, Chinatown and Strathcona before joining Highway One. Let's work together!"

Grabbing the attention of the English television, radio and newspapers, I successfully appealed to the larger community for their understanding and help. Larry would later help rebuild the community with his Strathcona Home Renovation Services Project.

The Strathcona Property Owners and Tenants Association (SPOTA) formed in November 1968 at a well-attended meeting where my father was elected one of three co-chairs. Mom was elected an Executive Member, and I was chosen as English Public Relations Officer.

Food was central to our strategy. At every SPOTA meeting, including the founding meeting, tea and pastries were served. Executive committee members—all women—made cookies or cakes. Others brought buns and tarts from Chinatown. Food lent a festive atmosphere to the meetings—social gatherings that cultivated a sense of belonging and community. Mom served tea and pastries along with large doses of political action.

"With the new Minister of Urban Affairs coming, let's have a Chinese banquet," Mom proposed. In addition to petitions, briefs and letters, SPOTA also employed banquets to raise funds and lobby decision-makers. "We could welcome the Minister and raise money for SPOTA at the same time. I can negotiate a good price with a restaurant—$125 for each table of ten, including tea, soft drinks and gratuity. If we sell tickets for $25, we'll make $125 a table. A little less if we want Scotch at the head tables."

"The Minister can meet our Executive and Board and see the broad representation of ethnic groups working together," added Harry, co-chair. "He'll see we're not just Chinese but also Ukrainian, Italian, Swedish and all different peoples."

"We should invite all the politicians—Mayor Campbell and Council, MLA's Herb Capozzi and Evan Wolfe, and Liberal MP Ron Basford, who has been so supportive," Sue, co-chair, said.

"I'll write the article for the *Chinese Times*," Dad offered. "They understand the synergy between Chinatown businesses and Strathcona homes."

"I'll help Bessie draft the invitations before I prepare the press release for the English media. We should have a press table at the banquet, too," I added.

The Hon. Robert Andras was our guest of honour. We were anxious that he share the view of his predecessor, the Hon. Paul Hellyer, that the community was worth preserving. Mr. Hellyer had placed a moratorium on "urban renewal" after his last dinner meeting with us, but resigned abruptly when his recommendations weren't adopted.

The serious business of lobbying three levels of government to stop the freeway was fueled by a sumptuous ten-course banquet at Ming's in Chinatown, lubricated with bottles of Johnny Walker Red Label Scotch at the head tables. The menu was a collaborative effort between Mom and the restaurant, selected to enhance the reputation of the restaurant and to reach the hearts of the politicians through their palates.

Before the eating commenced, Harry introduced all the politicians. Speeches were made and translated by our community organizer, Jonathan. Harry called on the government representatives to change their plans for the city. We were thrilled to hear Mr. Andras and Mr. Basford pledge their support for our community. Mr. Andras stated, "It is clear to me that housing is much more than bricks and mortar. It is about community and the people who live here. I will bring this message back to my Cabinet colleagues in Ottawa."

Now it was time to eat. We started with a platter of assorted BBQ meats—duck, chicken, roast pork, *cha siu*—all with the signature golden brown and red colours, with slices of orange and sprigs of cilantro. I served our guests before taking a bite of the duck with its juicy skin and meat infused with five spices.

Next came a tureen of steaming soup with cubes of clear, melt-in-your-mouth winter melon simmered in chicken broth and tidbits of crabmeat, shrimp, mushrooms, ham, lotus seeds, lily seeds, bamboo shoots and water chestnuts.

A light gingery platter of crisp stir-fried snow peas with crystal prawns followed.

Then came a personal favourite—sticky rice-stuffed de-boned, deep-fried chicken, crisp and golden on the outside, and chewy, garlicky on the inside.

Next, a childhood favourite—black shiitake mushrooms, slippery slices of abalone, and crisp green and white Chinese vegetables swimming in a light sauce.

For contrast, sweet and sour boneless pork—crisp pork pieces with red and green pepper squares, pineapple chunks slathered in a sweet and citrusy sauce.

Photograph courtesy of author.

A SPOTA banquet, 1969. From left to right—Faye Leung, Judge Orick, Mrs. Orick, Art Philips, me, Jonathan Lau, Mrs. & Mr. Lam.

The next dish was simple—sliced beef, marinated in soy sauce and garlic, stir-fried with crunchy *gailan*.

Not to be outdone was the whole steamed rock cod complete with eyes, with skin slightly crisped with hot oil, ginger and green onion poured over it as the finishing touch.

Finally, a heaping platter of fried rice with morsels of omelet, pork, shrimp and onions.

I have no doubt that the way to a policymaker's heart is through his or her stomach, and the women of SPOTA knew this, as they never did anything without food. After returning to Ottawa, Mr. Andras announced a change in national housing policy, forcing the city to abandon their urban renewal plans. Neither a third crossing nor a waterfront freeway would be built. Gastown, Chinatown and Strathcona were saved.

SPOTA's banquet drove home the message that Chinatown and Strathcona were neighbourhoods offering rich and rewarding cultural and gastronomic experiences, worthy of preservation. The urban renewal program, after much negotiating with SPOTA at the table, was replaced by a pilot project offering grants to renovate homes. My brother, Larry, through a federal employment program, hired and trained local residents to provide repair and renovation services to homeowners.

Mom noted, "That banquet for Mr. Andras was the turning point. We established goodwill through food and drink so our voices could be heard."

And we all agreed: saving our community through food was a family affair.

◈ ◈ ◈

Legacies

feeding legacies:
memories, recipes
preserved, pass from
mother to daughter; mother to son

motherless illiterate grandma
tutored by her grandma
'til parted by death
sold to serve

meals in gold mountain
made from memories
from dreams of grandma
of family, of china

ma—born in gold mountain
raised in middle kingdom
teacher, wife, mom,
dutiful daughter-in-law

menfolk gone
starving women and children
ma farmed land, mined courage
to feed her child, her village

dangling baskets of food, goods
on poles from shoulders
dodging bullets, running
to feed her village, her child

surviving—ma sought liberty
gold mountain opportunity
slaving in canneries, factories, cafes
tutoring chinese to feed her family

cooking from intuition
ma brewed perfection thru trial and error
no words, letters penned
for me who never tasted hunger

steamed rice with chinese sausage
memories of home: soups,
meats, vegetables, tart, tangy sauces
without words

hungry for home, flavours chinese
moved by memories, relying on
intuition—tasting, recreating
without words

another culture, another way
a gift of words printed, bound
i learned the words of cooking
of precision and measurement

stained, dog-eared pages mark
lessons learned in words of cooking
chewy brownies, dense cheesecakes
pies bursting with apples

oozing cinnamon, brown sugar, oozing
to stain pages capturing lessons
from memory, notations staining
margins   my legacies for you

Photograph courtesy of author.

Three generations of Chan women, in China, c. 1940. From left to right—my mother Mary Chan, my sister Jane Chan, my aunt Yim Lee, and my grandmother Lim Hop Lee.

◈ ◈ ◈

"Oh, hi, Larry! You're here already?" I greeted my brother with surprise on arriving at Mom's old house to celebrate Chinese New Year. Larry usually arrives last because of his busy naturopathic practice. His wife, Suelina, was keen to get underway: "Oh great! You're here! Let's *Bye Sun* and pay respect to the family spirits so we can all eat 'cause I'm hungry!"

"Sorry to be late," I apologized, "but we were making sticky rice at my house and without Mom's double-decker steamer, it took three hours to steam the two lots of rice."

"You made sticky rice? Really?" asked Larry in disbelief. "That's my favourite!"

"Actually, Seto Guo and Wylen made it," I said, "and Steve made Mom's favourite—BBQ ribs."

The warm reception from family members made it worthwhile to have spent the whole afternoon video-taping Mom's friend, Seto Guo, and cousin Wylen as they did the cutting, steaming and stir-frying.

Using Mom's preferred method, the five pounds of pre-soaked sweet rice were cooked in two batches, steamed in a cloth-lined basket set into a wok with water in the bottom, and covered with a large lid. Each batch took more than an hour to cook. During steaming, we monitored the water level in the wok, periodically sprinkling water on top of the rice and turning it with chopsticks. During the steaming, Seto Guo taught me how to fold gold ingots from the silver and gold foiled papers I bought from the Buddhist store on Main Street—ingots to be burned before dinner.

Seto Guo said,"Your ma used only California-grown sweet rice, making ten pounds at a time so there would be enough for leftovers for children and grandchildren to take home. The sausage, pork belly, mushrooms, onions and garlic would be diced the night before and refrigerated overnight; the rice soaked overnight; and she would rise at 5:30 in the morning to put the rice on to steam while she went outside to do some gardening."

"Why so early, when we didn't eat until noon?" I asked.

"She did the stir-frying later in the morning. Keep the rice warm, or you won't be able to budge it."

"No wonder Mom would offer to cook something else. I had had no idea how much work was involved or how heavy the rice was to stir-fry. Why do they call it sweet rice?" I asked.

"Because of the sugar content. I would scold your ma if she ate too much because she was diabetic."

"You *scolded* Ma?"

"I was the only person who could and did. No one else dared to, but she knew I cared about her, and it was for her own good," she said with a big grin.

Knowing my daughter, Emma, was coming to the potluck, Seto Guo first made a vegan version, leaving out the meats and using vegan oyster sauce. We didn't have a protein substitute, but I knew Nellie was bringing *Buddha's Feast* with tofu. When the vegan version was transferred into a small rice cooker to keep warm, the original recipe was prepared.

Arriving at Mom's house, I placed the rice on the counter and plugged in the vegan version beside it. For the first time since becoming vegan, Emma would eat sticky rice.

"Hurry up and come outside to *Bye Sun!*" Suelina urged. Joining other family members outside, I burned Hell Bank Notes and hand-folded gold ingots, whispering proudly,"Ma, today Seto Guo showed me how to make your sticky rice!"

Back inside, bowls of rice, glasses of whisky, and chopsticks were offered to ancestors at the table as incense burned. Formalities over, it was our turn to eat. Chicken chow mein, Buddha's Feast, whole chicken, whole

BBQ duck, Steve's BBQ ribs, stir-fried gailan, lotus root salad, Church's chicken, pastries and almond jello. More restaurant contributions than normal, but it was understandable as most people had to work.

"It is so great to have sticky rice tonight. Reminds me of when Ma was alive, and she cooked this dish for special occasions," Larry reminisced.

"It was great of Seto Guo and Wylen to bring all the ingredients and equipment to my house and show me how Ma made it. Tell me what you think," I said.

"Really good! The right balance of *lap cheung, lap yook*, dried shrimp, garlic, onion and rice. So this means you know how to make it now?" asked Larry hopefully.

"I have the list of ingredients and videotaped the whole process, so.... I guess so," I said.

"Did you steam the rice or use a rice cooker?" asked Suelina.

"We steamed it the way Ma did, in a cloth-lined basket in a wok. Seto Guo said that it is difficult to use the right amount of water in a rice cooker. It ends up heavy," I answered.

"Can you teach me how?" asked Suemay, Suelina's sister.

"You're welcome to view the tape, and we can make it together if you like," I invited.

"I had four servings. It's so like Grandma's! Garlicky bites of rice and preserved meats," said Karen.

"Thanks, Mom, for the vegan version! I love the bite of garlic, the crunch of onions, the squish of mushrooms and the pop of peas!" said Emma. "Best of all, it reminds me of Grandma even though she never made a vegan one."

"I'll box up the leftovers for you to take home. Be sure to thank Seto Guo, who made it especially for you."

The other leftovers went home with Larry. Happily, there was a bowl waiting at home for my son, Heming, who was in the U.S. that day.

Then Suelina surprised us with a bellydance—her first performance in twenty years! "Ma wasn't like other women of her generation," Suelina said. "She always supported my dancing, referred me to jobs at the community centre, the seniors group. I felt right dancing in her house tonight because I knew she would approve."

Mom's house. Mom's practice to burn offerings for ancestors out back. Mom's favourite dishes like the ribs and Church's chicken, her sticky rice recipe and even a bellydance. The dinner was a tribute to Mom, who was a forceful personality that influenced us all. She was a unique blend of traditional practices and modern ideas—an open mind, ahead of her time.

House of Chan Sticky Rice

The *House of Chan Cookbook* by Sou Chan, 1952. Shirley Chan, her story, and recipe bear no relation to the author of this cookbook.

5 lbs California sweet rice, soaked for 6-7 hours

½ lb Chinese sausages

½ lb preserved pork belly (*lap yook*)

6-8 Tbsp sunflower oil

1 large onion, diced

1 clove garlic, minced

Salt

8-10 large dried shiitake mushrooms, soaked for 2 hours, scrubbed with baking soda, then rinsed

¼ lb dried shrimp, washed

Dark soy sauce

Oyster sauce

2 tsp sugar

3-4 green onions, chopped

¼ lb frozen green peas, thawed

Chinese parsley and sesame seeds, for garnish

1.) Steam sausages and pork belly for 20-30 minutes. Cool to touch. Remove skin from pork belly. Dice sausages and pork belly.

2.) Line large bamboo basket with cloth and place in wok, with just enough water covering the bottom of the wok (do not immerse basket in water). Fill with half of strained pre-soaked rice. Steam at medium high heat for 1-1½ hours until rice is clear and plump. Sprinkle water over rice and stir occasionally. Transfer to covered dish, keep warm. Repeat for second batch of rice.

3.) Heat 2 tablespoons oil in wok, add onion, garlic, and one-half teaspoon of salt. Fry until onions are clear. Remove from wok.

4.) Heat 2 tablespoons oil in wok, add sausage, pork, mushrooms, shrimp to brown. Remove from wok.

5.) Heat 2 tablespoons oil in wok, add rice and stir in onion and pork mixtures. Mix carefully. Sprinkle soy, oyster sauces, sugar to taste.

6.) Add green onions and peas last to prevent mushiness.

7.) Remove to casserole dish or rice cooker to keep warm. Garnish with toasted sesame seeds and Chinese parsley, if desired.

A page from the *House of Chan Cookbook* by Sou Chan, 1952. Drawing by Siu Lan Loh.

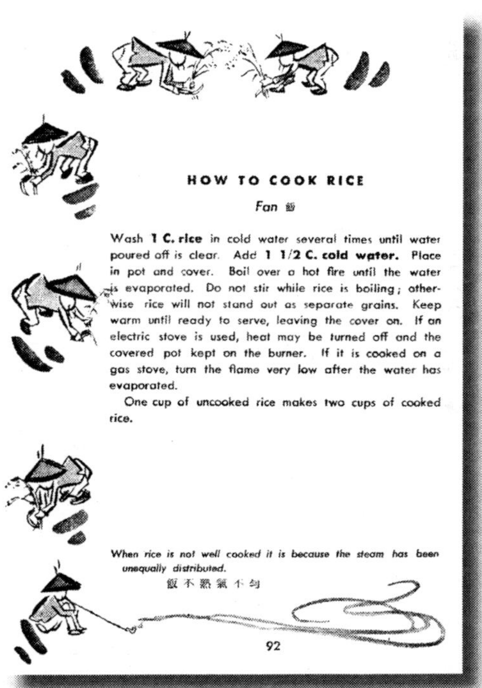

HOW TO COOK RICE

Fan 飯

Wash **1 C. rice** in cold water several times until water poured off is clear. Add **1 1/2 C. cold water.** Place in pot and cover. Boil over a hot fire until the water is evaporated. Do not stir while rice is boiling; otherwise rice will not stand out as separate grains. Keep warm until ready to serve, leaving the cover on. If an electric stove is used, heat may be turned off and the covered pot kept on the burner. If it is cooked on a gas stove, turn the flame very low after the water has evaporated.

One cup of uncooked rice makes two cups of cooked rice.

When rice is not well cooked it is because the steam has been unequally distributed.

飯不熟氣不勻

92

From *The Art of Chinese Cooking*, by the Benedictine Sisters of Peking, 1956.

Author's Note

Food memories are synonymous with family memories. Growing up, my dad ate at the family store in Chinatown before continuing into evenings at the Chan association. My mother and Jo Po (Grandmother) prepared the meals. Dinner preparation was not always harmonious, as the personalities and cooking styles of Ma and Jo Po were opposites. My role was limited to washing rice, slicing meat, or folding wonton. I shared clean-up duties with my sister but didn't cook until leaving home.

Feeding her family well was a priority for my mother, who had lived in China during the Communist revolution and the Japanese invasion. She had left the classroom to farm and braved enemy fire to trade goods for food to keep her family and the village of largely women and children from starvation. Returning six months pregnant to Canada, her birthplace, in 1947, my mother worked for her sister Lily and her husband Dick Gock Seto, a successful Chinatown merchant and their three children. Working at whatever was necessary to support her family in China and Canada, Mother saved to bring my father to join her. She also cultivated vegetables in our garden from spring to fall.

Mother met life's challenges head on. With a deep sense of fair play, she fought injustice. Faced with city plans to demolish our family home and neighbourhood, she did not hesitate to act. Twice she failed to stop the demolition, but she succeeded the third time when it became a family affair. (This does not diminish the roles played by neighbours and friends.) Food played a big role, with banquets and teas that built a sense of community and goodwill in our organizing and lobbying.

These stories are tributes to my Jo Po, who cared for us, and to my mother for her strength of character and formidable cooking skills. Until taking this workshop, I was afraid to make Ma's signature dish—sticky rice. I have included the recipe as taught to me by her good friend, Seto Guo, and aided by my cousin Wylen.

At home, my husband, Steve, does the cooking. He perfected my mother's BBQ spareribs to the point that she would request that he make it for her. I'm the baker, thanks to high school Home Economics and a recipe book from friends.

I wish to acknowledge Brandy for her encouragement and ability to weave together disjointed writings into a coherent whole, and the other workshop participants for their helpful criticism. Thank you to my husband, Steve, for his cooking and feedback. Thank you to my sister, Nellie, for sharing her memories on how she became a great cook of traditional family dishes.

Shirley Chan

Memories of Bamboo Curtains

Allan Cho

Part I: Gateway to the West

When I was a baby, I cried when I saw strangers, especially ones who touched my nose or pinched my cheeks. Father would pick me up, put me on his shoulders, and say, "Look at you, you're getting too heavy for me now."

I reached for a red envelope, a *lai see*, but a hand took it away from me. It was my first birthday party.

I gurgled, "Baba." He laughed and popped a fry into his mouth. We were celebrating my birthday at the McDonald's in West Vancouver, on Marine Drive and 16th Avenue.

I think most people would find it odd to consider McDonald's as part of the Chinese cuisine landscape. But to me, McDonald's has its own unique place in a Chinese Canadian context. For many immigrants who knew little or no English, like my parents, McDonald's was often the first point of contact to the West. It *was* the West.

It was also a refuge where there were other Chinese people. For immigrants concerned about convenience and economy, it provided a playground for kids whose family couldn't afford toys. And for the blue-collared working man, McDonald's was reasonably priced and didn't cater to any particular class.

For about ten dollars, any parent could order combo meals number one or two with dignity. They didn't need to learn any new words or be in fear of speaking incomplete sentences and mispronounced words. I fondly remember how my grandmother once took me to McDonald's during Expo 86 and ordered an ice cream cone for me, showing the server a tattered piece of paper with what seemed to be scribbles on it.

Things have changed. Bit by bit, piece by piece, McDonald's restaurants are being replaced by Starbucks and high-end cafés. A few weeks ago, I decided to visit the McDonalds' in West Vancouver, where I had celebrated my birthday.

Father was mumbling something about how his grandfather came to Canada during the railroad when suddenly everything became silent. We saw that our McDonald's no longer existed. In its place was a bicycle repair shop. We settled for another McDonald's in North Van near the Capilano Mall that day—but it wasn't the same. The lighting looked different. The people were different. But the memories of our McDonald's—they remained the same.

Part II: Red Eggs and Ginger

When my brother was a newborn, foreign food and strange people flowed in and out of the house. In Chinese culture a baby's first month birthday calls for a celebration. Proud parents introduce their latest addition to friends and relatives by holding a red egg and ginger party.

I lowered my head and touched the baby's miniature fingers. It clutched my thumb, much to its delight, giggling with little bubbles spouting from the mouth.

"Stop playing with your little toy," said Mother. "Come out to greet your auntie and uncle." I gently dropped my brother back into his crib.

"Such a big boy!" an old gentlemen said as he tapped my head lightly and grinned, revealing gold teeth. His cane made an annoying thump as he made his way to our kitchen. Already at the table was Ng Poh, Fifth Aunt, a grey-haired woman who waved me over and pinched me on the cheek. "Look at you—looks just like his father," she beamed and reached into her bag and took out a red envelope. My eyes widened.

"No, no," Mother interjected, "Your coming here is enough already."

Fifth Aunt laughed as she saw me stoop behind Mother and wrap my arms tightly around her legs. "Come over here," she said to me, smiling. Mother finally relented, nudged me over and told me to say thank you using my good Chinese.

"Have a seat, Ng Gong, Fifth Uncle," Father said in his thick Punyu dialect. "What kind of tea would you like?" I sometimes could not comprehend what Father said when relatives came to visit since they spoke a language different from the ones we spoke at home. I was often lost in the dialogue during these times, nodding to aunties and uncles if they nodded, and shaking my head when they shook theirs.

Ng Gong licked his lips. "Aiya, look at all this," he pointed to the dishes on the wooden oak table. "How can two old people eat all this?" He took his chopstick and snapped up a morsel of ginger fried egg. He opened his mouthful of gold teeth and slurped the egg, chewing slowly. Every now and then, his tongue would busily tuck in a piece of ginger that wanted to escape from the corner of his lips.

The food on the table was cruel in that it both intrigued and disgusted me. Its scent made my stomach knot in pain and my mouth water in yearning. My lips began trembling at the beautiful rainbow assortment of delicacies laid out in different shapes. But I frowned because I knew better than to try anything. Experience had shown me that it was all deceptive, nothing more than a mirage.

"Silly boy," Father threw back his head, unable to contain himself, laughing when I choked on the egg, which tasted nothing like the usual cooking that Mother prepared for dinner. "What's wrong this food?" he asked me, taking my bowl and eating the rest of the gingered egg.

Next came the soup, at which Father and Fifth Uncle both nodded their heads as they slurped. It was a dark thick broth, which looked like the kind of car oil that Father used. The pungent stench forced me to turn my head as the bowl was passed around the table. This, Father explained to me, is called *cho*, or vinegar soup. Ng Gong winked at me, placed a piece of pig's feet into his mouth, gnawing away mechanically.

I equally detested the sweet liquor, *teem jau*. Although it had a beautiful, airy scent and looked clear and sweet, it too tasted sickening. The name confused me because while it was supposed to be "sweet," it tasted like the spoiled milk that I drank from time to time when Mother forgot to clean the refrigerator.

My favourite food on the table was left untouched. I slipped from Father's arms, and slowly climbed onto the table, and reached over for a red egg, which I relished the most when I banged it on the table over and over until the shell crushed into what seemed like a million pieces of glass. Then I would make a fist and squeeze and punch up and down until it further turned to powder.

Mother shrieked, "Look at you! You're making a mess! That's your clean shirt, now I'll have to wash it! It will stain." Father and Ng Gong laughed. Ng Gong took me into his arms, and I sat on his lap. He wiped the red dye from my hands with a musty handkerchief he had taken out of his shirt pocket. He wiped away my tears, took my hands, and walked with me out to the back porch. It was sunset; the sky felt like it was going sleep. "You are like me when I was a small boy in China," he looked down at me. "Do you know why there are red eggs in China?"

I shook my head, still mesmerized by the old man's gold teeth. "Long time ago, most babies, like your brother, died very shortly after they were born. A baby who reached one month of age was very special." I blinked, looking up at the rivers of wrinkles stretching across his face. "That is why we celebrate with red eggs and eat together after the first month," he said. I smiled and jumped up, reaching for his sleeves. Fifth Uncle picked me up, and I sat on the ledge with him, grinding eggshells in my hands.

Photograph courtesy of author.

My mother and me at my parents' store, Granville T.V., in Vancouver, c. 1981.

Part III: Take out the Old, Bring in the New

To me, *leen goh*, or sticky cake, will always be associated with Chinese New Year's. As a young boy, I yearned for this chewy sweet along with the firecrackers and *lai see*, which were as synonymous as fruit cake and jingle bells at Christmas time.

My stomach moved as Mother stirred the gummy *leen goh* slowly. She told me it must be stirred counter-clockwise only. "Or else it would taste funny," she whispered. I always wondered why. Was it a superstitious Chinese New Year's tale to suspend the curiosity of a wide-eyed boy, who licked his lips and stretched out his neck in anticipation for this sugared treat, or did Mother really have some chemical mystery passed down from ancient times?

My favourite *leen goh* was not the freshly cooked batch that Mother flipped onto our plates, whirls of smoke coming from the crispy skin. Because it immediately melted in my mouth, I never liked that taste. "Eat up everything, you're a lucky boy today," said Mother.

"Can I eat something else?" I replied.

Mother shook her head and walked away from me and my steaming sticky cake. I would sit there for hours and watch my cartoons. I would wait, and wait, and wait some more until the *leen goh* would cool down to a more satisfying temperature. Clapping my hands, I grinned and grabbed the small square lumps, stuffing them in my mouth. I enjoyed the gluey texture of cold sticky cake, especially when there was a touch of egg yolk as dressing. The sweetness of the cake was even sweeter when Woody Wood Pecker pecked his enemy Wally Walrus on the nose, and slipped away from danger, heckling away with his famous laugh. I screamed even louder.

"Aiya," said Mother. "Look at the mess you made! No more *leen goh* for you," and before I knew it, my sweet sticky rice was replaced by the streaming saltiness of warm tears.

Part IV: A Map of the Forbidden City

Whenever I think of a Chinese restaurant, Kwangchow Lau (Canton Gardens) comes to mind. I still look for its whereabouts when I walk down Pender Street. But whenever I look up, I no longer see the bright neon lights that hung so magnificently in the sky. Instead, I see a tired and lonely brick building.

My cousin Irene, who was visiting from Toronto, asked, "Why doesn't Say Gong, Fourth Uncle, help Say Poh?" I saw the old woman waddle up the stairs. I looked down from the top and was startled when I saw how far it looked. Irene hustled to take my grandaunt's cane and lightly patted her on the shoulder, "Say Poh, do you remember me?" The old woman looked up and grinned.

Say Gong sighed and shook his head, "Hurry up!" He turned around, took off his fedora, snapped his shiny cigarette lighter, and puffed out a cloud of smoke. "Professor!" he shouted, and a man with bushy hair stomped out with his arms held out high above his head.

"Say sook!" he replied. They shook hands.

"Professor, we want a *sek ban*, rock cod," he stretched out his arms, "Big one that is still swimming." Both men shook with laughter, and each slapped the other on the shoulder. Even today I believe that there must be a story behind the nickname.

This dinner at Kwangchow Lau wasn't just a casual get-together. This was a historical ceremony which tied together generations, East to West. The daughter of my grandfather's older brother, my cousin Irene received a celebration not unlike an aristocrat from the Forbidden City during the imperial period. I still don't know whether she knew the implications of this dinner, but the men of the clan viewed this quite seriously.

According to the pieces of family history that I had managed to gather, my great-grandfather came to Canada as a young man to work on the railroads. Whenever our family did our weekly Chinatown grocery shopping, my father would point to a shoddy building as we drove along Powell Street and say, "My grandfather, your *tai yeh*, used to own that one." His remark had a hint of pride.

"It was hard in those days. He sold that house to build us one in China—a big one!" Father would exclaim. I'd rarely see him this excited, as if he was reliving his youth, his smile showing no age at all. "The threshold was this high," he stooped down, touching his shins. "I had to climb over it to get into the house as a young boy."

I never did find out what great-grandfather did in those cold, rainy days in Vancouver to earn a living after being laid off from the railroads. I wondered what he ate, now that I had all this food in front of me in Kwangchow Lau.

Before the eating began, the receptions always seemed to last as long as the meal. The adults walked from table to table, shaking hands, pouring wine, clinking glasses, lighting cigarettes, bursting out in laughter.

Mother opened her purse and took out a pen and a slip of paper. Mother always liked to teach me new things whenever she had a chance. She placed the menu in front of me. Pointing to the unfamiliar squiggles on the menu, she wrote a Chinese character. "A woman." She circled, "And a son." She continued, "Put together, means 'good' in Chinese." *Ho*. That was the first character I ever learned.

"Help yourself, help yourself," granduncle directed at Irene. "Don't be shy, everyone is family here," he said, and helped himself to a huge forkful of Peking Duck.

Irene shook her head, "I'm fine, I'm fine." The exchange would go back and forth until the kids at the table got frustrated and helped themselves first, much to the chagrin of the adults.

I chomped down on the crispy skin, its juice squirted across the table, which amused my cousins, who giggled. Then came the Shark's Fin Soup, which always proved to be a popular dish among the adults. The only time that our family would have this delicacy was for these special outings. "Shark's Fin Soup has significance," Mother whispered in my ear. "Indicates wealth because this is very expensive." Irene winked at me, and I almost melted in delight.

But the corner of my eye caught something out of place. Say Poh was sulking. It was the strangest sight that her daughter sitting beside her had to rinse all of Say Poh's morsels of food with the glass of brown tea before slopping it back onto her plate. I didn't really understand why she had to eat that way. Many years later, my own mother broke down into tears when the doctor told her she would have to eat her food the same way.

Part V: "White For Tofu"

We arrived at the cemetery. It had been eight years since Mother's return to the colony. The Queen had just a few days prior to our arrival signed for the return of Hong Kong to China. Mother bowed three times. I watched her and did the same. At the columbaria, rows of pictures faced us. My grandfather, Gong Gong, took out a bag of oranges and positioned them into a shape of a pyramid. I was tired, thirsty, and restless. Licking my lips at the sight of the fruit, I imagined how fast it would take for me to peel them all.

The Ching Ming festival, the day of the Third Moon, is also known as Grave-Sweeping Day. The Chinese characters mean "clear and bright." It is the time of the year when families visit the graves of their ancestors to clean the graveside and pay their respects. I was used to the damp, slippery grass in Vancouver, where it never fails to rain on Ching Ming. Mother would always tell me that when the gates of the underworld unlocked on this day, spirits would disperse to their graves scouring for burned incense and paper money to take back with them. But Hong Kong felt like the opposite. The only wetness I had felt was the sweat that slipped down my neck, staining my shirt.

Determined to pay the proper funeral rites for his beloved bride, Gong Gong solicited funds from neighbours and sold his camera equipment in order to pay for the meal. Mother recalled that Gong Gong spent much of his free time at home in a dark room developing photos, often late into the morning, until he came out smelling of sweat and chemicals, but beaming with pleasure. It was his hobby to take pictures of his family. Gong Gong would never again develop another photo after my grandmother's death.

Chow Mo Ngan, my grandmother, died in her early twenties, leaving behind a daughter of five, a son of three, and a young husband still ripe in love. In 1956, funeral parlours were street level. This particular one was in a predominantly busy section of Tsimshatsui; the funeral took place in front of a bus stop.

On the day of the funeral, some bystanders looked on. One woman sighed, lightly flapping her paper fan. "So unfortunate, look how terrible this is. All so young." She wiped a tear from her eyes. "Wave good-bye to *ah ma*." My grandfather scooped up both of his children into his arms and took them to their mother. My mother touched Chow Mo Ngan's face, the pure delicate features thickened with a white paste like a Cantonese opera singer.

Because working as a taxi driver could barely put three meals a day on the table for his family, my grandfather never brought much of a feast that other families did at Ching Ming. During these outings, father, daughter, and son would stand under the sun, eating mandarin oranges and drinking the kettle of *oolong* tea they had brought with them on the bus.

They watched as a family next to them unrolled a mat and placed dishes of *cha siu*, barbecued pork, *ham yu*, salted fish, and steamed vegetables onto the ground, while lighting paper money. "Let's eat, let's eat," a woman said as she reached into the bucket and scooped out the mound of rice into a bowl. The children gathered in a circle around their parents and chatted away. A smell of the feast and incense flowed across to the little girl, my hungry mother. She glanced over to the family, then sat down silently to finish her cup of tea.

Friends and relatives of the deceased would eat a seven course meal together—seven, or "*chut*," being a symbolic number for death in Cantonese culture—after the processions at the funeral parlour.

As I was growing up, Mother could still recite the vivid details of the meal, the assortment of vegetables and meat, the smell of the evening, which all strangely felt like weddings she would attend as an adult, except without the laughing and the cheering. The dish she savoured the most was the tofu because she rarely had it served at home. The slippery soft skin melted in her mouth.

Whenever we eat tofu at home, Mother tells us, as if she is also reminding herself, that tofu symbolizes whiteness and purity in the other world.

All photographs courtesy of author.

My grandmother, mother and uncle in Hong Kong, c. 1953.

My grandmother and mother in Victoria Park, Hong Kong, c. 1954.

My mother and her brother, Hong Kong, c. 1956.

My mother and her brother, Hong Kong, c. 1958.

Leen Goh, Sticky Cake

6 oz boiling water

⅔ cup brown sugar or 2 slabs (about 5 oz) Chinese brown candy (*peen tang* in Cantonese)

⅓ cup Chinese dates, softened in water, cut in half, pits removed, or ½ cup other dried fruit or ¼ cup dates and ¼ cup nuts

3¼ cups (1 400 g bag) glutinous rice flour

1 Tbsp milk

Water, as needed to make the dough

1 Tbsp vegetable oil or nonstick cooking spray

1 egg, beaten

1 Tbsp white sesame seeds

1.) Prepare the wok for steaming.

2.) In a bowl, mix boiling water and sugar, stirring to dissolve. Cool. Soak dates, dried fruit in hot water for at least 30 minutes to soften.

3.) Place sticky rice flour in a bowl. Make a well in the middle, and stir in sugar and water mixture. Add the milk and shape the dough. Add 1 tablespoon of water to the dough at a time, until you have a dough with a satiny texture. Incorporate one-half to three-quarters of the dates, nuts, or other dried fruit as you add water and work with the dough.

4.) Grease cake pan with vegetable oil or non-stick cooking spray.

5.) Steam cake in a wok over medium high to high heat for 45 minutes, or until the edges pull away from the pan. Remove from heat, cool.

6.) Use a knife to loosen edges, then remove cake. Wrap in wax paper, refrigerate overnight.

7.) To serve: cut the cake into quarters, and then into slices 2–3 inches long and ¼-inch wide.

8.) Dip cake slices in egg wash and pan-fry. Sprinkle on sesame seeds.

Author's Note

Born in Vancouver, I feel blessed to have lived through a unique period in which Vancouver had grown from a small municipality to a vibrant cosmopolitan city. Although many Hong Kong Chinese emigrated to Canada, they did so not out of desire, but of fear. Thus, my interest in Chinese diasporic history stems from my own experience growing up in the turbulent period of migration history. I wanted to learn about colonialism and its effects on a transient populace, where language, politics, and "home" never meant stability.

But in learning more about the past to understand the present with professional historians who study "authentic" history, I had neglected to learn about my own past—where I came from, how I got here, and why. Although I had signed up for this CCHSBC workshop hoping to learn more about the past, it wasn't until I heard my fellow writers' stories and vignettes of family gatherings that I got a real passion for understanding my own history. We wrote, we critiqued, we wrote some more, but we ultimately learned from each other through our own narratives, igniting hidden memories. What the workshop had taught me was that history from the "bottom up"—from those who experienced it—is very much as relevant and accurate as history from the "top down" written by experts in the field.

CCHSBC board member and UBC historian Henry Yu couldn't put it any better when he pointed out to us during one workshop that sometimes the best records are those of the human memory. Names, dates, and documents were often hidden, disguised, and "reused" in the past to protect the fragile positions of Chinese migrants. For those Chinatown addresses that were not recorded in directories, only those who had frequented or had known of those places can locate and retrieve things that were lost in the paperless annals of time.

I thank Brandy Liên Worrall for her tireless and diligent editing of all our work and all my fellow classmates for their wonderful feedback and for sharing their often intimate and wondrously fascinating memories of their past. Through my classmates stories, I was able to visualize Vancouver's bustling Chinatown as it was in the 1950s and 1960s, with its majestic Chinese restaurants, bowling alleys, and rhythms of Cantonese opera.

Interestingly, growing up in what felt like a schizophrenic period of history of Vancouver brings with it a somewhat bittersweet residue. The very issues I had studied about Hong Kong of the 1960s and 1970s, about dislocation and relocation, are the very ones I'm facing now in Vancouver. Just as ferociously as the movements of people from Hong Kong during the 1990s were to Vancouver—bringing with it culture, business, politics, and of course, food—these very same people are equally furious in their return to their native land. One by one, friends I've grown up with and acquaintances I've met along the way have left. The transience has become permanent.

Allan Cho

Authentic Chinese Canadian

Grace Chow

The Green Plate

My "green plate" is white with a light green edge. It is a little chipped but still usable. The sight of my green plate on the table meant that we were having a Western meal.

Anytime we had a Western meal at home, Mom, Dad, Maggie, and Peggy would use the brown and yellow plates. But Mom always gave me the green plate. Her reason was that it was slightly smaller, and she figured I couldn't eat as much.

"Gracie, you get the green plate because you smallest."

I always felt special using the green plate and considered it mine.

Our Western meal usually consisted of chicken breast or pork.

"Mom, what are you putting on the plates?"

"I put slices of tomatoes and cucumbers on the plates to make it look like Western dish, I think I saw that on T.V."

While Dad cooked and Mom assembled the tomatoes and cucumbers on the plates, I set the table with Lea & Perrins Worchester sauce, Heinz ketchup, HP sauce, Kraft BBQ sauce, and cutlery rather than chopsticks. Even though it was a Western meal, we still had our staple served on our plates—steamed white rice.

It was very important to Mom that all the major food groups were served.

"Important to eat all food groups, not just meat. Too much meat make you fat." She glanced at Dad.

We tried to take the focus off Dad and commented on his cooking. "Dad, the pork tastes good."

Dad beamed, as Mom put more vegetables and salad on his plate.

Over the years our family meals began having both Western and Chinese at the same time. But other than being chipped and faded, the plates themselves remain the same.

"Mom, you still have those plates?"

"Why wouldn't I have them? Do you know these dishes are older than some of you?" She looked at me and Peggy.

"They're so old and worn."

"If they don't break, why replace them?"

We use the same plates and knives, forks, and spoons, along with chopsticks, as our table setting. The same garnishes of tomato and cucumber slices are placed on the sides of our plates. Mom still gives me the green plate out of habit, although now I do need seconds and even thirds when I use it.

Authentic Sweet and Sour Pork

From 1984-1993 my father owned the Golden Wheel Restaurant, located on 872 Richards Street (between Robson and Smithe) in Vancouver. This was the second location of the Golden Wheel Restaurant. The original location was on Robson Street from 1976-1984. Due to its location in downtown Vancouver, the Golden Wheel served Western Chinese cuisine to tourists and non-Chinese. I helped my father from the age of six until the restaurant closed down when I was eighteen.

Photograph courtesy of author.

My parents in front of the Golden Wheel Restaurant, c. 1984.

Although sweet and sour pork was not considered an authentic Chinese dish, I enjoyed watching my father prepare it. It was always full of colour—red from the sauce and red peppers, yellow from the pineapple, green from the green peppers, white from the onions, topped with a bit of brown from the sesame seeds.

You could see the pork slowly turn golden brown as the oil sizzled. While the pork was being deep-fried, my father would gather up the vegetables and the sweet and sour sauce, and mix the ingredients in a wok. Then he would put the pork into the wok. Finally, he'd coat the pork and vegetables in the sweet and sour sauce, and plate it up or spoon it into a take-out container, giving it the final touch of a sprinkle of sesame seeds. I always insisted on sprinkling on the sesame seeds.

The first bite of sweet and sour pork: a crunch from the crispiness of the batter and vegetables, then a juicy tender centre, with sweet and sour sauce filling the mouth. Although we no longer have the restaurant, I still order this dish when I go to a Chinese restaurant—much to the dismay of my father, who never considered it authentic.

Jook (Congee): Comfort Food for All Occasions

My stomach is churning, my head is pounding, my face flushed, and my hands are ice cold. I just want to lie in bed or sit on the couch with my favourite blanket.

I want Mom to make me congee, but I am dreading calling her out of fear of all the questions and criticism: "What's wrong? You are sick! Do you have stomach problems, fever? I knew you weren't wearing enough warm clothes." In the end she agrees to make me *jook*.

Photograph courtesy of author.

Uncle and Aunt's house on 24th and Main, c. 1976-1977: front row—Peggy, Uncle Tom, and a family friend; back row—Maggie, Dad, me with Booboo, Mom, and Po-Po.

Mom's *bak jook* calls for adding three times the amount of water that you normally use to make rice, and then boiling it for a very long time. She prefers using a crock pot since she doesn't have to watch over the stove while preparing *jook*. Other than those basics, she never told me specifically how to make *jook*, as she's never very descriptive in her recipes.

Photograph courtesy of author.

Christmas 1994 at my parents' home: front row—Dad, Po-Po, and Mom; back row—Maggie, Silqun, Peggy, Conrad, and me.

The hot thick rice soup going down my throat is not exactly comforting. However, Mom insists that it is very nutritious. She says that we should eat it even if we're not sick.

Over the years Mom has adjusted how the congee is made for me and my sisters. I like my congee watery; Maggie likes it thick. Peggy isn't a fan of congee. My parents prepare congee with two major occasions in mind: sickness or celebration. The type of sickness congee depends on the severity of the sickness.

Bak jook (plain congee) means we're really sick with stomach problems, fever, and the possibility of not being able to hold down food. Mom, being practical, thinks if we can't hold the food down, then there's nothing wasted since it's just rice and water. *Jook* with *gongyiuhchyuh* (congee with dried scallops) means we are able to hold down the food. Mom has our relatives mail the expensive dried scallops to us from Hong Kong.

For our festive congee occasions, Dad makes the congee. The congee is prepared with meat, fish, or geoduck, and dried scallops with ginger and seasoned with white pepper, soy sauce, sesame oil, green onions, and shredded lettuce. Along with the *jook,* we'd have century egg, *youtiao* (salty donut), and pickled vegetables to compliment the congee.

Jook—for our health and happiness.

Po-Po's Visit

"Grace, did you clean your room? Peggy, did you put your things away? Did we forget anything from Chinatown? Did somebody check the flights coming in from Ottawa? Is it early? Hurry, we have to go to the airport, we can't let Po-Po wait!"

Mom's scampering signaled my grandmother's anticipated visit. Mom made sure everything was perfect, buying all Po-Po's necessities well in advance: food, yarn, Chinese videotapes, yarn slippers—although Po-Po always brought a pair just in case.

Po-Po stayed during Christmas with us for a few weeks at a time. It was a treat having Po-Po come visit.

Po-Po was a sturdy, spunky lady at five feet, three inches. Her theory was that since she was old, she didn't have anything to lose by speaking her mind. She was very proud of the four children she raised by herself since her husband passed away when he was thirty-eight years old.

Photograph courtesy of author.

Po-Po and Mom in Hong Kong in 1967.

Po-Po moved back and forth between Guangzhou and Hong Kong, finally settling in Hong Kong in 1958, before immigrating to Canada in 1972. She spent her first few years living in Victoria and Chemainus. Then she retired and moved to Vancouver in 1974 when my family immigrated to Canada.

Po-Po lived with Uncle Tom and Aunt Cecelia on 24th and Main Street in a three-storey house that is still in its original structure. In 1979, Uncle Tom got a promotion in the government, and my uncle, his family and Po-Po moved to the nation's capitol.

At Christmastime every year when Uncle Tom and his family went on vacation and Po-Po wanted to get away from the harsh Ottawa winter, we would see the same brown leather suitcase and a box that would arrive with her. The box contained Chinese videotapes that my uncle and aunt had borrowed from us and were returning, as well food and sometimes a new kitchen appliance, like a crock pot or a blender. Our eyes would open wide with anticipation when Po-Po unpacked her suitcase and box.

Photograph courtesy of author.

Po-Po as a young woman, c. 1947.

Po-Po pulled out the usual: a container of Vaseline, a red-handled hair brush, a few flowered polyester dresses and tops that she wore year after year, and a pair of yarn slippers just in case mom couldn't find the last pair she left in Vancouver. Then she pulled red envelopes out from her purse, gave them to us, and patted us on our heads. She would say, "You are now another year older. Do well in school, and be good to your mother."

Sometimes Po-Po brought along a Tupperware container. She would never open the container in front of us, but she would tell us that the Tupperware had a snake in it. We would always be curious, but she warned us not to open the container. She told us that the snake had no skin or head on it, and that we were too young to look at it. When we asked her if the snake was alive, she said, "Not alive, just sleeping."

I never knew where the snake came from and only found out recently. The snakes were imported into Toronto, some of which would be shipped to Ottawa. Ottawa had a large Vietnamese community in Chinatown. Vietnamese people would use snakes to prepare meals. So Po-Po got the idea to buy them in order to make soup for us.

After unpacking, Po-Po shuffled around the kitchen in her yarn slippers, finding a place for all her ingredients and gadgets. In the weeks that followed, she would be in a cooking and cleaning frenzy.

◈ ◈ ◈

Po-Po rolled up her sleeves and began soaking the *gongyiuhchuh* (dried scallops), *dunggu* (dried mushrooms), and *hamaih* (dried shrimps).

She noticed me watching her. "I am getting ready to make food for you to eat."

"What are you going to make?"

"I haven't decided yet. Maybe *lo bak go* (turnip pudding), *leen guo* (Chinese sticky pudding), *dou jiang* (soy bean drink), or whatever," as Po-Po shrugged her shoulders. "You will see when you come home from school tomorrow."

The next day, when I came home from school, my eyes widened with amazement. The kitchen was transformed into a multi-stationed cooking arena—no longer a typical family kitchen with a coffee maker and boxes of cereal on the counter. It had been completely taken over by a little old lady with large-rimmed glasses and a flowered dress and apron, moving about effortlessly in her yarn slippers. The stovetops were filled with steamers and pots. The counter was overcrowded with food that was ready to be steamed. Dishes that were ready for eating beckoned from the kitchen table. The tantalizing aroma of the *dunggu* and *laap cheong* (Chinese sausage) from the *lo bak go* made my stomach growl.

As the *lo bak go* was steaming, Po-Po stirred the snake soup on the stove.

"Snake soup—that's gross!" I said, wrinkling my nose.

"You don't know. Chinese medicine says eating snakes will warm you up in the winter, good for blood circulation and prevents arthritis. Snake meat tastes like chicken. I make this for your family, especially for your mom. She have bad blood circulation. Snake soup good for everyone."

"Why did you bring the snake from Ottawa? We can find them in the garden."

Po-Po shook her head. "This snake special for soup only, not the same snake found in the garden! You are lucky, you know? Snake soup is very expensive in China, and only rich people eat this," she huffed and continued to stir the soup.

Po-Po explained that to make the snake soup, you had to delicately peel the meat off the snake. The bones in the snake are very small, so it was important to do this carefully. Snake meat resembled chicken meat when it was shredded and peeled. Among the other ingredients in the soup were ginger, carrots, bamboo shoots, Chinese mushrooms.

During the weekend, Po-Po put me and my sisters to work. We would make dumplings and other dishes together. We would don our aprons and mix the dumpling filling or stir the ingredients to make the dough. The dough took time to prepare as the ingredients were stirred, then covered with a cloth so the dough could rise. When the dough was ready, Po-Po used her hands to roll the dough into a long tube, and then cut it into pieces. We would use a dumpling presser, which resembled a cutting board with handles, to press each piece of dough into round flat circles.

I can still remember Po-Po explaining the art of making dumplings: "You cannot put too much filling or too little. Too much filling in the dumpling will result in not sealing the dough properly. Too little mixture will result in too much dough. For a nice presentation, you need to put the folds on the dough when sealing the dumpling." She made the perfect dumpling and set it aside as the sample. My sisters and I would try to replicate the dumpling that she made, but ours never looked the same as the Po-Po sample. The folds were never even. Regardless of how they looked, Po-Po didn't mind. She would cook ours first.

Photograph courtesy of author.

Po-Po in the kitchen.

As we wrapped dumplings, Po-Po would tell stories, some about Ottawa and others about life in China.

I didn't learn too much about Ottawa, except her telling us that it was cold.

"I don't go out for six months during the winter, but I did go out once this past year. I walked to Chinatown to get my hair permed, and I only go out when your uncle drives me." As she told me this story, I could picture her layered with sweaters and scarves, walking to Chinatown all covered up and the only thing you could see of her were her glasses.

Po-Po also talked a lot about my two younger cousins in Ottawa, Silqun and Conrad. During her visits, Po-Po said the same things about them repeatedly, so that by the third or fourth time, I would mutter under my breath, "Not again."

"Your cousins are both taking swimming and piano lessons, so smart."

"Silqun has to wear special shoes when he sleeps—he special you know."

"Conrad is so helpful in the kitchen. He can make cinnamon buns and fudge all by himself."

"Little Conrad has eczema and has to use expensive cream at night."

She proudly beamed at the thought of Silqun and Conrad.

I always found it funny that when Po-Po showed me pictures of my cousins, she would point at Conrad and say, "Yen Yen (Grace), your eyes not the smallest now. Didi (Conrad) has smaller eyes than you!"

Then she would close her eyes and think back. "When you were born, I looked at you and said to your mom, 'Such small eyes.'"

Photograph courtesy of author.

My grandfather.

Her memory would go back even further, as she would divulge bits and pieces of her life before us.

"Before your Gong passed away, our family did well. We had servants to take care of your mom, aunts, and uncle."

Gong ran an import business, which was left to Po-Po's care after he passed away. But she lost the business when the communists took over in China. This was when she moved to Hong Kong, starting over with nothing and trying to raise her family on her own.

This is about as much as I know of my grandfather. Looking at our family photos, there seems to be only one picture of him.

When we finished making dumplings, you could tell which ones my sisters and I made compared to the ones Po-Po made. As they boiled in the broth, the ones that had too much filling broke open. You could see the chives and the bits of boiled filling floating around, while the pieces of dough sat heavily in the broth.

Po-Po cooked so much food during her visit with us that our freezer was packed to the gills by the time she got ready to go home. Satisfied that she did a good job as a mother and grandmother in leaving us with as much food as possible, she would turn her attention to stocking up so that she could provide for her son's family in Ottawa. She would go shopping for Chinese food that she couldn't get there—which meant a lot of food. She would pack everything into the same box that came with her from Ottawa—*laap cheong* (Chinese sausage), dried mushrooms, dried scallops, geoduck. Geoduck was not very common in Ottawa or Toronto, so Dad would have it prepared and put in a plastic container to be placed into the box of goodies Po-Po was taking back with her. Along with the food, she brought back videotapes of Chinese shows Mom taped for my aunt and uncle. Dad would carefully pack the box and weigh it a few times to ensure the box wasn't overweight. The snake stayed with us in Vancouver; the geoduck went back with Po-Po to Ottawa—a fair exchange.

Author's Note

My parents and my sisters Maggie and Peggy immigrated to Canada in 1974. Shortly after their arrival, I was born in Vancouver and became the first in the family to be born in Canada. I have spent most of my life in Vancouver. I studied at Ryerson University in Toronto, obtaining a Bachelor of Commerce degree. A few years ago, I lived in Beijing for two years, traveling, working, and learning Mandarin.

When Dan Seto, fellow workshop participant and dragon boat team member, let me know about this CCHSBC Food and Family workshop, I knew it would be a tremendous opportunity to learn how to develop my writing skills. At the same time I was very apprehensive. I had little experience writing narratives, and I wasn't even sure about my family history. Brandy emphasized that we may never know the truth because the past has already been lived. With her advice I have written about my experience, my own truth with the past. I found the experience invaluable, and I am inspired to continue writing.

One of my main goals for this workshop was to write a tribute to my grandma who passed away in 2003. For as long as I can remember, Po-Po spent most of her time in the kitchen cooking for her family. Cooking food was a way of showing her love. I hope the story about her displays how truly amazing she was.

Thanks to CCHSBC, my fellow workshop participants, Dan for the CCHSBC introduction, and Brandy for providing me support. It has been a pleasure and an honour to read all your stories!

Thanks to my family, friends, and God for providing this incredible opportunity! My love and thanks go to my family—Mom, Dad, Maggie and Peggy for a lifetime of love, support and encouragement; my dog Mulan for sitting beside me while writing; Uncle Tom and Aunt Cecelia for being my "Beijing parents"; and Silqun and Conrad for being the brothers I never had.

Many of my interests and hobbies are spent outdoors—running, snowboarding, dragon boating, hiking—and maybe now I have found an indoor interest in writing. I would like to continue writing about my family and about my experiences living in Beijing from a Chinese Canadian point of view.

Grace Chow

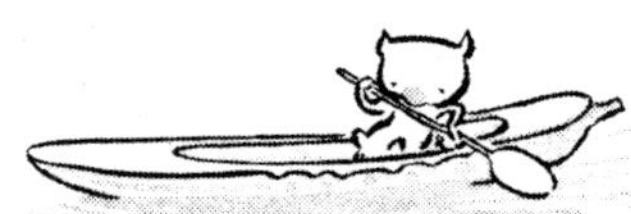

SAUTÉED SLICED PORK

Ch'ao P'ien Jo 炒片肉

Fry until done **3/4 lb. uncooked pork,*** cut fine. Add **1 C. onions,** coarsely chopped, and **12 dried mushrooms,** cut in strips. Cook a few seconds. Add **1 C. celery,** cut in 1-inch pieces, and **2 green peppers,** sliced. Cook a few seconds. Add **4 T. soy sauce, 1/2 lb. bean sprouts, 1/2 can water chestnuts** (336 grams), sliced, **1 T. fresh ginger,** chopped fine, and **1/2 C. water.** Thicken with **2 T. cornstarch** mixed with **2 T. water.** Heat thoroughly. Vegetables should be "crunchy." Serves 8.

*This recipe is good made with chicken instead of pork.

STUFFED CUCUMBER HALVES

Huang Kua P'ien 黃瓜片

Mix **1 lb. uncooked pork,** veal, or chicken, ground, with **1 T. oil, 1/2 t. salt, 1 T. soy sauce, 1 T. cornstarch, 3 T. onion,** finely diced, **1/2 C. dried mushrooms,** chopped, and **1 T. fresh ginger,** chopped.

Remove alternate strips of cucumber-peel lengthwise from **6 cucumbers,** each about 7 inches long. This helps the cooked cucumber to hold its shape. Cut in half lengthwise and then crosswise in 2-inch pieces. Scoop out seeds and refill with the meat mixture.*

In a large pan place **2 T. oil.** Arrange the stuffed cucumbers and add **1 C. bouillon.** Cover pan tightly and cook over moderate heat for 10 minutes. Lower the heat and cook another 35 minutes or bake in oven at 325°F. for 35 minutes. Remove cucumbers from pan. In the same pan blend together **2 T. cornstarch, 2 T. soy sauce,** and **1 C. water.** Cook a few minutes stirring constantly until sauce thickens. Pour over the cucumbers and serve at once. Serves 6.

* May be made in advance to this point.

From *The Art of Chinese Cooking,* by the Benedictine Sisters of Peking, 1956.

RICE, EGG & MATZOH DISHES

From *The Chinese-Kosher Cookbook,* by Ruth and Bob Grossman (all recipes authenticated by Rabbi Norman Siegel), 1963.

Initiations

Lilly Chow

1. Hard to Chew on

"Zoe. Just one bite."

My very young niece takes one look at the green object—a chunk of cucumber—and shakes her head. Her body starts to sag into the petulant position, and her lips press together to protest.

"Stop that—now. I don't want to hear it," her father tells her firmly.

Part of me flinches and curls up inside, as it does whenever I hear somebody being bawled out. (Can you imagine your boss reprimanding you like that? *"Close your mouth and obey me right now. Don't make me count to three."* Who would put up with that kind of degrading assault to one's dignity?)

Kevin drops his voice into an Old Testament timbre: "ZOE. Look at me."

Her eyes have widened and are locked on her dad's, mesmerized. Rasputin would have been familiar with this look.

"You know the rules. If you don't like it, you don't have to eat any more. But you have to try it first."

Reasoning with a twenty-four-month old child—often attempted, rarely successful. I marvel at Kevin's optimism.

"One bite. Just one."

Softly, she answers, "Yah."

Zoe opens her mouth, and Kevin smiles faintly as he manoeuvres the morsel inside with his chopsticks. We all watch her face. Sometimes, when he does this, the chewing gives way to a wrinkly grimace. Today, the surprise that dawns on her face makes us all chuckle. A shared joke.

"Do you want more of that?" Kevin asks.

"Yah!" Zoe nods sturdily, as she holds out her plate.

The grudgelessness of babies never fails to astonish me.

But then it occurs to me that Zoe doesn't have a dignity to defend. She doesn't yet tell stories about herself, such as "I am a person who doesn't eat X," or "I make my own choices." She can't lose face because she is pre-face. In fact, what my brother-in-law is providing her is structure, a scaffold around which she can develop a sense of self, a set of rules about how to *zuoren* (做人)—how to behave (literally: how to be a person). And in the process, young Zoe is given the opportunity to try a range of foods without prejudice. As much as I admire this malleability, I am several decades past it. My own food stories are fairly entrenched.

Photograph courtesy of author.

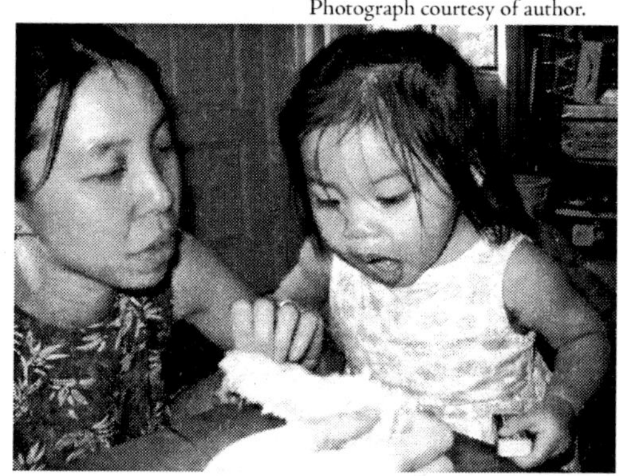

Zoe trying out—and apparently liking—corn, with my sister Lillian.

My mother also believed that her children should try every new food once, but we fought pitched battles over it. If a new dish appeared at the dinner table that instinct told us to avoid, we would steer clear of it—and hope that it would go unnoticed. Much depended on my mother's mood. Some nights, "Have you eaten this yet?" was phrased more as a suggestion. Other nights, she was less patient. If Mami specifically ordered me to try the liver (though it just as easily could have been oysters, or eggplant, or preserved eggs), and if I was dumb enough to balk, things moved quickly toward a standoff. This is the point in the Westerns when the bystanders start inching out of the saloon.

Mami set the rules of engagement. "You may not leave the table until you eat a piece of this." And with that, a sizeable chunk got plunked onto my plate. Any expressions of disgust from me would only harden my mother's position. I was slow to learn this.

Thirty minutes later, everybody else had finished eating. My sisters had tiptoed away from this tableau of pain (no gloating—tomorrow night it could be one of them).

"Are you going to eat it or not? Hurry up," Mami demanded.

"I don't want to!"

"You must eat it." She dumped the offending item into my rice bowl and took away the plate to be washed.

More time would pass. I continued the loneliest sit-in. The table had been cleared, the hot soapy smells of dishwashing filled the room, and the sounds of postprandial T.V.—oh, freedom!—leaked into the kitchen from the living room. And me, quietly weeping as Mami wiped down the table around my solitary bowl.

Finally, her language would shift. "I will not allow you to leave the table until you take one bite of it."

Sniveling as if physically ill, I lifted the liver (by now cold and congealed) to my lips and used my front teeth to tear off a tiny shred.

"Bigger than that," demanded Mami.

I sobbed harder as I complied. By that point, flavour or texture was irrelevant. After all that struggle, how could it be anything less than the most repulsive food on earth? And who could blame me for gagging as I swallowed that bite—and for honestly believing that my body itself was rejecting it?

A child makes submission palatable by seasoning it with passive aggression. A parent teaches respect for authority by setting rules and enforcing them. It was easy to forgive my mother, but I never forgave those foods.

II. Zongzi, San Francisco, 2003

When my friend Leon hears that my parents are planning to visit me for the weekend, he suggests that I take advantage of my mom's presence to get a hands-on tutorial in *zongzi*-wrapping. "Then, after she teaches you, you can teach me."

"Okay," I reply, "but it's going to be the straight-up *xianrou* (鲜肉) version. None of this Cantonese salty egg yolk nonsense." I'm a purist, and I make no apologies for it. Slow-braised fatty pork is virtually the mascot of Shanghainese cooking, and I have no patience for any other *zongzi* filling.

Leon holds up his hands to show he's not hiding anything. "Fine by me."

Like me, he has a dad who hails from the sweet Jiangnan (the Yangtze River Delta)—so he understands my strict *zongzi* minimalism. Also like me, he's a fan of "working mixers," where friends from different areas of your life merrily bond as they wrap raw ingredients side by side. He and I recently co-hosted a rousing dumpling-making party, and I think he is envisioning *zongzi* as the next logical step.

Mami is pleased to hear my request. I think we both remember her past attempts to teach me and my sisters how to wrap the rice dumplings. We were younger, our hands were clumsy and small, our squeamishness around drippy raw meat probably inevitable. Each of us would produce one, maybe two, gnarled leaf-packets. Mami would eye them dubiously, excuse us from continuing, and then finish up the entire lot (usually a couple dozen) on her own. This became our annual Duanwu Festival ritual. Did Mami untie our cramped, crumpled clutch purses and redo them from scratch? I can't remember ever eating any misshapen *zongzi*.

If you really want to learn, we'll start with the ingredients, she says. The day she arrives in San Francisco, we go grocery shopping in Oakland Chinatown. A bag of glutinous short-grain rice, a pound or so of pork belly (though nearly any cut that mixes lean and fat will suffice, apparently), cotton twine, and a stack of big crackly leaves, each one shaped like a bold vertical stroke of calligraphy. *You already have soy sauce and rice wine at home, right?* Mami asks me.

Photograph courtesy of author.

My mom, Julie, making zongzi.

I give her a look. Am I not my mother's daughter?

That night, we set the meat and the rice to steep in dark fragrant liquids. The leaves are revivified in a shallow water bath. The next afternoon, we stand at the sink, and she begins her instruction.

Curl the bottom of the hydrated leaf into a cone; cup it in one hand as you grab a handful of marinated rice with the other. Create a grainy bed for a jiggly chunk of flesh, and tuck it in with a pillow of fat.

Don't even think about leaving out the fat! Mami says. *I don't want to hear any "eeeuuuw, yucky" protests.* She is arguing with the younger version of me. Standing next to her, copying her movements, I have said nothing. The raw meat smells so sharply of the wine and soy sauce seeping from it.

Bury the meat under another scoop of rice grains, and then fold the top part of the leaf down sharply. Smooth back the flanking leaf "sleeveholes" like a straitjacket so that no grains can escape. Marinade will probably be dripping down your arm; pay it no mind. Without loosening your grip, layer another long leaf on top, fold over, pin snug, fold again and wrestle down the stem. Grab a length of twine and start binding.

Mami outpaces me two *zongzi* to one, and she can handle the string on her own, whereas I need an extra hand—but my creations do not embarrass me. Each one is a dense, satisfying handful: a squat prism with planed corners that run skew to each other, the drying leaves raspy and fibrous. It's clear that I have graduated from Zongzi University with a respectable GPA. Mami puts a big stockpot on the stove, packs the parcels in vertically, fills the pot with water. After it comes to a boil, she turns it down to the lowest possible heat and keeps it on a bare simmer overnight.

Since my parents have taken over my bedroom, I sleep on a futon in the dining room, adjacent to the kitchen. Over the course of the night, the flavoured steam of slow-cooked food fills the flat. It pushes its way into my dreams. *Zongzi* being cooked smell the way a Craftsman bungalow interior looks: hardwood floors and handcrafted cabinets that catch and hold autumnal sunlight. Warm and nutty. Cozy and honest.

Leon comes over the next morning for breakfast, all but rubbing his hands in anticipation. He greets my mom politely, then tells me, "I can't believe you breathed in that smell all night. I would have gone insane."

The plates clatter as I pull them out of the cupboard; we fish out a *zongzi* each from the boiler that has coddled them all night. At the table Leon and I both begin to disassemble the steaming green gift wrap, gingerly plucking at the taut damp string like kids playing cat's cradle. As the oiled leaves slide away from the dark rice body, the *zongzi* wobbles, then puddles on the plate.

"Uh, this usually doesn't happen," I said.

"It's like the cell walls have burst," Leon says, a little mystified.

We savoured every bite.

III. Breakfast in Shanghai

It is the autumn of 2003, and I am spending a few months in Shanghai with my parents. Our small apartment is located in the heart of Luwan district, which is home to trendy Huaihai Road as well as the historic *shikumen* rowhouses whose back lanes are havens for the old ways. Every day, Mami walks a couple of blocks to the outdoor produce stalls to buy vegetables, then goes next door to pick out a fish from the wet market. This is how she must have shopped in Hong Kong, and before that, in Taiwan: planning each day's meals while walking through the market.

Naturally, in her thirty years abroad, Mami had also mastered the art of North American grocery shopping. Every weekend of my childhood, my parents would pack me and my sisters into the station wagon, and we'd head off to Chinatown. While my mother shopped, Dad read the newspaper, and we three kids sat in the backseat of the car, singing and making up word games. Sometimes it would take an hour before we'd hear the knock on the rear door. That was our signal to pile out and help Mami transport a small flotilla of brown bags from the shopping cart into the back cargo area. Forty minutes later, when we pulled up in the driveway at home, the five of us ferried the bags into the kitchen, where Mami took another half hour to stash everything away in our two refrigerators. And later, there was the Costco infatuation that brought so many twelve-packs of croissants and ten-pound bags of tortilla chips into our lives.

Photograph courtesy of author.

My family enjoying ice cream in 1981. From left to right—my sister Jennifer, me, my sister Lillian, and my dad H.C.

Of course, Shanghai now has its hypermarkets and superstores as well. One in particular, Lotus Supercentre, has won Mami's loyalty with its free shuttle bus service. After a few visits, she urges me to accompany her. "Come with me," she says. "You should see this." While I'm no stranger to Chinese supermarkets, I am not prepared for the visual shock of entering the superstore's deli section, which is the size of a mall food court. In my family we like to tease each other with the phrase *xiangxiaren jincheng* (乡下人进城)—country folk entering the city—whenever one of us is momentarily fazed by new technology or some other striking development. And there, in the presence of Chinese foodstuff abundance, my inner yokel emerges. I stand slack-jawed at the multiplicity of seaweed, the panoply of pickled vegetables. Each station has its own uniformed attendant. The open freezers proffer big boxes of bulk frozen *jiaozi* (dumplings), *xiaolongbao* (small soup-filled dumplings), and *mantou* (steamed bread). To be able to mix and match from a selection of fifteen types of dumplings. . . . I pick up one of the cold white pebbles and stare at it for a while.

Sweets? Aisle upon aisle of bins are filled with every possible permutation of the flour-sugar-lard recipe. Some of these cookies and cakes are molded into flowers or animal shapes. Others emphasize content over form: brittle disks studded with sunflower seeds, crumbly cubes marbled with sweet bean paste, sturdy little drums blessed with sesame.

Over at the *bing* and *baozi* deli counter, the Chinese equivalent of a Western supermarket's bakery section, the pyramids of freshly steamed buns and deep-fried crullers and griddled pastries beckon. We ask the girl behind the counter to give us 500 grams of *dabing* (大饼). She pulls the stack of the flag-sized flatbread toward her, expertly cuts a multilayered wedge and tosses it on the scale. Sure enough, gravity exerts a neat half-kilo of force on this mess of pancake. The *dabing* girl smiles. She knows how good she is.

Is it not pleasant to partake of Lotus's air-conditioned door-to-door service? Indeed—but in all honesty, any commute is a hassle when we can buy food a few steps from our apartment's front gate. Every day, my parents wake up around 5:30 A.M. and head to the park for morning *qigong* exercises; on the way back, they buy breakfast in the neighbourhood alley. Sometimes, if I wake early enough, I join them. I love those smoky, dingy, scorchy, rusty back alleys, where all the surfaces look mended, and every object standing looks like it wants to sit down. Dough is rolled out on unlikely countertops—an old wooden writing desk with drawers, or perhaps a rickety Formica card table—a piece of furniture dragged out onto the street, then greased and floured. Woks seethe atop converted oil drums, and plastic basins and buckets stand by sullenly. Threadbare towels and rag mops are draped on the cement box sink. Red and blue tarp or streaky green corrugated siding serve as canopies. Above them, bamboo poles for laundry bristle from the *shikumen* windows. A silvery jangling, sweet but insistent, catches your ear. Your feet move instinctively to avoid the trike-trailer trundling by, laden with baskets of leeks. You look around and see tired white tile. You see bamboo steamers stained walnut by age and moisture.

Those are the exteriors. Now look inside. In the midst of all this grime, perfect *baozi* bloom—complexion creamy, moist as a baby's cheek. Next to them, glutinous rice *shaomai* sit askew on the woven mat like confused flower buds, sighing steam. A few feet away, salty radish-stuffed biscuits glisten loudly on the greased black proving ground of the griddle. One stall over, several dozen *shengjianbao* (pan-fried round dumplings) stippled with scallion and black sesame seeds, crustiness cracking where the juice has burst through, proclaim their solidarity: WE ARE LEGION.

Mami decides on what she wants, and I chime in. The treasures are plucked up, exchanged for coins so light they barely clink. We carry breakfast home in a thin polyethylene bag—a transparent sling pouch quickly rendered translucent by steam. The walk home is short, but in those few minutes, the crisp griddle cakes have started to turn damp and soft. Look inside.

Author's Note

As a recent immigrant to the city, I didn't realize at first that my fellow workshop participants were the community activists of Vancouver Chinatown. I might have met these folks eventually at some community event, but never like this—the intimacy of the workshop process made the connections much more meaningful. For them, the streets of Vancouver are as familiar as siblings—and I loved hearing them reminisce and gossip about how those family members have changed over the years.

Personally, I came to the workshop having already dabbled in food writing; trying to bring in family memories was the challenging part, because my strongest culinary memories were of meals I had cooked for myself or shared with friends. I was happy to acknowledge how extensively my food loyalties were shaped by the household in which I grew up, but I had never thought deeply about it. Because writing about family didn't come naturally to me, I figured that the discipline of "writing to the prompt" would be a valuable exercise. And discipline is what had drawn me to the workshop in the first place. I needed people to hold me accountable for writing.

The requirement of turning in weekly assignments worked. It confiscated all my excuses, one by one. On my own, I could occasionally trick myself into jotting down a few lines, but here, with deadlines looming, I quickly became reacquainted with the state of intense absorption that allows a prose piece to slowly take shape as the hours slip by. I also rediscovered the heady, ticklish anticipation of sharing a piece and hearing feedback. I realized that I wanted more of that feeling. I've been seeking out writing groups and partnerships so that I can continue the momentum.

Lilly Chow

Eating In, Eating Out: Five Decades of Food Memories

Betty Ho

"*Sut lay ee goo, Ma ma see goo*" (1950s)

I can still picture Dad. He combed his hair toward the back with short tuffs poking out at the sides, like a Chinese Dagwood of the 1950s comics. And he loved to cook and eat, which showed in his five-foot, six-inch stocky frame. All five of us inherited his flat pug nose, the ability to laugh at ourselves, and the appreciation for a good home-cooked meal.

Our family moved to a small corner store on Kingsway and Gladstone from our old store on Granville Street in Vancouver in 1952. My parents bought the store mainly for the living quarters in the back. My three sisters and I slept in a room so crowded that there was only a one-foot space between the double bed and bunk bed.

Dad didn't like us standing around while he cooked because of the lack of space. He told us, "*hahng hoy, hahng hoy*"—get out of the way. The kitchen, being in the back of our small store, measured about seven by six feet, with just enough space for a sink, stove, and small table. Cupboard space was minimal. I've always wondered how he managed to cook for the seven of us under such constraints.

Every trip from Chinatown brought us a feast of roast pork and fresh sole, later to be steamed with black beans and garlic. Our customers could always tell when it was suppertime because of the tantalizing aromas coming from the back of the store. We three older sisters alternated in serving customers while Mom and Dad took their breaks to have supper.

Dad liked to make a hotpot dish using arrowhead roots (*see goo*), braised pork riblets, shiitake mushrooms, and fried bean puffs (*doh foo*). *See goo* was a sign that spring would soon arrive. While preparing this dish, Dad sang, "*Sut lay ee goo, Ma ma see goo.*"

In early spring or anytime in January to March, I buy *see goo* to remind me of Dad and his little ditty. White steamed rice goes well with this dish to absorb the juices from the slow-simmered pork spareribs, cream-coloured *see goo*, brown shiitake mushrooms, yellow and white fried bean puffs, green onions and garlic. Each fried bean puff acts as a sponge, absorbing the gravy from the simmering hot pot.

If you're not sure what these arrowhead roots look like, imagine a white bulb with a short stem on the top end. I once heard that arrowheads symbolize the birth of little boys.

Simmered Springtime *See Goo* and Spareribs Hot Pot

1 lb pork spareribs, sweet and sour cut

2-3 garlic cloves

1 dozen *see goo* or arrowheads, peeled. Remove the hairy roots, slice each arrowhead into halves, or use the broad side of a chopping knife to smash them.

1 pkg Sunrise fried bean puffs, each puff cut into 3 pieces

5-6 shiitake mushrooms, soaked overnight, sliced into quarters

¼ brown sugar stick

1 green onion, chopped

1.) Braise spareribs and garlic in a Dutch oven at medium heat, then lower heat.

2.) Add 1½ cup of water, and simmer for 1 hour.

3.) Add sliced or smashed *see goo* to the pot, making sure there is enough liquid in the pot. Simmer for another hour.

4.) Half an hour before serving, add bean puffs, mushrooms, brown sugar stick. Stir all ingredients. Add chopped green onions, and serve.

Photograph courtesy of author.

Our wedding at the Marco Polo, April 22, 1960. From left to right—Pop, Art's sister Lucy, Art, me, my mother, my father.

Pop Tarts Time (1960s)

My father-in-law, Ho Kow, or Pop (as he was called by his sons), was ninety years old when he moved into our house in 1961, one year after Art and I got married. Art was the youngest son of eight boys and one girl. When Art's brother George and his family moved to Edmonton, we "inherited" Pop.

Pop wasn't very tall, only five feet, four inches. He seemed to shrink as time passed, becoming more and more bent as if the rain and sun over the years had eroded him away. With his long ear lobes and round benign countenance, he resembled a porcelain Buddha one could buy in Chinatown. The top of his head was shaped like a honeydew melon and was almost as shiny. Pop was a teacher in his village of Yen Ping in China, and in 1897, on a three-mast sailing ship, he immigrated to Canada by way of steerage.

As a second-generation Canadian Chinese who didn't know enough Chinese other than simple sentences, I couldn't carry on a meaningful conversation with him. However, I felt that he understood more than he had led me to believe, and that he knew everything that Art and I discussed around the kitchen table. He seldom displayed any temper, and he never interfered with the upbringing of our children, nor with how we handled our marriage.

Because Pop made his home with us, we became the centre of the Ho family get-togethers whenever any of the out-of-town brothers came to visit. After dinner, Art and his brothers liked to sit around the television to watch the B.C. Lions football team and yell at the players if they fumbled the ball. During the game, Pop would just sit quietly nodding, half sleeping in his chair, sometimes smiling as if he were thinking of himself in another time and place. Perhaps he reminisced of himself as the young immigrant who had raised nine children during the Great Depression and two World Wars.

He often sat at the kitchen table with his arms crossed to "supervise" me, teaching me how to cook his favourite foods. Under his direction, I, as a young bride and novice cook, learned how to simmer winter melon soup and make *yook beng* (steamed minced pork) and steamed lemon chicken. But before cooking these dishes, he, my three-year-old daughter Betsy, and I needed to buy the ingredients. We'd make the trek to all the fruit, vegetable, and meat stores located on the 200 block of Pender Street in Chinatown.

Our first stop was to the Dollar Meat store, where a whole roasted pig hung with its legs resting on bars and its snout facing a drip pan. "Cut me one of those ribs," Pop would say. As the woman sliced away at a chunk of pork, she would hand over a bite-sized piece of *cha-suey* (barbecued pork) to Betsy.

Next, we would walk to Yuen Fong for a piece of dusty light-green winter melon. We'd pick out a package of Farmer's brand dried turnip (*choong choy*), a bag of shiitake mushrooms, and a couple of fresh ginger roots. Jaywalking across Pender Street, I'd hold Betsy's hand in my right hand and Pop's arm with my left. We'd head for Fong Lee, the butcher who sold flank beef and T-bone steaks cut to order, then to Lun Chong, the chicken store where fresh-killed chickens were sold with heads and feet intact. At each one of these shops, the owners greeted Pop as if he were an old friend and commented on the weather.

One last stop before heading home was the Hong Kong Café, east of Main Street, where Victor Lum and his bakers made the best apple tarts, loaded with gooey apple slices, with the thin pastry encrusted with sugar. The timing had to be crucial because the apple tarts came out freshly baked around 2:00 P.M. If we arrived any later, we couldn't buy any tarts until much later in the afternoon.

When we returned home, I'd pour a glass of milk for Betsy, make a pot of tea for me and Pop, and lay out apple tarts for the three of us. Dinnertime would still be three hours away, so we'd have enough time for an afternoon tea break and for watching the Mouseketeers. It was a great time for three generations to enjoy the treats of Chinatown.

During the quietest time at night, on June 18, 1968, Pop died in his sleep at home, at the age of ninety-six. I was at his bedside when he died.

Photographs courtesy of author.

My niece Judy, my son Arnie, Pop, and Betsy, c. 1965.

A New Year's Eve celebration with Art, Betsy, and Pop.

Reasons to Celebrate (1977)

February 10, 1977 started out as an ordinary, uneventful day. Mr. Groundhog had already appeared in the newspapers, announcing yet another six weeks of winter. My husband, Art, had the day off before working his weekend shift at Eaton's department store, and he mentioned wanting to prune the apple tree that day. Suddenly, for some inexplicable reason, I felt that I had to come home before my shift ended at the private medical laboratory.

"Where's Dad?" I asked Arnie, our thirteen-year-old son, when I got home.

"He was pruning the apple tree, but he's gone to bed now."

That's strange for him to want a nap in the middle of the afternoon, I thought. I went to our bedroom and looked at Art. He seemed dazed and distant. He spoke as if he didn't understand what I was saying to him.

"What happened, dear?" I asked.

"I'm tired, I've got a lousy headache."

"You don't look well." I noticed an abrasion on the back of his head. "Where did you get this bump?"

Art mumbled something about falling, went to the bathroom, and threw up.

After cooking rice and stir-frying some beef and broccoli for Arnie and Betsy, I checked on Art a few more times. Disturbed, I phoned his doctor.

"Dr. Patterson? I'm calling in regard to my husband, Art. He fell from a tree. I don't like the way he's acting loopy. He has these black rings under his eyes, like a raccoon."

Dr. Patterson told me to get Art out of bed. "Don't let him fall asleep. He may have had a concussion. I'll call an ambulance to take him to St. Paul's hospital. I'll meet you in emergency."

Dr. Fairholm, a neurosurgeon, examined Art, taking several x-rays of his skull. He found a fracture on the left side. He also tried to get Art to describe what had happened to him, but all he got was only "yes" or "no" to his questions. Around 12:30 A.M., I was told to go home and get some rest.

Needless to say, I could not sleep. I eventually took some comfort from reading several passages from the Bible. Whether I had eyestrain from the small print or I was emotionally drained, I dozed off. Around 5:30 A.M. I got up to phone the hospital for news about Art. I spoke to a nurse in the post-anaesthetic room who put Dr. Fairholm on the phone: "Mrs. Ho, we were able to remove a clot from your husband's left skull, but we've found another clot in his brain. Your husband will be on the respirator for three to five days to allow the swelling in his brain to go down. This period is most crucial. After this time, we'll re-assess the situation."

I felt rather numb at hearing this news. I waited until 8:00 A.M. before phoning my supervisor to tell him about Art's surgery, that I couldn't come in to work, and to not expect me for a while. I got Betsy and Arnie up for school. I made them breakfast, then started to vacuum the hallway, living room, do laundry, but all the time, waiting for the phone to ring. I phoned Eaton's to let Art's staff know what was happening and that there were complications. Every time the phone rang, I jumped, expecting the worst, yet hoping for good news.

Much later, or so it seemed, a nurse phoned to say that Art would be moved to the intensive care unit and that I could visit him that afternoon. I barely recognized him with his hair all shaved and head partially bandaged, eyes closed as if the light hurt. He was hooked up to all those machines—heart monitor, pumps, three IV's. He was not able to speak for almost a week, and he didn't seem to be aware of what happened. But later, like the neat and tidy person he is, his hands started smoothing the bed sheets, and he was constantly wiping his mouth when eating, occasionally trying to take off his IV tubing. During the days that followed with him in the hospital, the demonstration of love and compassion by families and friends covered Betsy, Arnie, and me like a warm blanket. Chicken soup, sweet and sour spareribs, salmon, beans and beef, and rice were some of the food our families and friends brought to comfort and feed us at home.

Eventually, we discovered that Art had two congenital aneurysms, excessive localized enlargements of arteries, and that he had suffered an arachnoid hemorrhage which accounted for his swollen black eyes. His fall from the tree while pruning had likely precipitated a breakage much like popping of a blown-up balloon. For us, the spring of 1977 began when Art finally came home after fifty-one traumatic days, having survived two brain surgeries.

◈ ◈ ◈

I wondered if the eight-pound prime rib and the five pounds of chicken thighs and drums would be enough to feed the eleven of us: Bob and Louise, Roger and Bobbi, Tom and Janet, Mom, Betsy, Arnie, Art and myself. I also made a three-beans bake the day before.

"Mom, let me peel the carrots, potatoes, and zucchini. We're learning how to do vegetables in cooking class," Betsy said.

"Sure. Arnie, please help me with the extensions for the table, then set it for eleven people. No kids are coming, so we can all sit together. Art, will you bring up some extra chairs from the basement?"

"Why? What are we celebrating?"

"We're celebrating your complete recovery with a few friends. Later on, we'll invite both sides of the family for dinner at a restaurant to thank them for everything."

Art said, shaking his head, "I still really don't remember what happened. But I'm glad to be home and to see our friends."

That dinner was the first of many celebrations for 1977, building on lessons taught by my parents that family and friends take care of each other, and that food was one of the most important ways to do it.

Photograph courtesy of author.

Celebrating Art's recovery—Art, Betsy, me, Arnie.

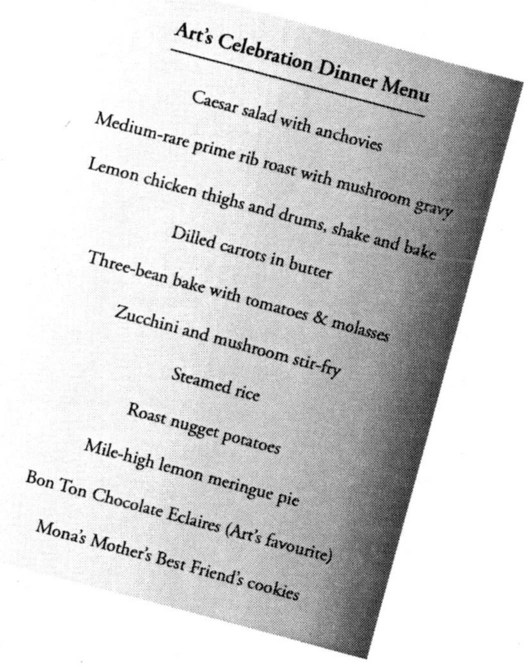

Art's Celebration Dinner Menu

Caesar salad with anchovies
Medium-rare prime rib roast with mushroom gravy
Lemon chicken thighs and drums, shake and bake
Dilled carrots in butter
Three-bean bake with tomatoes & molasses
Zucchini and mushroom stir-fry
Steamed rice
Roast nugget potatoes
Mile-high lemon meringue pie
Bon Ton Chocolate Eclaires (Art's favourite)
Mona's Mother's Best Friend's cookies

Only 89! (2006)

A magnet stuck on Mom's apartment fridge declares, "The kitchen stays a lot cleaner if you just eat out all the time." This partly explains why our family gatherings for the last thirty-seven years took place mostly in restaurants. Dad was the cook in our family with Mom always handling the business end of their lifelong partnership, whether it was a grocery store, a café, or eventually a small walkup apartment building. By the time Dad passed away in 1970, we had all married and were busy working and raising our own families. She found managing and cleaning a three-storey apartment block too much to handle by herself, so she moved into a secured strata apartment.

Another item worthy of attention in Mom's kitchen is her social calendar, usually marked up for lunches with friends or family at the White Spot on Broadway and Larch or at the Dutch Pannekoek House on South Granville where she is greeted as a regular customer. She also jots the dates down on the calendar when we're scheduled to visit her.

Even on her tiptoes, Mom barely measures four feet, ten inches. Her petite frame belies her spunky nature, especially when she worked as security for Sears (ladies' wear), helping to catch shoplifters, or when she was an extra in the occasional locally made movie. Her grown grandchildren get a kick out of hugging her and lifting her off the floor as high as they can.

She coordinates what she wears so stylishly that her married granddaughters want to borrow her clothes. The only thing is, they have to like her lime green, brown, burnt orange, or black clothes. No purple or red hats for this lady!

In 1945, she taught herself how to drive her first car—a used 1932 Ford—then a couple years later, taught Dad how to drive. She told me, "I just asked the car salesman to show me how the car works before I would buy it. Then I drove him and me back to the store on Granville street. I noticed by the time we got back, he had loosened his tie and had sweaty palms." In 2008 she hopes to receive a BC Auto Association certificate for her sixty years as a primary member. She was elated when she was able to renew her license so she could drive her Honda Accord at age eighty-eight.

This matriarch can claim an extended family that includes twenty-five grandchildren and twenty-four great-grandchildren. She's the glue that holds us all together.

At Mom's eighty-ninth birthday dinner, held in October 2006 at Sun Sui Wah on Main Street, there were three tables of just the Vancouver families. To keep things simple, we ordered the $268 set menu consisting of fresh fruit prawn salad, shredded conpoy or fish maw in chicken soup, taro seafood basket with vegetables, sautéed Dungeness crabs in supreme stock sauce, sautéed squids and scallop with vegetables, crispy skin chicken, deep-fried honey garlic pork chop, deep-fried sole fillet with sweet and sour sauce, pan-fried rice with shrimp and barbecued pork.

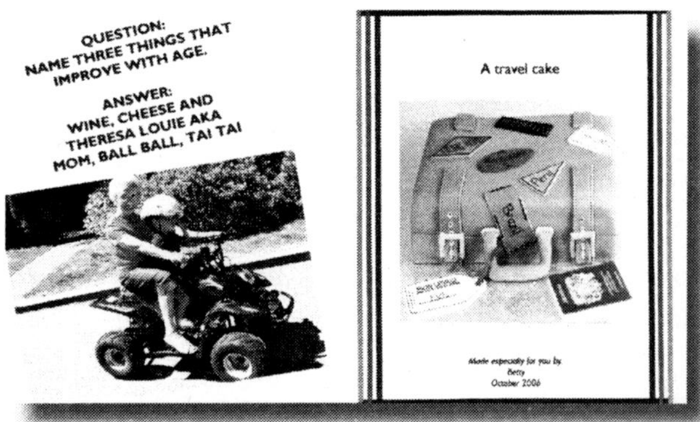

The invitation I made for my mother's 89th birthday party. Here she is, on an adventure with Nevin, one of her great-grandchildren.

Art exclaimed, "Good, there's fish maw soup on the menu!"

All of us love the little bits of fish maw, its white spongy texture with a slight fishy smell to it. There's a chewy yet slippery feel to it as it slides down your throat, softer than jellyfish, like edible sponges with a chicken flavour.

We asked for mango pudding for the dessert portion of the set menu and brought a Bon Ton Diplomat cake to celebrate Mom's birthday. A Bon Ton cake is a decadently rum-soaked sponge cake, twice layered with crisp flaky pastry sheets, topped with velvety butter cream icing and decorated with butter cream roses. One could put on five pounds just looking at it, but special occasions require a special dessert.

Art said, "I see your two sisters finally made it here!"

"Holly had to pick up Janny from the airport. She managed to get a flight out from Calgary at the last minute," I explained.

Deanna yelled, "Hey! Here come Uncle Nick and Tai Tai up the stairs!"

We all shouted, "Surprise! Mom! Ball Ball! Tai Tai!" Everyone surprised Mom, calling out the names she's known by (Grandma and Great-grandma).

Mom laughed, "Betty and Art, you should have told me this wasn't just family! I could have gone to have my hair done and dressed up a bit more! Arlene, Elaine, why didn't you tell me about this when I picked you up for lunch?"

"Thanks, everyone, for keeping it mum!" I told the crowd.

My sister Janny said, "Mom, we're taking you on a one-day mystery trip tomorrow. I've got it all arranged. Bring your passport. Think slot machines!"

Typical Chinese restaurants are noisy with laughter, loud conversations, and the clanging of dishes, and this one was no exception. When the squid and scallops were served, most of us already felt stuffed, so we asked for take-out boxes for the rest of the meal. However, we did manage to scarf down the Bon Ton cake. A good tip was mandatory to appease the restaurant staff for the mess we left behind. Mom was right—"our kitchens stay a lot cleaner if we all eat out"—and besides, leftovers taste better the next day.

Standing—my brother Nick, my sister Jan, me, and my sister Holly. Seated—Art and Mom.

Mom and her birthday cake!

Tai Tai and her grandchildren and great-grandchildren.

Photographs courtesy of author.

Author's Note

When my husband Art had his first Ho family reunion in 1992, and when I had my first Louie reunion in 2002, thoughts of writing about our respective families began re-surfacing. Taking this workshop is a continuation of my writing goals to tell personal narratives and stories. I believe writing is a natural progression from my passion for eclectic reading material and lifelong course studies. I am working toward a Bachelor in General Studies (BGS) degree as a mature student at Simon Fraser University.

The stories I wrote about Art, my parents, and my father-in-law (Pop) reflect important life lessons about family relationships, responsibilities, and memories of food and celebration. Art offers encouragement; Dad taught me a catchy little poem, his pleasure for cooking, and responsibilities for family; my father-in-law showed me how to shop for vegetables, fish, and meat and to be content; and Mom provides financial advice, and a zest for life and travel.

Art and I have been married for almost forty-seven years. Both Art and I are second-generation Canadian Chinese, born and raised Vancouverites. We have one daughter, Betsy, who blessed us with two grandchildren (Kendall and Deanna), and one son, Arnold, who teaches ESL in Hong Kong. I want to leave my family and extended families with favourite recipes and stories about us and the community around us. Carol Shields's *Stones* has been an inspiration to me; her novel is about an ordinary person living through extraordinary times, such as we all do today.

Thanks to the workshop for all the encouragement and camaraderie!

Betty Ho

Season to Taste

George Jung

Steamy Sunday

It was Sunday afternoon, and nothing was stopping us from reaching Elsie's place—not even nature's constant pelting of raindrops the size of grapes! Our arms were laden down with wet plastic grocery bags, and we didn't have a single spare arm to hold an umbrella.

Cynthia, her husband Daniel, his mom Mrs. Lee, and I had become friends during the past eighteen months as volunteers at various head tax redress events in Vancouver. We helped elderly Chinese widows compile information about their deceased husbands who had to pay a head tax to enter Canada between 1855 and 1923. Most of these seniors were in their eighties and nineties; a few were 100 years old, give or take a couple of years. Some spoke English, but most never had any formal education and are illiterate in any language.

Elsie's a ninety-three-year-old widow whose husband had paid the head tax. Her daughter Rosie and I had chatted many times by telephone. She said, "It's so difficult to track down family records. Mom never believed there would be any redress, and Dad's papers, including his head tax certificate, were destroyed during her successive rounds of downsizing."

Rosie didn't have much spare time after taking care of her family. Rosie's son, Brian, who just completed college, agreed to research his grandfather's arrival in Canada. I coached Brian: "Try searching the government's General Register of Chinese Immigration microfiche collection at the Vancouver central library."

Although it must have felt very much like searching for a needle in a haystack, Brian persevered and was eventually successful. Brian said, "I figured that Grandpa Jang Sun Foon must have arrived as a teenager and narrowed the search to certain years."

In the spring, Rosie confided in Cynthia that Elsie had been diagnosed with cancer. Because Elsie was advanced in age, no treatment would be taken. A few months later, Cynthia learned that Rosie had also been diagnosed with cancer. Just after the lunar new year, Rosie was slowly regaining her appetite and taste buds after chemo. She telephoned Cynthia and said, "I'm up to having visitors again. Can Daniel's mom show us how to make some of our favourite childhood Chinese snacks?" Daniel's mom, Mrs. Lee, offered to teach Rosie how to make a pork version of shrimp dumplings (*har gow*).

Photograph courtesy of Daniel Lee.

Mrs. Lee, Cynthia, and Elsie.

We unloaded the groceries onto the counter. Mrs. Lee poured a bag of wheat starch flour into a large mixing bowl and asked for boiling water. Mrs. Lee didn't bother measuring the hot water. We guessed it must have been four to five cups that she poured. As Mrs. Lee poured water into the bowl to cook the flour, she used a pair of chopsticks to stir the mixture. Gradually, the light flour was transformed in gooey clumps of cooked dough.

Mrs. Lee dusted the tabletop with tapioca flour and emptied the bowl of dough onto the tabletop. She squeezed a cup of pre-cooked tapioca paste into the dough. It was the secret ingredient that would lend more elasticity. She greased her palms with corn oil and proceeded to knead the dough for ten minutes. We marveled at how hot the dough must have felt. Then I remarked about the exfoliating properties of the dough that Mrs. Lee was kneading. Rosie and Cynthia giggled. Elsie watched all of us and joined in the giggling.

Mrs. Lee divided the dough into four pieces and formed them into four rolls. Then she divided each roll into lumps the size of golf balls. Using a homemade wooden press, Cynthia made small disks. Handing a piece to Rosie, I said, "Make four small pleats, then cradle the disk in your left palm and use your fingers to fold the four pleats into a miniature pocket. Then fill it with a spoonful of filling. Fold down the top flap and press both edges together to form a plump purse."

Some hands had more thumbs than fingers. Some dumplings were more shapely than others. Rosie was a good sport and persevered. Cynthia grimaced and scrunched up her piece of dough. Everyone soon mastered the pleating technique. Rosie's daughter Kori even tried her hands at forming a few pockets. With their hands firmly in their pockets, Brian and his father Barry declined on trying the pleating process. Daniel clutched his camera and avoided the dough. We learned that dough from one pound of wheat starch is enough to make about fifty dumpling skins!

We took turns arranging the pouches on a greased aluminum pie plate. Each dumpling was carefully spaced so that they would not stick together during the steaming.

The ladies cleared and wiped the table, and laid out eight plates and forks. Everyone was ready to feast. An extra place setting had been included for Elsie's youngest sister, Alice, who arrived stylishly late. As if on cue, she entered the kitchen just in time to see the freshly steamed dumplings being placed in the centre of the table. Each dumpling resembled a tiny purse in a shimmering translucent skin with a pearly grey tinge. We all agreed that our homemade dumplings were tastier, chewier, and larger than commercially made ones, which had creamy opaque skins. And because of the magic tapioca ingredient, none of the pouches had broken apart during steaming and now when all of us were picking them up from the tray.

Photograph courtesy of Daniel Lee.

Elsie.

Mrs. Lee also served Chinese sausages and radish cakes, which she had steamed earlier at home. Each square had the texture of pudding. She also brought homemade brown sugar sponge cakes. The table was laden with an old-fashioned feast.

Everyone was soon reminiscing about childhood days and about their favourite childhood treats. Rosie recalled deep-fried peanut and sugar crescents, which were made during Chinese New Year.

Rosie said, "I'm absolutely stuffed with *har gow* now! I'm sure I'll attempt to make them in the future, but I'll just enjoy them now while I can."

After gorging ourselves on savoury treats, our minds turned to Western-style desserts. We recalled the joys of eating Boston cream pies, which we had all enjoyed as teenagers. "I don't recall having any chocolate on the Boston cream pie—just lots of yummy whipped cream that actually taste like the real thing, unlike the stuff you get nowadays," Rosie said. Unfortunately, no one had a recipe.

Later, Rosie said to me, "If you can duplicate the delicious Boston cream pie like the ones they had at the Hong Kong Café, you are welcome in my house forever." I vowed to search my father's notes for a recipe, to bring to life more tastes of old.

❖ ❖ ❖

Pork *Har Gow* Dumplings

1 lb ground lean pork

1 cup minced water chestnuts

1 cup chopped Chinese sausage

½ cup minced Chinese mushrooms (optional)

1 tsp salt

¼ cup plucked fresh Asian coriander leaves

1 stalk green onion, thinly sliced

1 lb wheat starch flour

4-5 cups boiling water

½ pkg tapioca flour (for dusting of the table surface, and to make tapioca paste)

½ cup pre-mixed tapioca paste (tapioca flour mixed with cold water)

¼ cup corn oil

1.) To make the filling, stir-fry pork, water chestnuts, sausage, mushrooms, and salt. Let cool, then mix in fresh uncooked coriander leaves and thinly sliced green onions. Set filling aside.

2.) Put wheat starch flour in large mixing bowl. Add in pre-mixed tapioca paste. Slowly pour boiling water into the bowl while mixing. Continue mixing flour and water until you get a thick clump of cooked dough.

3.) Mix into the dough. Knead the dough until all the ingredients are evenly mixed.

4.) Divide the dough into four pieces and form them into four rolls. Then divide each roll into golf ball-sized balls. Flatten the balls into small disks.

5.) Holding the disk in the palm of your hand, make four pleats. Place a teaspoon of filling into the centre of the disk, then fold up the pleats to create a pouch.

6.) Lightly grease an aluminum pie pan with corn oil. Place each dumpling in the pan, carefully spacing them out so that they don't stick together while cooking.

7.) Place the pie pan in a Dutch oven or other large covered pot with water covering the bottom. Use a metal rack to place the pie pan in the pot for steaming. Steam for ten minutes, or until dumplings are cooked through.

Cake Walk—A Recipe Hunt

I was on a mission. I was on the hunt. Perhaps I would be lucky.

I dug into the bottom drawer of the chest that stood in the corner beside my mom's bed. That's where Dad's family papers were stored.

I set aside a framed sepia-toned picture of my grandmother with Mom and Dad as young parents. It must have been taken a few years after my brother Daniel had been born in 1937. Despite the civil war in China, the invasion by Japanese troops, and famine and starvation throughout the land, my father had not been able to bring his loved ones to the safety of Canada because of the exclusion act.

I flipped through a small stack of old restaurant menus. Some were stained, others were in pristine condition. These must have been the restaurants where Dad had worked. Most of the menus were from cafés along Granville Street where many movie theatres once thrived. Judging from the prices, these menus must have been from the 1950s and the 1960s. Apple pie cost less than Boston cream pie, which was between 20 cents and 35 cents.

Only a few menus showed a listing for Boston cream pie. I recalled having seen those cakes topped with freshly whipped cream in the New Moon Café, which Dad operated on Powell Street.

I scanned a small black booklet. It contained all sorts of information, some written in English, some in Chinese—all in his own handwriting. I even found an entry which indicated that Dad had paid the $500 head tax in 1913 when he arrived in Canada as a teenager. The certificate number, his name as it was transliterated (Jang Gan Hen) by an immigration official, the year, and the ship, the *Empress of Japan*. It was all there in black and white. And to think that I had spent two hours scanning the microfiche collection at the library.

I flipped quickly through a larger black booklet in which he had neatly printed various recipes. The thick ink indicated that he must have used a traditional Chinese brush that had been dipped into black ink.

No such luck. The elusive Boston Cream Pie recipe was not to be found.

Image courtesy of author.

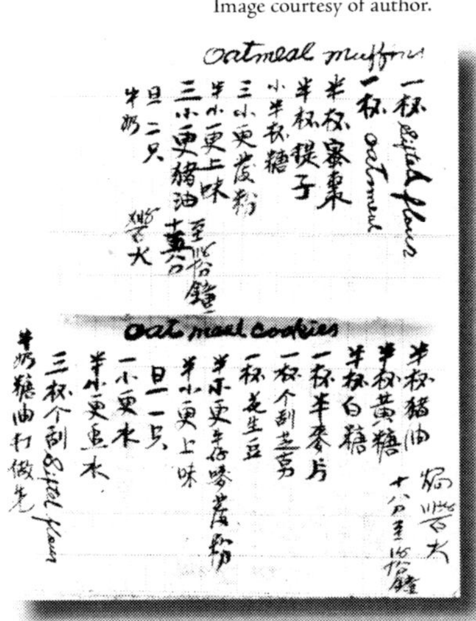

Oatmeal muffins

Oat meal cookies

A page from my father's notebook.

Applesauce

Through our head tax volunteer work, Cynthia, Daniel, and I had become acquainted with Mrs. Quon Chung Shee Der, a 102-year-old widow. She was a charming lady, who shuffled slowly on a four-wheeled walker. She was soft spoken, had sparkling eyes, and her mind was lucid for someone who was more than a century old.

On a rainy November day in 2005, Mrs. Der climbed two steep flights of stairs at the Quan Lung Sai Tong Society building in Chinatown with the assistance of two volunteers. As she was about to reach the peak of the incline, she called out, clear as a bell, "Where is the money, the refund for the head tax that my husband paid?" Everyone remarked on the clarity of her words.

After having won the thirty-ninth general election, the new prime minister requested a private meeting with living head tax payers and widows of deceased head tax payers. He wanted to hear for himself the needs and concerns of these seniors. His parliamentary secretary had been impressed by the seniors' stories, including Mrs. Der's remarks during an earlier meeting in Vancouver.

Mrs. Der said to Mr. Kenney, "Many persons have asked me about the secret of longevity. Would you like to know too?" With a sparkle in her eyes, she looked at him and said, "My husband paid the head tax, and I am determined to live long enough to see a just redress. I want to eat it, to have a taste of it, before I die." Mr. Kenney told her that he hoped the government would do the right thing and that she would have a long life.

Mrs. Der was seated next to the prime minister during his meeting with head tax seniors at the Strathcona Community Centre. Mrs. Der said to him, "Look at my arm. I cannot lift it because I've injured my shoulder. Despite my poor health, I came to the meeting today."

Photograph courtesy of Gabriel Yiu.

Mrs. Der, me, and Prime Minister Stephen Harper during his visit to the Strathcona Community Centre.

In the autumn Mrs. Der's strength failed her. She had fallen several times while doing her daily regime of leg exercises. Cynthia often visited her in hospital. After much coaxing Mrs. Der would, without dentures, savour a few spoonfuls of applesauce that had a smooth texture and a pleasing balance of sweetness with just a hint of sourness. She enjoyed the coolness of the applesauce. She also liked clamping down on peach jello, sometimes orange jello with tiny slices of canned mandarin oranges. These were some of her favourite treats.

On March 16, 2007, Mrs. Der died of pneumonia. She didn't live long enough to eat with satisfaction, to have a long-awaited taste of justice. What would she have treated herself to? What favourite treats would she have shared with her eighty-four-year-old daughter and her middle-aged grandsons? Although she had applied for an *ex gratia* payment which the Canadian government offered to living spouses of deceased head tax payers, the symbolic payment process had been implemented much too slowly. With justice served and her husband's money refunded, would Mrs. Der have discovered treats that might have become new favourites?

Staple on My Mind

I've just returned from Ottawa. It's eight o'clock, and all that my weary bones can feel is the numbing coldness of winter. The black ice during the evening commute was frightful. My entire face was frozen during the trek home. The driveway still needs shovelling.

Oh, how I crave for a bowl of slowly simmered soup that my mom used to serve with every meal. The steaming warmth from the soup would work wonders to melt away the stressful knots in my stomach, in my shoulders, all over.

Just one spoonful of her papaya peanut soup. The layers of flavours are as complex as those of my favourite single malt scotch. The tingling spiciness of ginger. The hint of orange peel. The crispy almond halves, the mushiness of boiled peanuts. The surge of juicy chunks of sweet papaya. The first mouthful is always the best.

May's Winter Soup

Photograph courtesy of author.

Winter 1958—my sister May, Jane, Grandpa Wong Kwai Jew, Ernie, Dennis, May's husband Gordon.

Gordon's words of protest hung in the air. "If no one in the family wants to organize dinner for Chinese New Year, then do what you will. I will simply make do with a sandwich and a tin of soup."

It was 2006—the year of the dog—and it was a dog of a year for Gordon. It was a trying time for him and his children. He said, "I'm weary of cooking by myself and eating alone." He longed for the comfort of a traditional home-cooked dinner with his family.

The day after Mother's Day in 2006, my sister May and her husband Gordon were shopping in Chinatown and were returning to their City Gate condominium by a different route. They stood waiting for a traffic light to change at Keefer and Gore in Chinatown. A young man jaywalked and shoved his way onto the street corner. Gordon watched as my sister was thrown aside and onto the roadway. He chased after the man, as May lay on the asphalt. She was hospitalized for fractures to the wrist and thigh bones.

For eight months, Gordon shopped for fresh meat and vegetables every morning. He cooked May's favourite foods, then he ate lunch by himself. Come rain or shine, he traveled by bus every afternoon to the hospital to bring dinner to May. He wanted to spare her the tastelessness of Uncle Ben's rice. Every evening, he watched as May ate the food and drank the soup he prepared for her. On those days when May lacked an appetite, he hid his disappointment. Instead, he diverted her attention by chatting about happier days. He wracked his memory trying to remember her other favourite meals which he could cook later in the week.

On Christmas Day we ate dinner at the hospice. While May and Gordon's children, Kathy and Barry, were getting take-out food, May's breathing became more laboured, and the doctor put her on oxygen. May gasped for her last breath of air. We stood still, hoping and willing that May would stop gasping for air like a fish out of water. We continued to stand and wait silently. May stopped struggling and seemed to be asleep. Individually, we took note, and yet no one spoke. We waited for Kathy and Barry to return with dinner.

Gordon went to get a cup of tea. His son Ernie followed. Eventually, Kathy and Barry returned with Chinese noodles. While the others ate dinner, I sat with my sister, waiting and watching guard. A nurse passed by, and I asked her, "Can you check my sister's pulse?" Soon, other nurses joined the first nurse to assist her in using several methods to check for a pulse, which they could not detect.

Gordon and the children reassembled in May's room to hear the nurses confirm the unmentionable. May had indeed made a graceful exit and was finally at rest. And the family was beside her.

I slipped out of the room to have my dinner. I told Gordon that the rest of the kids where on their way: "Dennis and Jane are already driving over here, and the roads are wet. Let's not distract them with a telephone call." He nodded in agreement. Soon enough, they were able to say goodbye to their mom.

A week later, on the first day of the new calendar year, January 1, Gordon and the family gathered to share a hot pot dinner at home. The meal fed the body but not the soul. It didn't seem to hit the spot for Gordon.

A few weeks later, Gordon said that during the lunar new year's eve dinner, one should be surrounded by children and grandchildren—at home and not in a restaurant. He wanted to savour traditional dishes synonymous with luck and prosperity. Chicken and fish—complete with heads, feet, and tail fins—symbolize plenty from start to finish. Dried oysters (*hao see*) braised with strands of hair-like lichen (*fat choy*) and napa cabbage (*sui choy*)—their names are homophones for a thriving business and longevity. For the new year, he wanted to push away sadder memories of cooking dinner alone for his wife.

"It's really important to him," I said to my nieces and nephews. "Can you rearrange your schedule to have dinner with your dad?" Most agreed to come to this gathering, and a new menu quickly fell into place. Some said they would come with pre-made dishes, others promised to arrive early to help cook.

I went to Gordon's house the following morning and pressed the buzzer. "I'm downstairs. Are you ready?" We walked toward Chinatown. We planned on an early start to avoid being swamped by battalions of grannies on a mission. They might appear petite, but their sharp elbows are lethal. Soon enough, each and every granny would have elbowed her way to the front of the long queues at barbecue meat shops.

During lunch, Gordon and I witnessed these scrimmages firsthand from the safety of ringside seats at Hon's restaurant. We watched as we ate. I said, "Look, three freshly roasted suckling pigs have already been sold in less than one hour." Like sandbags, one- and two-pound bundles of roasted pork were carried out by grey-haired grannies.

With our bellies full of noodles, wontons, and brisket, we reluctantly joined the fray. We secured our bundles of roasted pig and continued in our search for frozen prawns, pork loin and bones, and ginger root. After we secured our groceries, we trundled toward home. The winter melon soup had yet to be started and required four long hours of simmering.

Back at the condo, we headed toward the kitchen. Gordon said, "It's time to start the soup. I've already prepared most of the ingredients this morning."

Gordon reached into the cupboard for a pot. He filled it halfway with water and placed it on the stove, turning the knob to high heat. He turned his attention to the ginger, which he crushed with the side of his cleaver. Then he dumped the ginger into the pot of boiling water.

He reached for a second pot. He explained, "The pork should be blanched separately to avoid transferring any fatty scum to the main soup pot." He boiled water in the second pot and placed the pork loin into it. After it quickly turned grey, he transferred the pork to the main pot. He repeated the process with the pork bones.

Gordon prepped the winter melon and dried scallops and added them to the soup, along with the red beans, almonds, and tangerine peel. He looked distantly into the pot while stirring, as if the aromas from the soup were prompting memories of May.

I had never seen Gordon making soup before. I've often seen him making tea. More recently, I've seen him preparing rice and stir-frying vegetables. But never soup. Soups had always been made by May.

As I watched Gordon, I sensed that cooking together would be therapeutic for both of us. A time to reconnect—to both the past and the present.

George Jung

Winter Melon Soup

2 whole dried scallops

2 leaves of dried tangerine skin

2 Tbsp dried almonds, "north" and "south" types

1 Tbsp red adzuki beans

2-inch knob of ginger, peeled and crushed

2 lbs pork loin, cut into 4-inch chunks

2 lbs pork bones, pre-cut by butcher

2 lbs winter melon, washed, de-seeded and chopped into 2-inch wedges

1.) Soak dried scallops, tangerine skin, dried almonds, and red adzuki beans in separate bowls until plump, 3-4 hours. Drain and set aside.

2.) Fill a large stockpot halfway with water and bring to a boil. Add ginger to boiling water.

3.) In another stockpot, boil water and add pork loin to blanch it. When the pork turns grey, remove it from the pot and transfer it to the main stockpot. Repeat the process for pork bones. Discard water from the blanching process.

4.) Add winter melon to stockpot.

5.) Flatten dried scallops between your fingers. The scallops will separate into strands. Add them to the stockpot.

6.) Add red beans and almonds to the pot.

7.) Scrape the white matter from the tangerine peel. Add the cleaned peel to the stockpot.

8.) Reduce heat and simmer for two to three hours. Salt to taste.

Author's Note

This writing workshop was not easy. It demanded plenty of focus and discipline. I found that forcing the first word to appear and remain on the page was the most difficult step. Where to begin? Which thought to capture? What to say? My mind would freeze. In anticipation of this, our workshop leader had provided a series of weekly assignments that contained an essential array of techniques to pry open our imaginations and to help us explore, develop and hone our thoughts.

The workshop also demanded time management and planning. A solitary page required lots of my time that often stretched way beyond the last of the evening news. Despite coaching from our workshop leader—"You can always try getting up earlier in the morning and do some writing before you go to the office"—I fell into the habit of reworking tired strings of words until that rooster had already crowed ever so faintly in the fog of my sleep, being hunched over a keyboard.

Seeking recipes by telephone was surprisingly challenging. Friends and family rattled off the lists of ingredients, but the instructions became more vague when I pressed them about precise quantities. I would often hear, "Use half a scoop of cornstarch, and a spoonful of oyster sauce." Would that be a silver teaspoonful or an Asian porcelain spoonful? My sister would say, "Fill the large pot half way with water." Later, I would discover that the largest pot in my cupboard would not even be as big as her smallest pot since she usually cooked for a family with seven hungry mouths.

Increasingly unpredictable and uncooperative are my rapidly fading memory cells. My sudden flashes of ideas or insights are not in short supply, but those brilliant thoughts generally evaporated before a scrap of paper and a pen could be found. Hopefully, a notepad and pen in an accessible pocket will remedy this challenge, even on an overcrowded Skytrain.

Researching for this workshop, I have rediscovered the joys of simply preparing and sharing food and reminiscing with some seniors. I wish to work with them to capture some of their stories that form such an integral part of our community's collective history. Every one of them has faced and overcome life challenges that new generations would find unimaginable. Many of our seniors had more than their fair share of hardships, hunger, loneliness, poverty and separation from families and friends. Their experiences are replete with stories that must be captured on paper, on tape, on any medium, before those stories evaporate.

I enjoyed learning collectively in a group. Our gatherings allowed us to share and to learn from each other. Our workshop leader always had words of encouragement for everyone. And our fellow workshop participants were always ready to offer an encouraging word or a helpful insight, all of which were better than a hug.

George Jung

This was a booklet produced by La Choy Foods in 1957. The inside cover page proclaims: "La Choy brings you delicious, different Chinatown meals—quickly and easily!"

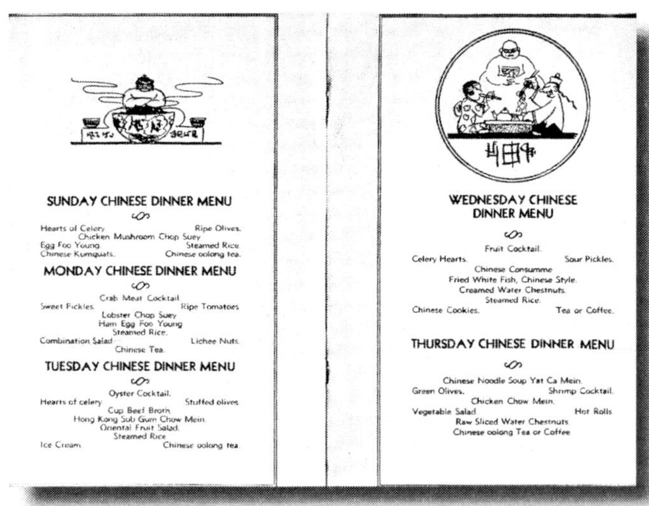

SUNDAY CHINESE DINNER MENU

Hearts of Celery. Ripe Olives.
Chicken Mushroom Chop Suey
Egg Foo Young. Steamed Rice.
Chinese Kumquats. Chinese oolong tea.

MONDAY CHINESE DINNER MENU

Crab Meat Cocktail.
Sweet Pickles. Ripe Tomatoes
Lobster Chop Suey
Ham Egg Foo Young
Steamed Rice.
Combination Salad Lichee Nuts.
Chinese Tea.

TUESDAY CHINESE DINNER MENU

Oyster Cocktail.
Hearts of celery. Stuffed olives.
Cup Beef Broth.
Hong Kong Sub Gum Chow Mein.
Oriental Fruit Salad.
Steamed Rice
Ice Cream. Chinese oolong tea.

WEDNESDAY CHINESE DINNER MENU

Fruit Cocktail.
Celery Hearts. Sour Pickles.
Chinese Consumme
Fried White Fish, Chinese Style.
Creamed Water Chestnuts.
Steamed Rice.
Chinese Cookies. Tea or Coffee.

THURSDAY CHINESE DINNER MENU

Chinese Noodle Soup Yat Ca Mein.
Green Olives. Shrimp Cocktail.
Chicken Chow Mein.
Vegetable Salad Hot Rolls
Raw Sliced Water Chestnuts.
Chinese oolong Tea or Coffee

From *Madame Chiang's Chinese Cook Book (Translated in English): Prepare a Delicious Dinner in Your Own Home and Surprise Your Friends*, by the Chinese Cook Book Company, 1941.

Chinese Home Cooking

Table Etiquette

In olden times the seating of guests at the dinner table and at banquets followed very definite and rigid rules. Today this custom is only adhered to at State banquets and at the marriage feasts of the wealthy and socially prominent families.

Square tables were used with each seat numbered and the guests seated according to their importance of rank, age, etc. Although today the round table has, for the most part, replaced its square predecessor, the "honor seat," the one facing the door is still traditional. This seat is reserved for the honored guest. If there is more than one honored guest the eldest one is given the preference. The Chinese people have great respect for their elders, age connotating wisdom and experience.

Generally, a young person would not accept the Honor Seat in the presence of elder persons, and a wise host would not create such an embarrassing situation. With the exception of the Honor Seat, the other guests are seated in any manner which the host thinks will tend toward congeniality and the pleasure of the entire party. Guests always wait by their chairs until the host starts to take his seat.

After the guests are seated, the serving starts. One dish is brought in at a time and placed on the center of the table. Each guest should serve himself and should take from the dish that portion of food nearest him. The young guests wait until the elder people are served, but it is the duty of the host to see that the plate of everyone is heaped with the choicest part of the food. The guests, on the other hand, do not necessarily have to finish all the food which is piled on their plates. In fact it is considered good manners to leave some food to show the abundance of the dinner.

After chopsticks have been used, they never should be placed on the table cloth. They should be rested on their little rack or on the plate at the end of the meal as well as between courses. It is considered poor manners to be eating all the time.

The tea pot remains on the table throughout the meal and the guest is at liberty to drink all he wishes. During the dinner it is permissible to comment on the excellence of the food, but it is a mistake to show greediness by eating too much from one dish.

From *Chinese Home Cooking: Recipes of Cantonese Dishes*, by the Chinese Committee, International Institute, Y.W.C.A, Honolulu, Hawaii, 1941.

Everyday Tastes: A Food Album for My Sons

Jackie Lee-Son

"Come and eat, supper's ready!" I've prepared curried chicken with pineapple, red and green peppers, and cashew nuts.

"How do you make this, Mom?" My sons Dave and Jon always ask me how to make the meals I cook, as they look for ways to spice up their instant noodle repertoire. Their curiosity has inspired me to pass along recipes in a meaningful way.

I decided to compile a cookbook especially for them. Each page describes a recipe along with a memory or anecdote from when I grew up in South Africa. I hoped that the recipes and stories, even though from a different time and place, would still be relevant in my sons' lives.

Dear Dave and Jon,

I want to share some of our favourite recipes, memories, life's lessons, and practical "how to's" to make each day easier for you. I hope you will always eat well. . .

Sweet Tonic Tea (*Leong Cha*)

Soon after I was born, I became very ill. Mom was our Florence Nightingale and had nursed many members of the family with great strength and compassion. I appreciate the care she gave me when I was a sick baby. Mom's mother, my Por Por, lived in another city and flew to Kimberley to bring me Chinese medicine. My father's mother made me *leong cha*. A photograph on my dresser of Mom holding me in her arms is a constant reminder never to give up hope.

Photograph courtesy of author.

Me and Mom, 1955.

Saturday Afternoon Congee

Congee was the first dish Mom taught me how to make. Everyone worked in the shop, and in those days shops closed for half the day on Saturdays. So I would prepare a pot of congee every Saturday for everyone's lunch.

After the shop closed Mom cashed out the registers. A'ya supervisied the re-stocking of shelves and inventory. Dad met with salesmen. When everyone completed their work, we ate a late lunch together. Some Saturdays, I would have preferred to play with the neighbour than to cook a pot of congee.

It is not always convenient or fun to help out. But I've learned life is not just about receiving or about what others can do for you. It's about giving back and doing so with a willing heart.

Photograph courtesy of author.

At my fifth birthday party, I'm preparing for my speech.

Whipping Up Secret Ingredient Icing

From the time I was five years old, I can remember the birthday parties my parents organized for my brothers and me. Back then we didn't have prenatal classes or preschools, so we didn't have the usual parties with little alumni. My parents invited the small Chinese community. Mom did all the cooking and baking herself. After blowing out the candles, we'd stand up on the chair and make a speech: "Ladies and gentlemen, boys and girls—thank you for coming to my party. Thank you for all the lovely presents. I hope you enjoy yourselves." Even in front of my friends and family, I was a bit nervous. This was my foray into public speaking.

In 1985 I was mortified at the task of greeting the audience at an inaugural concert of a concert series. I decided if I could make a speech as a little girl, I could deliver a greeting in front of a theatre audience. Over the years I've learned to transfer skills and experiences. When nervous about new and challenging situations, draw on positive energy of past successes and experiences. The new experience will be the icing on the cake.

Secret Ingredient Icing

Jello pudding (any flavour)

Whipping cream

1.) Make pudding as per instructions on Jello pudding box, substituting whipping cream for milk.

2.) Spread over cake and enjoy.

Photographs courtesy of author.

I enjoy making shape cakes for special occasions, and here are two that I made for my sons—a piano and a hamburger.

Chow Mein Comfort

Photograph courtesy of author.

Jack making a speech at my parents' golden wedding anniversary in 2001.

Jack Mmetseng first came to work with our family when he helped Dad wash the car. Dad asked him to come back and help with other chores around the house and the shop. He worked with A'ya, then with Dad, then my brother, until he retired in 2004 after fifty-one years with the family. He is very proud he knows the entire family, even those who left South Africa many years ago.

Jack helped A'ma in her corner store. He bottled the vinegar and paraffin used as fuel in the kerosene lamps and prepared the funnel-shaped sugar packets. He loved A'ma's cooking. He especially loved A'ma's chow mein. It was one of his favourite meals—one of his comfort foods associated with our family, which also became his family.

When a devastating storm wreaked havoc on many of the homes in our town, much of Jack's home was ruined. A'ya told Jack to go to the shop and take some groceries home.

Jack remembers A'ya's final hours. He went to the hospital to visit A'ya, and when the hospital staff asked him what he was doing there, he said, "I'm here to visit my father." At that time hospitals were racially segregated, but Dad asked the staff to let Jack spend some time with A'ya.

Jack said he knew A'ya could hear him speak, he knew when A'ya was close to dying. Jack was so proud to make the speech at A'ya's funeral. He told me it all came from the heart.

A'ma's Papaya Soup

A few years after my grandparents set up their corner store, my father started a supermarket business a few blocks away. We lived in the home attached to the shop. When I looked outside the kitchen window, I could see the narrow path that led to the shop. The store was our playground, but A'ya soon put us to work. We packed shelves and later helped behind the counter. Those were the first lessons in customer service and building lifelong friendships with our customers.

Some days A'ma asked us to come for supper after the shop closed. I enjoyed the walks to my grandparents' home, which was next to the shop Chan Yan & Co General Dealership. Their home was small. I remember the kitchen with the half doors. We would open the top half so the fresh air and sunshine could stream in, and leave the bottom half closed so the dogs and cats (and chickens if they escaped the coop) could not come into the house.

We always had soup, rice, and a meat dish. The table had a glass top. Underneath the glass were family photos. Even though we saw them all the time, after we cleared the table and removed the tablecloth, we'd look at the photos.

Photograph courtesy of author.

Chan Yan & Co, the shop beside my grandparents' home.

There were so many favourite treats that came from A'ma's kitchen. A'ma made papaya soup—steaming hot clear chicken broth soup with soft, sweet papaya. And she made the best *lupcheong*—big, plump sausages. She'd cook them in the steamed rice, and the juices from the sausages would seep into the rice. After dinner we'd often enjoy grapes from her grapevine. We would squish these plump, juicy grapes in our mouths. A'ma also had orange and lemon trees. She'd send us home with bags of fruit. Mom made lemon madeira loaf from the juice and rind of the lemons.

A'ma taught me that sometimes you don't have to leave home to experience the best things in life.

Papaya Soup

½ chicken

10 cups water

1 Tbsp salt

2 carrots

1 papaya

1.) Cover chicken with water, and boil with salt for 1½ hours.

2.) Remove chicken from broth. De-bone and shred.

3.) Peel carrots and slice.

4.) Peel papaya, cut in half, and remove the black seeds. Cut into two-inch pieces.

5.) Add papaya and carrots to broth, and cook for another half hour.

6.) Add 1 cup shredded chicken.

Serve.

Old and New Tastes

The Mother Superior announced the Holy Family Convent was closing its doors at the end of the term. There was a shortage of nuns. They would build up the bigger convents at the expense of the smaller ones. My small hometown of Kimberley would lose its only private school for girls. During that apartheid era, the Chinese were not permitted to attend the public schools. We had no choice but to look for a school in another city.

My best friend's father drove my friend, her younger sister, and me to Johannesburg to look for a boarding school. We drove from school to school until an Anglican private school accepted us. We were the first Chinese girls at this school.

The first time I left home for boarding school, I remember the chicken with winter melon being my last home-cooked meal. A'ma grew the winter melon in her garden just as Dad does now. We sat around the dinner table in our usual seats. We shoveled the rice from the bowls into our mouths with our chopsticks. We didn't say much. It was soon time to leave for the train station.

As the train pulled away, I watched my family standing on the platform waving goodbye. I can remember the feel and sounds of the train's clickety-clack on the railroad tracks. The clickety-clack still reminds me of the empty feeling I had in the pit of my stomach when I left home for boarding school.

We ate in a dining hall reminiscent of Harry Potter. The prefects arranged the seating—ten to a table, usually a mix of girls from different grades. Each week at lunch we rotated to give each table the chance to sit with the Headmistress. We looked upon this with more dread than joy. The first time I sat down to a meal at school, I didn't know how to use a knife and fork. More food landed on my lap than in my mouth.

The best part of the boarding school meal was undoubtedly the desserts. During dessert time the prefect took the mail to the head table, and the Headmistress read out the names of everyone who received a letter. I remember gripping my hands so tightly and wishing so hard I would hear my name called. Fortunately, Mom wrote me a letter every week, and friends and family also wrote frequently. They made a difference to my days.

While at school, I always seemed to be living in the past or in the future—either thinking about the previous school holidays or counting the days till the next school holidays. I didn't know how to enjoy the present. I've since learned getting there is just as important as the end result.

Buttermilk Rusks

Mom always had a large container filled with buttermilk rusks ready to eat when I came home from boarding school for vacation. I craved Mom's cooking so much when I was away at school. Although we were not allowed to take food back to boarding school, Mom always made a care package for me. Rusks were always part of this package. They seldom lasted beyond the first week back at school. Apart from perennial hunger pains, we always ate these snacks very quickly before the matron snooped amongst our clothes and found them. We were devastated when she confiscated the food supply we smuggled.

Perhaps because I always had to leave friends behind, I put extra energy into maintaining friendships. The boarding school years were tough, but we learned to live together. We forged friendships that have endured over the years. Friends are like windows through which we see out into the world and back into ourselves.

Buttermilk Rusks

2 cups sugar

A pinch of salt

3 lbs self-rising flour

1 lb butter

2 eggs

1 pint buttermilk

1.) Mix sugar, salt and flour.
2.) Rub in butter.
3.) Beat eggs with buttermilk.
4.) Combine the flour mixture with the egg mixture.
5.) Bake in two bread tins for about 1 hour and 10 minutes at 375 degrees.

6.) Remove from oven, and cool completely before cutting into biscotti-sized pieces.
7.) Place on rack in oven to allow the air to circulate around the rusks.
8.) Dry for about 5 hours in the oven at 200 degrees.
9.) Cool and store in an air-tight container.

A Golden Recipe

In 2001 Mom and Dad celebrated their golden wedding anniversary, and I made a trip back home to South Africa. The smell of diesel was overwhelming as soon as we disembarked the plane in Johannesburg. Then we arrived in Kimberley and saw the vast expanse of arid land and the unique outline of the thorn bushes and prickly pear plants, silhouetted in the setting sun glowing through a haze of red sand. That night we enjoyed a family reunion and heard the familiar sound of crickets chirping.

We ate great food and shared the joys of being together—one of the greatest lessons from food and family that I could ever hope to pass onto my sons.

Author's Note

In 1955 in Kimberley, South Africa, a pregnant lady struggled up the stairs of a hospital. It was her second child, so she knew it would not be a long labour. Despite this lady's apparent pain, the admitting nurse asked, "White ward or non-white ward?" Oddly enough, I never learned in which ward I was born. I am second-generation South African-born Chinese and moved to Vancouver in 1974.

I'd like to dedicate this sampling of food memories to my family.

My mother taught me to cook; she's always been able to produce a wonderful meal for unexpected guests as though she had spent days preparing. My father enjoys entertaining and is always the gracious host—he taught me the value of customer service and being a good friend. My older brother shared his childhood memories of growing up together. My younger brother is the gourmet cook of the family. A'ma, my father's mother, made the best *lupcheong* I've ever tasted. A'ya, my father's father, always came to our home next door to the shop and called us to work when we weren't at school. Por Por, my mother's mother, raised and educated five children on her own, and she ran her Sophiatown grocery store and often volunteered to cook for Hong Ning Chinese Old Age Home.

I never had the opportunity to meet Kung Kung, my mother's father, as he died when Mom was about eight. An uncle offered to take me to the village in China where the house Kung Kung built still stands. I feel I must begin to plan for that trip today.

Finally, my sons inspired the creation of their personalized cookbook, which in turn inspired some of these vignettes. My older son was married this past April, and my younger son is engaged to be married next year. They, together with their partners, are about to begin another important chapter of their lives. Creating personal histories is the greatest gift we can leave our children and the generations to come.

Jackie Lee-Son

Every Little Bite Helps

Roy Mah

Beef on Rice

Of all the dishes that she made, none came close to beef on rice. It was everyone's favourite dish. The one-dish meal was simple, nourishing, and economical—and symbolic of an early immigrant's struggles.

She could afford only the very basic ingredients, and preparation time was limited. Besides working long hours as a seamstress, she also peeled shrimp on the dock and worked on farms picking potatoes. Despite these conditions, she managed to prepare this simple dish. I can see her now. . .

Mom cuts the beef flank steak into thin slices and marinates it with oyster sauce. She soaks and dices black mushrooms. When the water in the rice is almost evaporated, she sprinkles the beef and mushrooms over the surface of the rice. The rice is left simmering until done.

When the rice is cooked and the cover is opened, a steamy aroma arises from the mixture. The sweet and somewhat salty smell of the oyster sauce and beef flood the air. She adds diced green onions and more oyster sauce. Then she stirs the rice and mixes it up with the beef, green onions, and mushrooms. Mom leaves the rice simmering a bit longer to give it a crust at the bottom.

We always fought to eat the crust, especially when it was thin and crispy. We scraped the crust off the bottom and sprinkled on salt. Sometimes we also added water so that the crust was both crunchy and moist. The dish was even more of a treat when we got to stir shrimp paste into it. This was comfort food at its best.

In order to appreciate my mother's process and care, I tried to make beef on rice myself. What a disaster! Instead of slicing the beef, I diced it. I sprinkled on the beef and diced mushroom just as the water evaporated. After about ten minutes, I added the green onions but no more oyster sauce, believing there was already too much. For a more delectable taste, I added a small amount of preserved turnips onto the rice.

My rice was too soggy and slightly burned. It tasted like very thick beef congee. The oyster sauce did not have the same taste—it had an overpowering oil and artificial flavour. Although the saltiness of the turnips came through, the rice was still not that palatable. I almost broke my teeth when I bit into the crust.

It definitely was not the one-dish wonder I remember. Now I only have the fond memories of Mom preparing this dish at a most difficult time in her life.

Chicken, Chicken, Chicken

Photograph courtesy of author.

My father, Bing, c. 1950s, Hong Kong.

Chicken always made an appearance at important celebrations such as birthdays and New Year's; it was also a dish that fed us on a budget. For Dad, no matter how special or mundane the occasion, chicken was his favourite food—and one that happened to be representative of the progression of his Canadian life.

In the early days, a whole steamed chicken was his dish of choice. He might have learned how to make this when he worked at Wayen Diner (now known as New Town Bakery) in Chinatown. With scarce finances and tight time constraints, this dish made economical sense. Preparation time was minimal, as the chicken simmered in hot water. When he chopped the chicken into pieces and arranged them into a shape of chicken, it was a simple, elegant dish. He made a dipping sauce of green onion, ginger, and five-spice salt in hot oil.

Dad loved chicken thighs and legs, and he took great pleasure in chewing the meat off the back and neck bones. I can still hear him slurping as he spat out the tiny bones.

During the grocery store days, when Mom and Dad were really too busy to cook, the chicken meal became a bucket of Kentucky Fried Chicken and a big hillbilly jug of A&W Root Beer, supplemented with the usual Chinese vegetables such as *bok choy* or *gai lan*. Take-out chicken was relatively inexpensive and was the quick "Canadian" way of feeding a large family, especially in an emergency situation.

I remember one time when we gathered around the dinner table, and Mom served a hot meal in a glass bowl. Just before we began to eat, the glass bowl shattered. We all looked up to the ceiling, thinking that something fell down onto the plate, but it was just the heat of the food that caused the bowl to shatter. It was a frightening moment. Dad was quick to send one of us to Kentucky Fried Chicken to get dinner, and Mom quickly prepared some vegetables. Something good (we got to eat fried chicken) came out of something bad (broken bowl). But I can still remember the saddened look on Mom's face when the bowl burst into pieces.

Dad's idea of the ultimate chicken dish was sticky rice chicken. Dad considered this dish to be a magnificent platter. It was expensive and labour-intensive to make, but now and then, Dad just had to splurge on it. A whole chicken was de-boned and stuffed with sticky rice. Then it was deep-fried and cut into pieces.

Dad took pleasure in the sound of the crusty outer layer as he took a bite. After the initial crunch, the stickiness and chewiness of the rice and meat came through. He sniffed at the aroma of the earthy mushroom sauce that came with the chicken. He tilted his head, laughed, and picked up another piece of chicken. Needless to say, there were no leftovers.

These chicken dishes mirrored the progress that Dad had achieved during his working life as an immigrant. From him, I've learned to appreciate these dishes, but I now avoid Kentucky Fried Chicken due to health concerns. Chicken with sticky rice is still desirable but hard to find, as restaurants do not have this tantalizing dish on their menus anymore. But I still love the steamed whole chicken and make it often, always with thoughts of Dad in mind.

Steamed Chicken

1.) Rub salt on outside of chicken and wash in cold water.

2.) Slowly immerse the whole chicken in boiling water with couple slices of ginger. Return to boiling.

3.) Turn heat down to low. Cover and simmer for about 1 hour.

4.) Take out the chicken, and cool before cutting.

5.) Chop the chicken into neat pieces.

6.) Serve with dipping sauce.

Dipping Sauce

1 onion, chopped

Ginger, minced

Five-spice

Hot oil

Mix the ingredients, and cook with hot oil over medium heat for a few minutes. Oyster sauce can also be used.

Photograph courtesy of author.

Steamed chicken, with head partially intact.

Past and Present at Chinese New Year

Clang! Clang! Clang! The noise of banging pots and pans woke me up, and I knew instantly that my wife, Lynne, was already starting the New Year's preparations. Although we consider ourselves third-generation Chinese immigrants from Toishan village in Guangdong province, we've tried to keep some traditions alive. So we always celebrate Chinese New Year's with traditional dishes and an ancestor worship ceremony. The ceremony unites the past and present, and re-affirms our sense of family loyalty and lineage.

My mother's insistence on completing the ceremony before noon was the reason for our haste to prepare and cook. In recent years, Lynne has chosen eight dishes to symbolize blessings in longevity, riches, and virtue. I can't recall when we changed to completely vegetarian and seafood dishes, but that's how our ceremony has somehow evolved over the years.

The menu included steamed fish, large bean sprouts with green onions, prawns with ketchup sauce, *fat choy* (black moss) in an egg omelette, stir-fried vermicelli with *siu choy* (Chinese cabbage), bean curd soup with red dates and dried oysters, a vegetarian dish consisting of diced black mushrooms, dried oysters, celery and water chestnuts, and finally, lettuce leaves for wrapping.

Fish symbolizes abundance of good fortune, while bean sprouts ensure roots in the family. In Toishan dialect, the word for prawns sounds much like the word for "having a very lively existence," and vermicelli represents long life. *Fat choy* and dried oysters signify wealth and prosperity. Dried bean curd is a homophone for fulfillment of wealth and happiness. Lettuce leaves gather all the blessings into a unified hope.

The preparation actually began a week before New Year's day, when the dishes were chosen. We bought the dry ingredients such as dried bean curd, packages of vermicelli, frozen peeled prawns, black mushrooms, and dried *fat choy* at T&T Supermarket. Later, we got fresh ingredients, such as the tilapia fish, large bean sprouts, and lettuce. Two days before New Year's Day, we soaked the black moss and dried bean curd, and diced and stored mushrooms, water chestnuts, celery, and dried oysters in individual containers. We defrosted the prawns the night before. We soaked a package of vermicelli on New Year's morning. We finished all the cooking just before noon and presented the dishes at the altar to give our ancestors the first bites.

The altar is a homemade pine shelf with decorative edges, about ten inches deep by twenty-four inches long. It faces south and is mounted two-thirds up the wall. At the back of the shelf is a gold picture frame with images of Grandfather Dock, Grandma Fong, my father Bing, and Uncle Kun. To the left sits a figurine of a colourful and smiling Buddha surrounded by five children. Buddha holds a gold bead chain draped over his arm. The Buddha of Fulfillment will bring many joys into the home and also guard the young and innocent.

Two miniature red light bulbs peek out from the top of gold electric candle holders. A round ceramic incense holder contains three sticks of incense to purify the surroundings. Below the altar is a table for displaying offerings.

Photograph courtesy of author.

Our ancestral altar.

We placed three miniature cups filled with Johnny Walker whiskey at the front of the altar, along with three pairs of wooden chopsticks and three bowls of rice. We stood in front of the altar with paper money in each of our hands. We intoned in unison our wishes for the coming year.

"Please keep us safe. Help us grow and prosper. Wealth and health in abundance. *Tsut Yap Ping Hon. Bo Bo Go Sing. Tai Gut Tai Lay.*"

We bowed three times in respect of those who came before us, struggled for us, and sacrificed for us. Then we burned paper money in million-dollar denominations for their use in the afterlife. We also burned paper replicas of cell phones and designer clothing. We left the food on the altar for about five minutes. (Tradition calls for the food to be left out for most of the day, but we've decided that our ancestors are fast eaters.) Then we bowed again and prayed to our ancestors for blessings.

As I lowered my head, I stared into Grandpa's face and marveled again how he had braved the immigration trail. He arrived in Victoria on June 14, 1913, at the tender age of twenty-seven, after a long journey on the ship *Chicago Maru*. During his forty-three years in Canada, he went back to China a couple of times, got married, and had two boys—my father and my uncle Kun, who died at age eighteen. Because of the head tax and the Chinese Exclusion Act, Grandpa and Grandma remained separated across the ocean until she passed away in 1951.

Grandpa became a Canadian citizen on June 2, 1954. Little is known what work he did, but it must have been the usual labour-intensive types. Near the end, he managed a merchandise store on Hastings Street, east of Columbia Street, in Chinatown. He was buried under the name of Dock Oy Mah at Mount Pleasant Cemetery in Vancouver on April 1, 1956. (The name Dock Oy was his given name after his marriage, a practice prevalent at the time.) My father became the sole heir to the name, thereby immigrating to Canada.

Now looking into my father's eyes in his photograph, I almost had to laugh at all the vegetarian dishes spread out on the altar. He would've had a fit since he was a "meat and potatoes" type of person. He developed his taste in food when he was waiting tables at Wayen Diner in Chinatown. With his hair slicked back and glistening with Brycream, he was popular with customers and got good tips.

I remember how he relished his chicken on the rare side, with a just a bit of blood trickling out of the meat. He always said the meat was much smoother and juicier this way. He'd chew on his toothpick and smack his lips in enjoyment. Food was one of the few pleasures in his life as he toiled in the grocery store business for twenty years until he retired in 1985.

We finished the ceremony and took the food to the dining table. Our eyes focused on the lazy Susan, as it was barely large enough to contain all the dishes. My son Raymond already started lapping up the ketchup sauce along with the prawns. The sweet and sour aroma of the ketchup hung in the air.

The fish had a gingery and sharp green onion smell offsetting the fresh fishy taste. The fish tasted very tender and smooth. Mom sucked at the eyeballs and a bit of the fishtail. She said the eyeballs were going to give her good sight.

Photograph courtesy of author.

Mom and Dad in the 1970s in Vancouver.

My son Christopher searched for the biggest lettuce leaf to make a big blessing wrap. He then slopped on the bean sprouts and vegetables, and angled the wrap into his gaping mouth, as juice dripped onto his place. My daughter Sharon used her chopsticks to lift up the stringy vermicelli, trying to place them neatly into her bowl of rice.

"If you want to prosper and grow, you have to eat *fat choy* omelette and bean curd soup," Lynne encouraged everyone.

"But the *fat choy* is so hairy. It gets stuck in my teeth!" Sharon whined.

"Every little bite helps you. That is what New Year's all about," Lynne said.

I smiled at Mom, who had the last word, "Our ancestors are at peace."

Author's Note

This is the second workshop that I've attended. I had hoped to further my family history writing. For such a topic as food and family, writing should be simple and straightforward. Yet I had great difficulty in connecting food and family memories. There was a disconnect that I struggled to overcome. One technique that I learned to use in the drafting process was to write in the present tense to make the stories seem more immediate and accessible to my senses. This helped in writing about my father's favourite dish and my grandfather's early journey into Canada.

New Year's is an important Chinese celebration, even for long-time Chinese Canadian immigrants. Therefore, I wanted to document this important occasion and why we observe certain celebratory protocols. I also wanted to recognize my family's long history of being a part of Canada.

For an engineer, creative writing is a foreign art form. The supportive atmosphere of the workshop provided excellent suggestions and useful critiques. It was interesting and entertaining to hear how our food experiences and tastes related to our family histories. And of course, the camaraderie evident at each class was a bonus.

I also thank my siblings for providing some of the details in the stories. Their memories are much better than mine.

I hope that everyone keeps writing, reading, and eating!

Roy Mah

CHICKEN VELVET

Chi Jung 鷄茸

To **1/2 C. uncooked chicken breast,** ground, add **1 t. cornstarch, 1/4 t. salt,** and **1 unbeaten egg white.** Mix well and slowly add **1/4 C. water,** a few drops at a time. (If water is added too fast, the mixture will not hold together.) Beat **4 egg whites** until stiff and gradually fold into the chicken mixture.

Heat pan, add **2 T. oil** or chicken fat, and let it heat only to melting if solid fat has been used. Pour the chicken and egg white mixture into the pan, remove from fire at once, and stir the mixture rapidly. After the fat is stirred into the mixture, replace on fire, and cook until firm but not browned. The mixture should just "set."

The gravy may be prepared beforehand. Pour the hot gravy over the Chicken Velvet. Heat thoroughly and serve hot. Serves 4.

Gravy

Mix **1 C. rich chicken stock, 1 t. sherry, 1/4 t. salt,** and **1 T. cornstarch;** heat thoroughly.

Notes: May be prepared in advance and reheated. If chicken fat is used in place of oil, Chicken Velvet is an excellent dish for an invalid.

27

From *The Art of Chinese Cooking,* by the Benedictine Sisters of Peking, 1956.

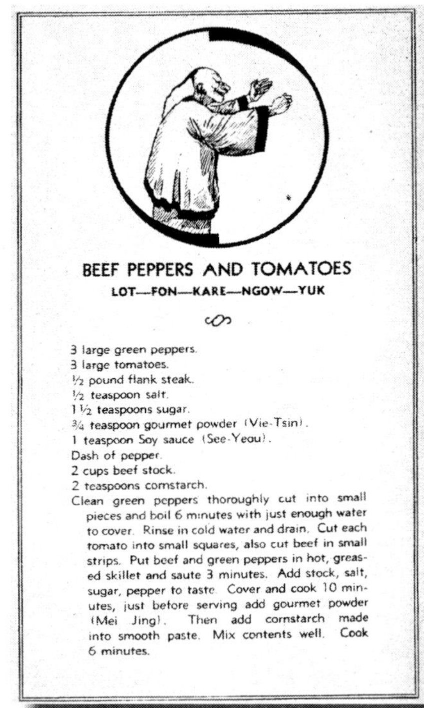

BEEF PEPPERS AND TOMATOES

LOT—FON—KARE—NGOW—YUK

3 large green peppers.
3 large tomatoes.
½ pound flank steak.
½ teaspoon salt.
1 ½ teaspoons sugar.
¾ teaspoon gourmet powder (Vie-Tsin).
1 teaspoon Soy sauce (See-Yeou).
Dash of pepper.
2 cups beef stock.
2 teaspoons cornstarch.

Clean green peppers thoroughly cut into small pieces and boil 6 minutes with just enough water to cover. Rinse in cold water and drain. Cut each tomato into small squares, also cut beef in small strips. Put beef and green peppers in hot, greased skillet and saute 3 minutes. Add stock, salt, sugar, pepper to taste. Cover and cook 10 minutes, just before serving add gourmet powder (Mei Jing). Then add cornstarch made into smooth paste. Mix contents well. Cook 6 minutes.

From *Madame Chiang's Chinese Cook Book (Translated in English): Prepare a Delicious Dinner in Your Own Home and Surprise Your Friends,* by the Chinese Cook Book Company, 1941.

Warming Up: Community & Family Fare

Gordy Mark

Kendo New Year Potluck

Photograph courtesy of author.

Our kendo class, from young to old.

"Heels up, pressure on toes, left hand—pressure on last two fingers, right hand soft, shoulders relaxed, back straight, stomach out!" Ryuji shouts.

"Hai!" the class yells in unison.

"Five *shomen subari* (head strike) going forward, three *shomen subari* backward, all one breath. Five times each, following my pace!"

"Hai!"

As we move forward and backward, we count out loud our strikes.

Uchi, ni, san, shi, go.

"I want more KIAI! This is not a library!"

"Hai!"

Kiai is very important component of kendo. It is more that just a loud form of vocalization or "yelling." The stronger your *kiai*, the more you are able to control the state of your mind and project your inner spirit and power. Fear, prejudice, and doubts weaken your mindset. With a strong *kiai*, you will be able to dominate and defeat your opponent. And the greatest opponent that you must overcome is yourself.

Ryuji makes us do more drills until he is satisfied that we are performing the techniques correctly with enough spirit and determination. Finally, Ryuji signals an end to our warm-up. The class and Ryuji bow to thank each other for their participation in the exercise. George, our *sempai* (most senior student), yells, "*Sei retsu!*" We quickly line up for opening.

It's only nine o'clock, and sweat is already pouring from my forehead. My heart is pumping so hard I can hear it thumping in my head.

George yells, "*Mokuso.*"

The brief meditation period allows me clear my mind, catch my breath, and regain some energy.

All the instructors push us to our limits. They know if you are not working to your full potential. Some of the kids are whacked on the side of the head or pushed to the floor if they slack off. They are expected to get up and fight back with greater spirit, effort, and determination. Training in the dojo is hard, but it helps prepare you to face and deal with the realities of life.

Displaying a strong *kiai*, I find that I have enough energy to execute not just one more strike but five additional strikes. I don't want to waste any energy delivering a poorly executed technique.

George yells out, "*Sei retsu!*"

We quickly form a line for closing. Today, our workout lasts only one hour and fifteen minutes. It is shorter but still a tough workout. We go to each of our instructors and bow to each other to show mutual gratitude for today's practice.

I started studying kendo in fall 2003. After attending a few weeks of practice, Ara sensei told me that the class celebrates New Year's by having a potluck lunch. Ara sensei invited me and my family to attend this annual celebration, and since then, we've always looked forward to attending it.

Today is our first kendo practice for the New Year, which is why we ended early—so we can have our potluck celebration. We quickly put away our equipment, change our clothes, and prepare for lunch.

Everyone helps to unfold the tables and chairs. We arrange the tables in two long rows along the length of the dojo. We place three tables near the kitchen door for the food. Some of the parents help to line the tables with white paper, and others put out the food, plates, napkins, and utensils.

I seat myself next to Yuki, one of the associate instructors. Ara sensei will be speaking in Japanese, and I can ask Yuki for the English translation.

One of my classmates puts cups on the tables, and one of the parents fills them with steaming green tea. Everyone is given a warm bowl of soba noodles in a clear broth, sprinkled with green onions. I quickly drink my cup of tea and then my soup. The broth is slightly salty. I slurp my noodles. This doesn't satisfy my thirst, so I grab a bottle of water and pop, polishing off both.

Ara sensei thanks the participants, parents, volunteers, and instructors for all their hard work in keeping the Renbu Dojo going. The fundraising activities have been a success. We applaud those participants who are awarded certificates of achievement and outstanding effort and performance. Then Ara sensei invites us to join in sampling the various types of food we have today.

I join the queue and begin filling up my plate. I take some herring roe and red salmon roe. A bit of mixed green salad with sweet vinegar, soya sauce, and sesame oil dressing. Some teriyaki chicken.

Someone in the line asks, "Did George make these California rolls?"

"Yeah, I made them. Two containers of them at the restaurant—so you better eat them!" George shouts.

There's the cooked shrimp ring I brought this year. I bought it from Costco and thawed it this morning.

Dean asks, "How was today's workout?"

I say, "It was good. Even though it was short, it was tough. I don't think I had an easy workout yet. I keep coming hoping that the next workout might be easy."

Everyone laughs.

I excuse myself so I can visit the dessert table. Japanese rice crackers, chocolates, hard candies, cheesecakes, cookies, jello.... I see some of the fruitcake cookies that I baked. They are similar to the fruitcake my dad used to bake, except they are not as dark in colour.

The potluck is wrapping up, and everyone pitches in to clean and put away the tables and chairs. The kids are still bursting with energy. They haul out the hockey nets and set one up at each end of the dojo. Time to play some indoor soccer. If I were younger, I probably would have the energy to participate.

When I first started learning kendo, I attended the Sunday morning class.

Ara sensei asked me, "Why do you want to study kendo?"

"I want to study kendo for exercise and also as something that I can continue when I'm eighty years old."

"How old are you?"

"I am fifty-four."

"You are quite old to be studying kendo."

"I have the determination to learn."

"Mark-san, I have some bad news for you. At your age, you physical strength and speed will continue to decline. However, you have an opportunity to develop your spirit. You are not too old to learn."

Sitting in the dojo, finishing my potluck meal, and watching the young people playing soccer, I have more confidence that I'll never be too old to keep learning.

My Father's Fruitcake

Photograph courtesy of author.

Me and my father, Mark Yu Wah, Stanley Park, Vancouver, 1958.

Mark Yu Wah stood in front of the hot grill. His mind drifted back to China, where he used to enjoy his mother's home village cooking. He saw chunks of winter melon floating with the sliced black mushrooms and whole shrimp in a steaming pork broth. The bitter melon and tender slices of beef were smothered with a layer of black bean sauce. He could smell salted fish, duck egg pork patties, and roasted duck. It made his mouth water just thinking about it.

No time to daydream! He had customers filing into the café for lunch. They wanted their fast food—hamburgers and French fries.

After a long day operating the café, Yu Wah looked forward to taking the bus home. His wife, Li Ying, would have dinner ready. Although Li Ying was a third-generation Chinese born in Canada, she learned village-style cooking from her mother and grandmother. She spoke several dialects of Chinese, including his own village dialect of Taishan hua (台山话).

Early Sunday morning, his two sons, Gee Ho and Gin Gee, greeted Yu Wah.

"Hi, Dad. Are you making fruitcakes for Christmas?" Gin Gee asked.

"Yes, I am. Do you want to watch?"

"Sure. . .can I lick the bowl?"

"No, I get the bowl, you get the spoon!" Gee Ho quickly said.

Yu Wah made a compromise. "Since Gee Ho is the eldest, he gets the bowl, and Gin Gee, you can lick the wooden spoon."

His sons nodded in agreement.

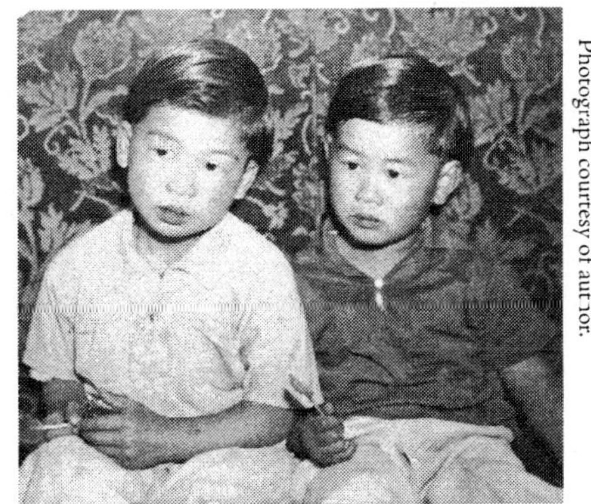

Photograph courtesy of author.

Me and my brother John, 1954.

Yu Wah made fruitcakes for Li Ying's family every Christmas. There wasn't enough money to purchase gifts so he baked fruitcakes instead. Her father, four brothers, and one sister would each be given a cake. He also baked two extra cakes for his family. It took a full day to make all the cakes.

"Why do you leave the butter and eggs out?" Gin Gee asked.

"So that they will warm up to room temperature. When you cream the butter, it will be lighter and fluffier than if you took the butter right out of the fridge."

He added sugar a bit a time into the creamed butter. He beat the eggs into the mixture, one at time. Then he incorporated flour, green, red, and yellow candied fruits, and nuts into the batter.

With a confused look, Gee Ho asked, "What's that white stuff on the nuts?"

"I coated the nuts with flour so they won't sink to the bottom of the pan when the cake is baking."

Gee Ho and Gin Gee helped to cut and oil brown paper bags to line the loaf pans. Yu Wah filled each pan two-thirds full with the batter. No need for a spatula—he simply used his curled index finger to extract the remaining batter clinging to the mixing bowl. He left some behind for Gee Ho.

Yu Wah slammed the filled pan against a folded towel lying across the counter top.

Wham! Wham! Wham!

Looking puzzled, Gee Gee asked, "Why are you smashing the cake?"

"This helps drive the trapped air bubbles out of the mixture and spread the batter evenly across the pan."

"Can I try smashing the cake"?

"Maybe when you are older." Yu Wah finished filling all the loaf pans and said, "Now you and your brother can have what is left on the bowl and spoon."

Gin Gee took the wooden spoon and retreated to the living room. He plopped down on the sofa. With the bowl Gee Ho sat with his legs folded on the floor. He could smell rich butter and egg in the batter.

Yu Wah put the fruitcakes into the preheated oven and let them bake for about one hour. Then he removed the cakes from the oven and placed them on kitchen table to cool. The cakes had a rich colour, well bodied with fruit. Candied red and green cherries, bits of oranges, raisins, pineapples, pecans, and almonds dotted the cake's surface.

"Dad, can I have a piece of cake?" asked Gee Ho.

"I want a piece too," Gin Gee echoed.

"No, you'll have to wait until Christmas."

But they were all happy they got to have a little baking treat before the presents could be opened—and eaten—on Christmas day.

My Mother's *Hung Siu Sek Baan Yue* (紅燒石鱭魚), Barbecued Rock Cod

Today, Li Ying is making her mother's village-style *hung siu sek baan yue*. Translated literally into English, it means "red-fired rock cod." Even though the fish is deep-fried, it somehow it got translated as barbecued rock cod. Perhaps in the village, the stove was fired red-hot so that the fish could be cooked in a wok filled with oil. Her mother says the rock cod in Guang Dong province (廣東省) are not as big as the ones in Canada. Fortunately, Li Ying can go to Chinatown and buy a fresh rock cod.

The fish store has a fine selection spread over its counter. Li Ying selects the fish with the clearest eyes, the one whose gills are still flushed bright red with blood. She presses her finger into the skin of the fish to make sure the flesh is firm. The fish merchant places the fish onto a scale to weigh it. He guts the fish before wrapping it in brown paper and newspaper. Li Ying also purchases a bottle of sweet pickled mixed vegetables.

At home, she unwraps the fish and places it in the sink. Bright red blood oozes from the body cavity. She turns on the cold water tap and rinses the fish until the water runs clear.

She lays the fish across a cutting block. Using a meat cleaver, she trims off the dorsal, pectoral, and anal fins. She scores the fish across the body with a downward motion, making parallel cuts from the head to the tail. This breaks the skin and exposes the white flesh. Then she scores the fish at a ninety-degree angle in the opposite direction, creating a diamond pattern. She repeats this procedure on the other side of the fish.

She pats the fish dry, then dredges it over a plate covered with flour. She partially fills the wok with corn oil. When she sees the oil bubbling and starting to smoke, she gently slides the fish into the oil with a wire ladle. A sudden sizzle and a large burst of steam—the water is driven out of the fish.

Li Ying fries the fish until the flesh is no longer transparent and becomes a milky white colour. She opens the door a bit to help draw out the deep-fried oil smell. After four minutes, she carefully turns the fish over on the other side using the ladle. When the flesh is white to the bone and the skin a golden brown, she removes the fish and places it on a paper-lined plate to drain.

Photograph courtesy of author.

My brother John, Mom, me, and Dad, 1958.

She transfers the fish to a serving platter and tops it with a layer of sweet pickled vegetables, along with cilantro and green onions.

"Yu Wah, remember to not turn the fish over when you debone it. You know what they say—if you do, the fishing boat will overturn."

She gives her sons some pieces from the tail, where the bones aren't as sharp. Li Ying takes a small piece of fish from the belly. There is a crispy layer of skin with sweet, juicy flesh inside.

Yu Wah prefers to eat his fish with rice. The boys like a lot of pickled vegetables on their fish.

Eventually, only the bones remain on the plate. Li Ying is happy that she learnt her mother's village style of cooking. It is peasant cooking, but it allows her to prepare delicious meals with simple ingredients.

Liu Family Reunion

My grandfather, Liu Tien Hsiung (劉天雄), was born in 1884 in Victoria. He was the eldest of five children, all born in Victoria. My grandmother, Loo Sung Young (盧笑容), left China in 1904 to marry my grandfather. They had ten children.

Photograph courtesy of author.

My grandfather Liu Tien Hsiung.

In the summer of 1998, I attended the funeral service for my uncle Herb. He was my second uncle on my mother's side of the family. After the service, I had an opportunity to speak with many of my first cousins whom I hadn't seen since we were kids.

"It seems like the only time we get together is when one of our parents dies. Why don't we meet for a happy occasion?" I asked them.

Kevin suggested, "What we need to do is to organize a family clan celebration."

Mayme said, "That's a great idea."

Kevin, Mayme, and I had several reunion planning meetings. We mulled over many questions. Where should we meet? How would we contact everyone? What type of food would we have?

Kevin said, "We should go somewhere with lots of cheap food." Kevin became responsible for finding a location.

Photograph courtesy of author.

First cousins, from left to right—Nancy, David, Shirley, Owen, Anne, Sadie, Kevin, Mayme, and me.

Mayme looked after the reception and decorations. She brought glass jars and vases filled with blooming chrysanthemums picked from Mrs. Chu's garden. The floral arrangements and balloons decorated the tables.

My job was to contact everyone. Twenty-nine people ended up attending the family reunion. Anne, our oldest first cousin, made the journey from San Mateo, California. Mayme's daughter Melissa and husband Chris came from Calgary. Kevin's son Bradley and wife Julie Lee came from Alberta Beach. Most of the other Liu family members lived in the Vancouver area.

We held a buffet brunch at Yic's in North Vancouver. It provided a wide selection of Canadian Chinese and Western food. There was chow mein, sweet and sour spareribs, fried rice, and other Chinese Canadian dishes. For those who preferred Western food, there was selection of fried chicken, French fries, sausages, salads, fresh fruit, cold cuts, other hot and cold dishes, and pies and cakes.

I saw that my son Eric had polished off his sweet and sour spareribs, most of his chow mein, half of his fried chicken, and almost all of his fried rice.

"The sweet and sour looks awful, and all the vegetables are over-cooked," my wife, Virginia, remarked. Although the ribs were smothered in a thick, red sauce, they looked dry and very tough.

I found most of food to be on the greasy side and barely acceptable. Before I ate any sausages, I used a napkin to wipe off the excess oil. I managed to find some crispy bacon and fresh-cut fruit.

Not everyone shared the same view about the food. For others, the volume of food choices was the greatest draw. Some people raved about the excellent quality and selection.

After an enormous lunch, we opened our photo albums to share memories. I realized that there was a wealth of information at the reunion, coming out in bits of stories during our show-and-tell.

I found out that our great-grandfather had sailed on a junk boat from China to San Francisco in the late 1800s. He later traveled to Victoria and set up an employment agency. My eldest cousin shared her experiences about growing up following the Depression and visiting our grandparents in Chinatown. Kevin even found out that his hairdresser was the wife of his first cousin, Owen!

Despite the difference in opinion among the three generations about the food itself, we all agreed that the reunion was a great success. Food turned out to be a good topic for conversation—and a catalyst for digging up memories and unknown connections.

Sweet Pickled Vegetables

2 cups sugar

1 cup white vinegar

1 ½ cups water

1 *gai choy* (mustard green), salted for 30 minutes, then rinsed with boiling water

2 carrots, peeled and julienned

½ cucumber, thinly sliced

½ red bell pepper, thinly sliced

½ tsp red pepper flakes (optional)

Sweet chili sauce (optional)

1.) Mix sugar, vinegar, and water in a saucepan. Heat and stir until sugar is fully dissolved. Let pickle solution cool.

2.) Add mustard green, carrots, cucumber, bell pepper to the pickle solution, and leave in the refrigerator overnight.

Author's Note

When I first enrolled in the writing workshop, I wondered if I made the right decision. The topic was not one with which I felt comfortable. My father passed away when I was sixteen years old, and my memories of him weren't clear. I also had difficulty remembering the food that my mother made when I grew up. How could I possibly write about food and family?

Holding the writing workshop in a non-traditional classroom setting—in a café—took me away from the type of writing instruction that I had been taught in school. What also helped was how my fellow writers provided me with inspiration, encouragement, ideas, and support. Meeting weekly to review each other's drafts was something that everyone looked forward to. It was an opportunity to get positive feedback for improvement. And it was a time that you could laugh and joke and have some fun.

Brandy's acute insights provided me with direction to improve my style and clarity. Freewrites were useful in helping me generate ideas and possible areas for development. I also got a lot out of writing in different perspectives, as the writing presented here demonstrates. Writing in the third-person perspective allowed me to gain some insight and intimacy on my father's and mother's thoughts and stories; writing in my own voice helped me recall memories that I might have not have given much thought to previously.

I also discovered that in writing about both family and community food memories, I was able to make connections in how I've come to view the fellowship created out of sharing food. There is great significance in the way that people have come together over sharing meals or teaching friends about one's own food culture, both historically and personally. Communities have been built and friendships made during potlucks and other gatherings, and this was even evident during the six-week workshop. I hope to continue the work that I've started here.

Gordy Mark

Love, Patience, and Garlic

Amy Perreault

Chicken Soup in Mom's Kitchen

"Mom! I'm hungry! What's to eat?"

I pace around the kitchen, watching each step Mom takes, looking at her baby blue satin Isotoner slippers Dad bought her for Christmas.

"Chicken soup," she says sternly, glancing at me out of the corner of her eye. I stare up at her, squinting my eyes and scrunching my nose.

"Oh. Do I like chicken soup?"

Mom ignores all my pestering questions and asks, "Well, are you going to help me? The veggies are in the crisper."

She lets me help her wash the carrots, potatoes and green beans. Mom has a vegetable scrubbing brush that looks like a potato. It's easy to hold in my small hands. I want all the vegetables to be perfect, no dirt or nubby moles on the potatoes, no white hairs on the carrots, and I make sure to snap off the ends of the green beans. I want Mom to notice how good I am at cooking so she lets me do more interesting things than wash the lousy vegetables.

"Amy, can you grab three cloves of garlic? On second thought, make it four!"

◆ ◆ ◆

I don't have many memories of Mom feeding me chicken soup when I was younger, but what I do have are three tried and true ingredients that I swear by: love, patience, and garlic. I know the first two sound painfully corny, but it's true on so many levels. It wasn't Mom's chicken soup that made me feel better when I was sick—it was knowing she loved me enough to cook meals that came from her heart. She also had the patience to let me help her cook even when it would have been easier to do things herself.

I know when a meal comes from a person's heart because it always tastes better. Whenever I stayed at a friend's house for dinner, the food never tasted the same as at home. I believe this is why people often have stomach troubles when traveling for long periods of time. They are eating unfamiliar foods—bad chi prepared by unfamiliar people.

Memories of my mother have been the main ingredient in the dishes I now prepare for the people I love. I have learned a lot about relationships from Mom's philosophy of "Love, Patience, and Garlic."

When my boyfriend David's mom was away in Korea, I could tell he was missing her by the way he kept talking about Korean food. I guess this is proof that the heart and stomach are more closely related than I thought. Children grow up and become independent from their parents but still remain attached through the umbilical cord of food and taste.

"You know what would be good right now? *Yuke jung*! Mmm.... really spicy with lots of shredded meat and *bap* (rice).... Remember when my mom made the *daeji-bulgogi* (spicy pork)? Oh my God, that was so hot my ears were ringing! Hey, did you ever try my mom's chicken soup?"

So the first time I tried his mom's chicken soup was the first time I tried to make it for him as she would. Since then, chicken soup in my household has morphed into something that looks nothing like the soup made in my mother's kitchen. It's great that soup can bring together people of very different backgrounds, but to be honest, I enjoy making this version because I don't have to peel any vegetables!

Meeting Uhm-ma

Forget what they say about the quickest way to a man's heart being through his stomach; you have to get past his mother first!

I have to admit our initial meeting did not go according to plan. I went to David's house, Brown Betty in hand (that usually wins them over—I make a mean Brown Betty), and nervously said hello to his mother, aunt and grandmother. To my disappointment, I didn't see her for the rest of the night. I remained on the perimeter of the kitchen—*her* kitchen. On the car ride home, I was so upset that when we finally got to the front of my house, I blurted out, "Your mother hates me!"

I ran in the house before David could see me crying like a fool. I was used to being welcomed with open arms. This was very different—this was going to call for something better than a Brown Betty! I phoned my mom, and she consoled me with her usual humour, "Maybe she doesn't like sweets?"

A few days later, I received a phone call from Mrs. Bae (that's how I referred to her back then). She asked if I had time and wanted to meet her for dinner. I was scared out of my mind. Our telephone conversation ended with her saying, "Don't tell David I phoned you." I was playing out possible scenarios of what might take place during our first and possibly last meal together. Oh my God, was this woman going to murder me for stealing her son?!

Photograph courtesy of author.

Uhm-ma and her sons, David and Andrew.

Well, I am still alive, and dinner was delicious. She just wanted to get to know me, and I am grateful. I wanted to know more about her family, so over the years, I have gotten to know the laws of Uhm-ma's kitchen.

Making *Mandu*

I remember the first time that I made *mandu*, Korean-style dumplings, with Uhm-ma.

Gathering the ingredients was like hunting for treasure. She had a specific store in mind for each ingredient, and if it was too expensive at one place, she always had a backup plan.

We got the garlic stem in Chinatown. I don't remember the exact store because we went to three (plan A, B, and C). This was a key ingredient in Uhm-ma's recipe. David's family does not like *kimchi* in the *mandu*, but according to Uhm-ma, this is usually the way you prepare it. Uhm-ma uses the *mandu* recipe she got from her mother-in-law: lots of garlic stem, no *kimchi*. Our families do have something in common!

We went to Sunrise Produce to purchase the tofu, and to Kingsway to get the wonton wrappers because they had the best deal. Our last stop, for the ground pork, was on Carrall Street at a Korean-owned butcher. Uhm-ma spoke Korean to the owners while I stared at a sectional 3D plastic model of a cow on the wall. I am not fluent in Korean, but I understand context, so I know when I am the subject of conversation. This time was the usual explanation of why she had a white girl with her, and they joked about how I liked to cook Korean food. The butcher asked if I could eat such spicy food, and David's mom laughed, hit his arm and said that I was able to make *Yuke jung* (fire beef soup).

When I look back at the first time I met Uhm-ma, I realize that a mother's kitchen is a space that one has to be invited into when the time is right and you know each other well enough to share.

I sat across the kitchen table from Uhm-ma and watched her meticulously and patiently fold each wonton wrapper, holding it all together with just the right amount of garlic-stem. But our *mandu*-making sessions have served up more than family home cooking; they have also been the perfect opportunity to learn embarrassing details about David's childhood. However, unlike the *mandu*, these tidbits never leave Uhm-ma's kitchen.

Mom's the Word

Cooking your first turkey dinner has got to be one of the most strenuous kitchen experiences. *The Griswald's Family Christmas* plays in my head over and over—especially the scene where the turkey comes out of the oven glistening and golden brown. But when the knife makes the first incision, the entire carcass deflates, and as my father would say, it was as dry as a popcorn fart.

Two years ago I cooked my first turkey dinner. The occasion for this tryptophan-induced dinner? Thanksgiving. I was knighted into turkey chefdom by David's mom.

"Amy, it is Thanksgiving tomorrow, so we probably should have dinner," Uhm-ma said.

Oh yum! I thought, as I remembered my mom's moist stuffing, wild rice, celery, sage, and the gravy that held the dinner together like heavenly brown glue—tasty glue, of course!

I was beginning to salivate when Uhm-ma said, "So let me know how much everything costs, and I will pay you back for the groceries." Her request—no, declaration—broke me out of my reverie.

Did that just happen? I stared at her straight in the face, stepped out of my body for a brief moment, and gave myself a swift kick to the butt. I still had an imaginary ring of my mom's gravy around my mouth. The weight of the holiday had just been placed on my shoulders.

I stammered, "Uh, Uhm-ma, don't worry about it. I'll take care of everything."

"I will tell everyone that dinner is here, so make sure you get a big enough turkey."

Just like that, she chasséd out of the kitchen and left me standing there, smiling like an ass. I was contemplating my next move when David popped his head into the kitchen.

"Grab your coat, we're heading to Superstore to grab the dinner stuff." He stopped and looked back at me. "You know what you're doing, right?"

God, the nerve! *You know what you're doing, right? Me-me-me-me-me. . . . blah blah blah.* Well, one thing we will never question is the fact that you know what you are doing, David—just sitting there and enjoying it all and acting surprised when it comes out perfect. Grrrrrrrr!

"Amy, let's get going—it's gonna be a zoo in there. Thanksgiving is tomorrow!"

I sat silently in the car, calculating, worrying, and playing out the Griswald scene in my mind. I began making a mental shopping list. I closed my eyes and thought about Thanksgiving dinner tastes and what types of ingredients those tastes translated into. I knew the basics from eighteen years of watching Mom prepare our family's turkey dinners, but it was the magic and experience I lacked.

Photograph courtesy of author.

David and my pièce de résistance—the only help he usually provides is in eating all the food.

The intensity in Superstore could easily be compared to the chaos in a toy store on Christmas Eve. I saw several other young couples frantically milling about—boyfriends blankly pushing the shopping cart from aisle to aisle, and girlfriends, some staring at crumpled pieces of paper, some on cell phones asking questions like, "Mom, but what is *in* the sweet potato casserole?" Maybe they were trying to recreate their childhood memories too.

We made it through Superstore unscathed with all the ingredients. As soon as David dropped me and the groceries off, I made a frantic call to Mom.

"I have to cook a turkey dinner tomorrow, and all of David's family is gonna be here, so I don't know what I am gonna do. . . !"

"Amy, hello! Okay, okay, slow down! Do you have the turkey? How big is it?"

"I don't know! It's pretty huge!" I manoeuvred the slippery carcass while balancing the phone between my ear and right shoulder.

"Well, if it's eight to twelve pounds, it's going to take three and a half to four hours at about 325 degrees. It is thawed, right?"

"Oh my God, Mom, there weren't any fresh turkeys left!" I wailed while punching the twelve-pound frozen mass in front of me. Ouch!

"Well, Thanksgiving's tomorrow. . ."

"Mom, I know! I know!"

There was a brief moment of silence. Then I heard Mom step up on the stool in front of the fridge to reach for her faded blue duo tang, filled with decades of recipes, advice and family memories.

"All right, leave the turkey overnight in the sink, and in the morning check to see if it's thawed. If it's still frozen, trickle some warm water over it until it is thawed. Don't worry, honey, it will all be okay. Do you have a pen and paper?"

The Cabbage Connection

Photograph courtesy of author.

The Perreault family.

My family flocked from the prairies to the interior of British Columbia when I was young. The reason I say flocked is because prairie people never stray too far away from each other.

My dad's extended family is massive, and historically, they have been travelers. My family's Métis heritage explains the Perreault kinship sprawl across the prairies and into other provinces. Let's put it this way—if you closed your eyes and pointed to a map of the prairies, your finger would probably land on a town where we had relatives. Large gatherings were not uncommon, and family had a tendency to just show up. I think this is why the food portions at these gathering were huge—you never knew who would be there to eat.

My memories of the prairies are mostly from road trips during summer vacation. Family reunions meant at least three full days of feasting. It was prairie potluck-food and family recipes that had migrated from various parts of Canada. The variety of food displayed on checkered plastic tablecloths was a spectacular sight. One thing that always stood out was Grandma Perreault's cabbage rolls, carefully wrapped and covered in tomato sauce. I think this recipe has been traveling a long time from the Ukrainian side of our family and is now a permanent fixture at every gathering.

Grandma Perreault always orchestrates the prairie potlucks. She has had lots of experience raising four children while running a small greasy spoon in Saskatchewan. She drives Dad crazy because she refuses to sit still once the food is on the table. Perched on the edge of her chair, Grandma scans the table for the blueprint in her mind and says something like, "Shit, I forgot the green beans in the microwave!" She still insists that Dad eat four eggs and half a pound of bacon every time we go to visit her in Kelowna. She knows how everyone likes their bacon and eggs cooked, and whether their toast is dry or buttered. I think she misses the house being full. I miss her cabbage rolls and their perfect balance of beef, rice, cabbage, and tomato sauce.

When I first met David, he introduced me to *kimchi*. I instantly fell in love with this spicy, garlicky, cabbage mixture. Uhm-ma watched me devour the *kimchi* and looked over at David with a surprised look on her face.

"Wow, she really likes *kimchi*! This is strange for a *Hiyen-saram* to enjoy it so much!"

I laughed and thought to myself about my love for cabbage that has been cultivated throughout the years. As I sat at the dinner table with David and his family, I began to think about the migration—and evolution—of food again. I was still part of the cabbage connection, whether in Vancouver or back on the prairies.

The strength of my family comes from women—Grandma, Mom, Uhm ma wrapping up layers of memories for their families to savour. Now that I am older, I see the importance of family gatherings and food. And I see the migration of food and recipes as a way of mapping out where my family has been.

I have started composing symphonies in my own kitchen, making everything from Korean dishes to turkey dinners for David and his family. But my turkey dinner is definitely a matinee compared to my grandmother's epic headliner performances.

I wonder. . . . does *kimchi* go with turkey?

Amy's Chicken Soup (my version taken from Uhm-ma's kitchen—sans David's opinion)

1 whole roaster chicken (*d'ak*)

1 head of garlic (*man-uhl*), cloves peeled and separated

Half a white onion, finely chopped (*yung pa'h*)

Salt (*soogim*)

1 bundle of green onions (*pa'ah*)

1 tsp black pepper (*who-chuu-garru*)

1 Tbsp crushed garlic (this is in addition to the one head of garlic)

3 Tbsp crushed roasted sesame seeds (*geh*)

Love (*sarang-hey*)*

Patience (still learning the word slowly—maybe lost in translation)*

1.) Wash and remove all of the skin from the chicken. I usually use scissors and do this under running water.

2.) Remove any organs inside the chicken. I do this with a spoon and look away. (This is a very emotional thing for me. I always apologize to the chicken for scraping out its internal organs.)

3.) I usually remove the wings, but you don't have to. Be warned that the first time you do this, it may be traumatic. (I still feel as if I am breaking a smile child's arm every time I remove the wings. I apologize at this point too.)

4.) Place chicken in a Dutch oven or large pot, and fill it with as much water as you can. As the water boils away, add more because this soup can be eaten for several sittings, and there's always a shortage of broth.

5.) Boil the chicken with the garlic cloves, white onion, and salt to taste. I usually add a bit of salt at the beginning and a bit at the end after the broth has formed. Do not over-salt—there are weird people out there who will automatically add salt without even trying the soup you have so lovingly prepared for them. Do not make a fuss—you can't change this absurd behavior. Just put salt on the table and watch. Sometimes it is therapeutic to tsk-tsk and say "high blood pressure" under your breath.

6.) Once the chicken is cooked (no pink and the legs pull easily away from the body), remove the chicken and set it aside in a bowl. Remove the soup from the heat. Once the soup cools, you can easily skim the fat off the top.

7.) If you are in a hurry, you can run the chicken under cold water until the meat is cool enough to touch, or you can place it in the fridge to let it cool.

8.) Pull the chicken off the carcass and place it in a bowl. Tear off pieces the size of your pinky finger, and place them in a separate bowl.

9.) Add a handful of thinly chopped green onions, black pepper, crushed garlic (if you don't like garlic you should have never attempted this recipe), and crushed roasted sesame seeds to the chicken shreds. Massage all the ingredients together (while thinking lovely thoughts) and taste. Now this part is for you to decide: add more of what you need—it's up to you and your family's taste.

10.) Re-boil the broth.

11.) Add the chicken mixture to a bowl for each family member, and top with a ladle of broth. Serve with steamed rice. The soup tastes good if you add the rice to it at the table. For a spicy version, I usually have Korean red pepper flakes (*goh-chew-garew*) on the table as a condiment.

12.) Serve with your favourite side dishes (*banchan*). I usually serve this with *nappa kimchi* (*baechu-mock kimchi*) and dried anchovy sauté (*meddruchi bokum*).

13.) See below for the notes on the ingredients Love and Patience.

Enjoy!

*Notes on Love and Patience (How to Cook for Your Boyfriend)

1.) Don't ever think that your cooking will be better than your boyfriend's mother's. Be patient enough to hear him out. His comparison of your cooking to his mother's is his subtle way of being sensitive and showing his respect for that "other" special woman in his life. Embrace it.

2.) Try not to be offended when your boyfriend attempts to correct your cooking techniques so they will be more like his mother's—even if he rarely steps foot in the kitchen. It is easier to go along with it. The more you agree, the more quickly he will leave the kitchen and be out of your way. Smile and thank him for his groundbreaking insight on how to correctly slice green onion. After he exits the kitchen, wait three seconds and exhale. Continue as before because you were doing it right in the first place. And don't forget to LOVE the fact that you *are* right!

Photograph courtesy of author.

"Don't tell me how to cook, David!"

3.) Remember: Love, patience, and garlic. My mom said that garlic breeds good, honest, healthy people. If you order garlicky food on the first date, it will keep the creeps away, and the nice guys will offer you gum! So it is entirely up to you to decide if it is a three- or four-clove kind of day.

Author's Note

You can take the family out for food, but you can't take the food out of family!

I wanted to take this workshop to learn how to write a narrative using food. I knew that food had the power to go beyond the dinner table.

I wanted to document my experience of coming into my partner's family—a Korean immigrant family—using the kitchen as an entry point. I have been shopping around for a cookbook that explains a few things about Korean food preparation and protocol, but I never found anything that told the whole story or got personal enough to make sense to me. There are experiences that simply cannot be found in recipes alone. Some of the best dishes I have made came from recipe deviations or a fusion of family secrets. Whether it's through a phone conversation with Mom or a hands-on lesson from Uhm-ma, I am beginning to create food memories that are flavoured with a variety of influences.

As a university student, I have been taught to look for dates as pivotal moments in history, but after taking this workshop I have found that the everyday process of sharing a meal together holds more meaning and should not be taken for granted. This workshop has given me a space to write about my experiences of cooking, experimenting, and getting to know David and his family, while rediscovering my own family memories found in the food we prepare, the food we eat, and the food we share.

Amy Perreault

The Spirits of Food

Dan Seto

Mom's Foo Yi

When I was growing up in High River, Alberta, we lived above my grandfather's restaurant, the New Look Café, which only served Western food. My mom would often take my brothers and me downstairs for a visit. We'd watch the cooks in the kitchen grill hamburgers, smother French fries with thick brown gravy, and deep-fry battered fish. In the dining room I'd watch the waitresses serve huge wedges of Boston cream pie, splitting cream puffs and filling them with whipped cream, or scooping vanilla ice cream onto slabs of apple pie. But we rarely got to eat the restaurant fare. Instead, Mom would lead us back upstairs and cook Chinese food for us. This was food that we didn't know the names of—food that no one else in our school ate. And some of the food was particularly stinky, not appealing in any sort of way. One of those foods was *foo yi*.

◈ ◈ ◈

Photograph courtesy of author.

My grandfather's restaurant, the New Look Café.

I am seven years old. Mom is slicing up some meat and putting it in a bowl. Then she goes to the fridge and comes back with a jar filled with yellow squares floating in cloudy water. Mom takes out a few of these squares and mashes it into the meat.

I put my nose to the jar. Whew! It's so stinky! The squares look like the soap I saw at the Chinese laundryman's place. Mom puts the bowl of meat in a pan filled with water and covers the pan with a lid. I hear the water bubbling. I'm bored of listening to water bubble.

My brothers and I go watch television. We forget about dinner until Mom calls us.

Photograph courtesy of author.

My mom and my youngest brother, Wayne.

"Set fun la," Mom says. It's time to eat!

Mom takes the lid off the pan and a big rush of steam billows out of it. She puts the bowl of meat on the kitchen table. She scoops out the meat and gravy, and puts some in my bowl of rice.

I take whiff—it's not smelly anymore. I paddle some meat and rice into my mouth. The rice and meat squish between my teeth. The salty gravy is hot and smooth.

As we're eating, Mom tells us in her Hoiping dialect, "In China, we didn't eat much meat because we were so poor." I notice that she's not eating much of the meat now. Instead, she goes to the fridge and uses her chopsticks to pick up one of the cold yellow squares from the jar and puts it on her rice. She must really love eating this stuff—she eats it without cooking it.

I take another big bite of my meat, gravy, and rice.

◈ ◈ ◈

When I was older, I found out what those yellow squares were. They were fermented bean cake, known as *foo yi*. Mom still makes this pork and *foo yi* dish for us—a taste that connects me back to my childhood. And as I got older, I began to realize why Mom has always eaten *foo yi*, cold and plain on rice.

We five brothers often drop in unannounced to enjoy Mom's cooking. Even when she cooks other dishes, she still seems to enjoy eating the *foo yi*, one or two squares. I tried eating the *foo yi* plain on rice when I was young. I didn't like it. As an adult, I tried eating it like that again, and I still didn't like it.

One day, we were having grilled steaks for supper—big juicy steaks, over a pound each. Mom grilled them perfectly for each of us, according to the way we like it, usually medium or medium rare. Always cooked with one flip on each side to lock in the juices.

She cooked the last steak for herself. I could tell she was looking forward to eating it.

We sat down to eat.

"How are the steaks?" Mom asked.

"Ho yeh, ho yeh," we all said. Mom was pleased. She was preparing to take the first bite of her steak. Just then, my cousin walked in.

"Have you eaten yet?" Mom asked him, as she got up to greet him.

"No, not yet," he said. He sat down where she had been sitting. He began eating Mom's big, juicy steak on the plate in front of him.

"How's the steak?" she asked, as she walked over to the fridge and reached for the jar of *foo yi.*

Steamed Pork with *Foo Yi*

1 lb pork, cut into 1-inch squares

5-6 *foo yi* squares

½ tsp salt

2 slices ginger root, chopped

1 tsp light soy sauce

½ tsp sugar

1 tsp garlic

1 tsp cornstarch

1.) Put pork slices in a large bowl. Coat the pork with *foo yi* and salt.

2.) Add ginger, soy sauce, sugar, garlic, and cornstarch. Lightly stir with a spoon or spatula.

3.) Place the bowl of pork in a large pan filled with water. Cover pan with lid. Steam until meat is cooked and tender, about 30 minutes.

4.) Remove bowl from pan, and serve directly from bowl.

Approximately 4 average servings or 1 serving for Dan.

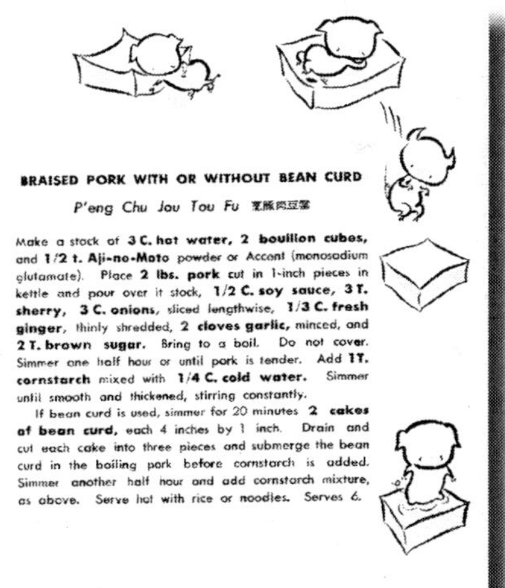

BRAISED PORK WITH OR WITHOUT BEAN CURD

P'eng Chu Jou Tou Fu

Make a stock of **3 C. hot water, 2 bouillon cubes,** and **1/2 t. Aji-no-Moto** powder or Accent (monosodium glutamate). Place **2 lbs. pork** cut in 1-inch pieces in kettle and pour over it stock, **1/2 C. soy sauce, 3 T. sherry, 3 C. onions,** sliced lengthwise, **1/3 C. fresh ginger,** thinly shredded, **2 cloves garlic,** minced, and **2 T. brown sugar.** Bring to a boil. Do not cover. Simmer one half hour or until pork is tender. Add **1 T. cornstarch** mixed with **1/4 C. cold water.** Simmer until smooth and thickened, stirring constantly.

If bean curd is used, simmer for 20 minutes **2 cakes of bean curd,** each 4 inches by 1 inch. Drain and cut each cake into three pieces and submerge the bean curd in the boiling pork before cornstarch is added. Simmer another half hour and add cornstarch mixture, as above. Serve hot with rice or noodles. Serves 6.

From *The Art of Chinese Cooking,* by the Benedictine Sisters of Peking, 1956.

Dad's Thanksgiving Congee

Photograph courtesy of author.

My dad at the New Look Café in the 1960s.

We always look forward to Thanksgiving because Dad cooks a great roasted turkey dinner, perfected after many years of working in and owning restaurants. He is always enthusiastic to cook this dinner because we enjoy it so much.

In the last few years another tradition was created. The day after we have roast turkey, Dad makes turkey congee. At first, making congee the day after was perhaps just an afterthought—he found a good use for the turkey carcass. But these days he seems just as excited about making the turkey congee as the turkey dinner the day before. He always reminds us to come back the next day for congee.

He boils the carcass in a pot of water with a handful of rice. Then he picks off the leftover turkey meat to serve in the congee. He adds other ingredients, such as ground pork, beef, prawns, or pig stomach. For garnish there are chopped duck eggs, green onions, parsley, Chinese radish, and white pepper. Served with Chinese doughnuts, we all feel this is Dad's Thanksgiving congee. But to my dad, congee has always had a special meaning.

It was late 1948. The Chinese Communist rebels were trying to recruit Dad to fight for them. One of Dad's distant cousins approached him to join them in their fight to overthrow the Nationalists. Dad thought it was no big deal. He wasn't politically motivated, but he joined so he could get fed and have better living conditions.

One late afternoon, Dad and his squadron were walking along a street in the village. As they approached the corner of a building, rapid machine gunfire erupted. The Nationalist soldiers set up machine guns on top of a building. They were poised to shoot to kill.

Six of the members of Dad's squadron turned the corner, right into the machine gunfire coming on their right side. Dad, with two other members, were a few steps behind. They had not turned the corner and could not be seen by the Nationalists manning the machine guns.

"Stop! Don't run yet!" Dad told his two comrades.

The other six members of the squadron had jumped down an embankment into some rice fields. From there they kept running. The machine gunfire followed the six into the distance.

"Run, now!" Dad yelled, as they ran toward the embankment to jump into the rice fields. The line of fire was coming back toward them from right to left.

As the bullets ricocheted off the embankment, Dad and his buddies slid into some sweet potato hedges growing in the field. These hedges were about three feet high and provided excellent cover. In addition to the gunfire coming from the right, there were also six or seven Nationalist soldiers with rifles shooting from ground level on the left side.

There were six farmers scattered throughout the rice fields. To avoid the gunfire, they began crouching as well. Dad pulled out his handgun and pointed it at the farmers.

"Stand up, or I'm going to kill you," he said. The farmers stood up. Dad hoped the Nationalists would stop shooting if the farmers stood up and got in the way.

He was right. The shooting stopped momentarily, and Dad and the other two members were able to escape the gunfire. They crossed the stream behind the rice fields and disappeared into the mountains.

It was getting dark. The three of them kept walking for two hours, when it started to rain. They huddled together with their backs toward each other under a tree, taking turns sleeping while the rain continued to pour.

Fearing the Nationalists would still be after them, they started out early in the morning. They found a path leading up the mountain. When they reached the top, they saw a farm at the bottom on the other side. They walked down the mountain toward the farmhouse. They were exhausted and cold but kept going.

As they reached the farmhouse, the farmer greeted them. He ushered them inside and offered each of them a bowl of hot, steaming congee. Just plain congee.

In recalling this memory, Dad knew he had a lot to be thankful for. That bowl of congee ultimately meant his survival.

As he pats his stomach and finishes telling his story, a big smile comes over his face. "That was the best meal I ever had."

Dad's Thanksgiving Congee

1 cup rice

12 cups water

1 tsp salt

2 slices ginger root

1 turkey carcass (you can substitute turkey or chicken wings or drumsticks)

1.) Soak rice in water for 2 hours in a large pot.

2.) Add salt, ginger, and carcass. Bring to boil over medium to high heat.

3.) Reduce heat, and cover with lid.

4.) Cook for at least 2 hours, stirring occasionally, until you have your desired consistency.

5.) Remove turkey carcass, and scrape off turkey meat into congee. You can also add ground pork, beef, pig stomach, prawns, or whatever else you desire. Add these ingredients in the last 30 minutes of cooking.

Optional garnishes: green onions, parsley, chopped duck eggs, Chinese radish, peanuts, Chinese doughnut.

Communist Soup

"Have you eaten yet?" Mom asks when I walk through the door.

I sit down at the kitchen table. Before I can even answer, Mom brings me a big bowl of communist soup. I can't remember when I first heard of the term communist soup, or *goong chun gung*. I believe it's synonymous with *lai tong*, which refers to daily soup.

Tonight, the communist soup contains pork spareribs with lotus root. I remember eating lotus root as a child because I thought they looked like wagon wheels floating in the soup.

Mom always serves my soup in my own special bowl—it's larger than the bowls the rest of my family eats from. I pick up one of the spareribs with my hand and dip it in soy sauce. I take a big bite as the tender meat separates from the bone.

"Did you visit Uncle Rat while you were in Toronto?" I ask, taking a bite of the lotus root.

Mom says, "We had dinner with him and his wife, and I just found out that he..."

Dad interrupts, "Let me tell you..." Whenever Dad says "let me tell you," it always means he's going to tell me one of the stories from his past—a story we've all heard countless times.

"You know Uncle Big Mouth? The one with such a big mouth that the Communist rebels wanted to kill him? You remember him?" Dad prods me to make sure I'm paying attention.

I nod while I continue eating my soup. In fact, I know this story quite well. The year was 1949. The Communist rebels were hiding in my dad's village. They were worried that if Uncle Big Mouth exposed them to the Nationalists, their lives would be endangered.

"So one night the Communists rebels set up some guys on the lookout. They knew the route where Uncle Big Mouth walked home after work every night. When they saw him, they signaled to the sharpshooter to shoot him," Dad continues. "But they shot the wrong guy!"

"Such a tragedy to shoot the wrong guy," Mom adds, as she often does at the end of this story.

Someone had warned Uncle Big Mouth that he was set up to be killed that night, so he went into hiding. The guy that got killed happened to be at the wrong place at the wrong time. But what did this story have to do with Uncle Rat?

When my parents visited Uncle Rat in Toronto, for some reason they told him the story of Uncle Big Mouth. All of a sudden the past caught up with the present. A secret that had been buried long ago in China came unraveled.

"I was one of the guys on the lookout for him that night!" Uncle Rat revealed.

It had been over fifty years since Uncle Rat was on that lookout to have Uncle Big Mouth killed. In the subsequent years he has visited Uncle Big Mouth in Vancouver, stayed at his house, and accepted his hospitality—all without Uncle Big Mouth knowing.

The stories always seem to change just a little. So does communist soup. As I finish my soup, I wonder if my mom could make communist soup with oxtail the next time. I haven't had that in a long while.

Communist Soup with Lotus Root

1 lb fresh lotus root

1 lb pork spareribs

6 Chinese red dates

12 cups water

2 slices ginger root

1 Tbsp soy sauce

1 tsp salt

1.) Wash and clean lotus root. Cut into ¼-inch slices crosswise so they look like wagon wheels.

2.) Cut spareribs into small slabs. Combine spareribs, lotus root, Chinese red dates, water, and ginger root in pot. Bring to boil. Skim surface with a spoon to clear the broth.

3.) Lower heat, cover with lid, and cook for 1 hour.

4.) Add soy sauce and salt. Simmer for 5 minutes.

5.) You can substitute pork spareribs with beef short ribs, oxtail, or any other beef or pork bones.

Photograph courtesy of Wayne Seto.

Mmm. . .communist soup!

Fong Leun Tong New Year Banquet

I am attending the Fong Leun Tong Chinese New Year banquet. I have never been in a room with so many Chinese people. As I sit down at our designated table, I scan the room.

Big bulging eyes are staring at me. Those eyes are looking into mine, like they're looking into my soul, searching for the truth. Those eyes are looking at me as if to say, "Have you done wrong against the Fong Leun Tong? Have you brought shame to the name of the Fong Leun Tong? If you are guilty, are you ready to deal with the Curse of the Fong Leung Tong?"

The Fong Leun Tong is open to members worldwide with the surnames "Seto" or "Sit." The Canadian chapter of the Fong Leun Tong was set up in 1959, with its head office in Vancouver.

The next year, four elders traveled across Canada to raise money. My dad put up $1500 for a debenture. The money raised was used to buy a clubhouse where members socialized. The members also bought revenue property to generate income for the association. The income generated went toward disadvantaged clan members, charities, and scholarships, as well as toward hosting a lavish clan New Year banquet every year.

"這四個伯有靈—*Koi thai goi buk yu lain*," Dad would say. For a long time, I didn't know what he meant, but it sounded mysterious. What my dad meant was that although the four elders were deceased, their spirits lived on and continued to look over the clan. If clan members behaved properly, their spirits would look out for them. If they didn't conduct themselves appropriately, their spirits would put the Curse of the Fong Leun Tong upon them.

I stare into the bulging eyes again. The head is huge with a large forehead, with steam coming out from the top of it. The wide body is draped with yellow slivers and green flecks, lying in a pool of hot dark oil. "Are you afraid of the Curse of the Fong Leun Tong?"

I am not afraid of the Curse of the Fong Leun Tong because I have not stolen or conducted myself improperly. I am an honourable member of the Fong Leun Tong.

I take my chopsticks and plunge them into the throat of the steamed rock cod, its bulging eyes staring at me as I tear out a chunk of meat, along with the bones that hold it. I take a big bite—its meat is firm and smooth, topped with ginger and green onions, lightly coated with soy sauce, oil, and its own juices. I know I will have good luck in the New Year after I eat this fish.

It may seem improbable that a curse could be brought on by four dead men. Or that a rock cod could bring good luck. But tell that to Chinese people who have strong beliefs, especially those who believe that you are what you eat. That eating fish can bring abundance. That eating oysters can bring prosperity. That eating whole Chinese black mushrooms can bring wishes fulfilled. That eating *fat choy* (sea moss) can bring great wealth. That eating long life noodles at Chinese New Year will bring long life.

One time, in the meeting room of the Fong Leun Tong clubhouse, a clan member stood up, shook his fist in defiance at the pictures of the four elders hanging on the wall. . .and dropped dead. Is this curse or coincidence? You be the judge.

Another time, my dad was having tea with a cousin, who was visiting from overseas. The cousin was spouting some negative things he had done within the Fong Leun Tong years ago when he was living in

Vancouver. Then realizing he had said too much, he said, "I'm not going to say anymore." He made a motion with his hand, as if to zip his lips. A few months later, he dropped dead. Another time. . .

Chinese people don't like to talk about curses—especially at New Year. They would rather talk about good luck, good health, prosperity, and happiness.

But for those who go against the goodwill of the Fong Leun Tong, may I suggest that you eat an extra helping of long life noodles, just in case.

Chinese Canadian Professionals New Year Banquet

This year, I was asked to be the featured speaker at a Chinese New Year banquet sponsored by the Association of Chinese Canadian Professionals. Many in the audience were young and optimistic with bright futures ahead of them.

Photograph courtesy of author.

My family in High River, Alberta in the 1960s, from left to right—me, Hopland, Mom, Hopman, Dad and Lewis.

I see a familiar face. A face I had met at a Chinese New Year banquet several decades past. Still proud and majestic but more modern. Almost hip—wearing red shades covering the eyes and a coat in bright red to match.

My speech was on growing up with different cultures living in a small rural Alberta town during the 1960s. My family was one of the few Chinese families in High River. I spoke about Chinese customs, quirks, and superstitions.

I talked about how my mother would put green onions in my pockets when I went to school—because in Chinese the word for green onion and the word for smart sound similar. The audience laughed when I described how my teacher pulled out big stalks of green onions from my pockets.

What I didn't say in my speech was that my mother was also a realist. She put green onions in my pockets for a little extra luck in getting good grades, but she also knew that getting ahead would still be a big struggle. She told my older brother when he was growing up that as Chinese Canadians, we would never be accepted as equals. She never told this to me—maybe to protect me from the harshness of reality.

I greet the familiar face from the past. The rock cod of old has undergone a few changes. Its big bulging eyes are now covered by red cherries. Its body still wide and sturdy, but perhaps a little bit smaller in stature. It is deep-fried in hot oil instead of gently steamed.

When I finished my speech, I sat down at my table with a group of young Chinese Canadians. One young lady lived in Squamish when she was about seven. Her dad, an immigrant from Hong Kong, took a job as an engineer because it offered him the best job opportunity. She remembered that there were only three Chinese families in town and how people looked at her because she was different.

I asked a young Chinese Canadian man how he coped living on the east side of Vancouver when he was growing up. He said he found it pretty easy because the majority of the kids were Asian. But when he joined the working world, he found it more difficult. He looked as if he was going to say something more, but then he abruptly stopped.

The waiter cut off the rock cod head. Because no one else wanted it, he gave it to me. I look at the head. The cherries covering its eyes were pink, like rose-coloured glasses. I removed the cherries, fully expecting to see eyeballs. I was quite jarred to see the eyeballs had been scooped out, and now in the fish head were empty sockets. The window to the soul was missing.

The rock cod had its mouth open as if to speak. I picked up the rock cod head and bit into its skull. It was light and crispy. I bit off the jaw and was surprised that it was slightly soft. I tore out its throat and munched on it, savouring the tangy tomato sauce coating it.

Author's Note

I was fortunate to be part of the first-ever CCHSBC family history writing workshop in 2006. This second workshop has given me an opportunity to continue writing more stories. My thanks go to my fellow participants, who gave me valuable insight and shared their knowledge and experiences. A special thank-you to Brandy, our facilitator who kept me focused and whose judgment I totally trust.

The highlight of this workshop was having a potluck lunch where everyone brought a food dish and told a story about it. I talked about my search for the old-fashioned cream puffs I had as child—the kind that were light and crispy, filled with real whipped cream. Recently, I made sixteen attempts at baking cream puffs, using various recipes, but have not been able to duplicate the cream puffs of my childhood. If anyone knows of a recipe for crispy cream puffs, please email me at **vanrocket69@yahoo.com**.

My family history in Canada begins with my grandfather coming to Canada from Canton, China in 1910 as a head tax immigrant. He sponsored my dad in 1949. Later, my dad went back to Hong Kong to marry my mom. My early years were spent growing up in High River, Alberta before moving to Vancouver.

The Fong Leun Tong is our clan society comprising of people with the surname Sit or Seto. In 1952 my dad visited the clan headquarters in Vancouver when it was located on Union Street. The headquarters were later moved to a house on Georgia Street. After the four elders raised the money from their fundraising drive, two buildings were purchased in the early 1960s. A house located at 718 East Pender Street became the headquarters from the early 1960s to 1999. The building purchased at 9 East Hastings Street is a commercial building, where the headquarters were relocated upstairs from the year 2000 to the present.

I have visited the headquarters at 718 East Pender Street and 9 East Hastings Street on many occasions. While there, I have had many animated discussions, with ongoing oral histories being told.

There has been a movement in and around Chinatown to maintain or renovate buildings which various family clans own. Whether they renovate or not, many clans will never sell their buildings. Chinese people often think of their clan building like a family home—it's the last thing they would want to sell.

However, times have changed. I was saddened to hear that the former headquarters at 718 East Pender Street was sold on March 20, 2006. Recently, the Board of Directors of the Fong Leun Tong Society has given notice to discuss the motion to sell the headquarters at 9 East Hastings Street.

Because of our physical headquarters disappearing, it's even more important to document the memories we have of those times.

Dan Seto

In Hot Water: Cross-Cultural Food How-To's & Lessons Learned

Bob Sung

Comfort Food

A rainy, dark, and very blustery winter evening. I've just arrived home feeling totally out of sorts. Nothing would be better now than stick-to-the-ribs comfort food—the kind of heartiness that reinforces a feeling of wellness and a soothing warmth to my body and to my soul. Robust Indian curry chicken stew, tangy Mexican *chile con carne*, luscious Italian *bolognese* meat sauce with pasta, savoury Chinese beef brisket and tendon stew with hot white rice—these dishes invoke strong memories that exemplify profound life lessons.

Racial Comfort

Curry chicken stew is reminiscent of correcting the negative perception of East Indians that I had in my younger years. A good friend invited me to his girlfriend's family home for dinner. They were an East Indian family with a great love of food. As soon as I arrived at their home, they got me making *chapati* and preparing the curries. As well as the curry chicken stew, the menu consisted of okra curry, *dahl*, tandoori lamb, and butter chicken. Their willingness to teach me made me humble and ashamed of my prejudicial notions. Imagine! My prejudice defeated by curry spice, chutney, and *chapati*.

Risky Comfort

I used to be in the wholesale produce business, a career which entailed buying trips to the U.S./Mexican border town of Nogales, a distribution point for fresh fruits and vegetables from Mexico. One memorable buying trip occurred during the raucous Cinqo de Mayo festivities.

I went to a little cantina called La Caverna, which was built in a mountainside cave. There, the cook showed me how to prepare fiery *chile relleanos*, massive pulled pork *tortas*, overflowing beef *enchiladas* with refried beans, and *mole* chicken. We annihilated the meal, washing it down with mescal, a very potent spirit made from agave, mescal plant, and a worm in each bottle.

The next day, I woke up in the Nogales Hospital after having my stomach pumped. Too much food, too much mescal. Was the risk worth it? I don't know if I can answer that question, but in the end, it was still a truly remarkable culinary memory.

Flexible Comfort

Italian bolognese meat sauce and pasta reflects my willingness to be open to a realm of possibilities. Everyone has their own meat sauce recipe, and I'm sticking to my guns and do not want to deviate. But one time, while I was fixing a big batch of sauce for my family, a young start-up (no names mentioned—even if he is my nephew!) threw in spoonfuls of miso paste and sesame oil. He looked at me and said, "Give it a try, Uncle, you'll like it!" There was nothing I could do but to taste it. And. . . . Wow! An added dimension! For now, my culinary mantra is "Flexible taste. . .flexible life."

Photograph courtesy of author.

The comfort of a Sung family get-together.

Forgiving Comfort

I associate Chinese beef brisket stew with forgiveness and connection. When I was younger, it was always "look but don't touch" in Mom's kitchen. Sometimes, the fact that the kitchen was her domain that was off-limits to me would get to me, and I would lose my temper. Finally, I said, "Mom, I'm sorry for showing my temper, but I want to cook!" In the days that followed, a loving trust was in initiated in the kitchen, and the first cooking lesson Mom gave me was beef brisket stew.

She told me, "Make sure the tendons are tender, full of flavour. The brisket should be a dark red colour, the *lo bak* firm and pungent. Get all the spices and soy ready. Let the ingredients slowly braise and simmer, with the aromatic perfume of the sauce eventually rising."

Although gone from my life, she still talks to me about recipes and ingredients.

Chinese Beef Brisket Stew

3 lbs beef brisket

5 Tbsp vegetable oil

½ tsp fermented red bean cake

4 Tbsp hoisin sauce

5 Tbsp dry sherry

5 Tbsp light soy sauce

2 Tbsp garlic, minced

1 whole star anise

2 tsp Chinese five-spice powder

7 cups water

1 large *lo bak* (Chinese white radish/daikon), chopped

1.) Cut brisket into 2-inch strips, then cut strips into cubes.

2.) Heat a wok, add 3 tablespoons of oil. Brown brisket cubes. Set aside meat.

3.) Add remaining oil to wok. Crumble up red bean cake and put in wok. Add hoisin sauce, dry sherry, light soy sauce, garlic, star anise, five-spice powder, and water. Bring to a boil.

4.) Add meat to the wok and reduce heat. Simmer for 2 hours.

5.) After 1½ hours, add the Chinese white radish. Cook for another 30 minutes until beef and radish are fork tender.

Serve immediately with steamed white rice.

SEE YOW GUY: HOW TO BE A BIG BOY

You must picture me as a lippy and arrogant sixteen-year-old. These were the years marked by my invincible, "who cares about anyone else" attitude.

July 1966, the end of the school year and the start of summer vacation. Because I was a good student that year, my parents decided to reward me with a trip to California to attend a two-week sports camp at Stanford University. Football, baseball, tennis, swimming, golf! And for the first time in my life, I was going to be traveling alone and making my own arrangements to get to the camp.

My father was testing my limits and abilities, but at the same time, my mother was freaking out with worry. I tried to reassure her by saying, "Don't worry, Mom—I'm a big boy now!"

Day of departure. The journey to San Francisco was a two-hour flight. During this time, I befriended a Chinese boy named David. He was the same age as I, and traveling on his own to see his relatives in the Bay area.

Upon arrival into San Francisco Airport, we decided to share a cab into town. We jumped into the back seat of the cab and noticed that our driver was African American. As we pulled away from the airport, I got David's attention, pointed at the driver, and candidly refer to him (in my lousy Cantonese) as "*see yow guy*."

All of a sudden, while driving on the freeway, the driver jammed on the brakes, swerved to the curb, and stopped. He turned around with eyes full of anger and yelled, "Don't you be calling me *soy sauce chicken*!"

He drove to the closest freeway turnaround, headed back to the airport, got out of the car, and threw our bags onto the sidewalk. He called us "little chink bastards," then took off in a haze of blue smoke from the spinning tires.

David threw me a look of total disgust, picked up his bags, and saying nothing, disappeared into another cab. I stood there speechless, in complete shock and disbelief. The instantaneous shame that I had for my arrogant blunder felt like a film of oil that couldn't be wiped clean. I was also ashamed because I just used a racial slur—something that I would react to the same way as the driver had.

I sat on the airport curb trying to understand my mistake. Chalk it up to experience and learn from such a hurtful remark. Be respectful of others.

The term and the dish "*see yow guy*," or soy sauce chicken, will always have significant meaning for me. It will always remind me of the ugly airport incident—a lesson to be a big boy now.

See Yow Guy (Soy Sauce Chicken)

1 fresh whole chicken (2 to 3 lbs dressed)

3 ½ cups dark soy sauce

5 Tbsp Worcestershire sauce

3 cups water

¼ cup brown sugar

2 loonie-sized pieces of ginger root

3 star anise

4 Tbsp alcohol (gin, Scotch, vodka)

3 scallions (cut up to ½-inch lengths)

1.) Select a pot in which chicken can fit easily but not loosely.

2.) Combine soy sauce, Worcestershire sauce, water, brown sugar, ginger, star anise, and alcohol in pot. Bring to a boil over low heat.

3.) Add whole chicken to the pot. Simmer over low heat for 15 minutes.

4.) Turn chicken over and simmer 20 minutes. Remove from pot.

5.) Cool and chop into serving pieces. Arrange on serving platter. Sprinkle with scallions. Spoon sauce over the chicken and serve.

A Lesson in Communication

It's June of 1970. I'm starting my very first romantic relationship with a pretty girl named Mary. Love is in the air—so how do I celebrate? A special dinner at Foo's in Chinatown, consisting of all my favourite dishes! Careful planning is in order.

First, I must prepare a list of all my favourites—chicken chow mein, garlic fried crab, *gai lan* with oyster sauce. I'm getting very hungry while making this list, but I'm also looking forward to this great dinner date.

Second, because I don't speak a word of Cantonese, it's important that I learn how to order my favourite dishes. After all, I want this evening to be a totally authentic one to really impress Mary (who is Caucasian)!

All week, for one hour each day, Mom and Dad have been drilling in me how to pronounce the correct tones. I'm retaining it all very well—man, am I going to impress Mary or what?!

Saturday finally arrives. I am looking so cool in my tan bell-bottoms, tan elevated boots, indigo long-collared shirt, and rose-tinted wire glasses. I pick Mary up, and she's looking really hot in her red miniskirt, white knee-high leather boots, and frilly white blouse.

When we get Foo's, the place is extremely busy and teeming with a lot of people, the clicking of chopsticks, lively conversation, and awesome aromas coming from the food. Getting to our table, I start to lose my nerve and break out in a cold sweat. After all, how can I fake speaking Cantonese in front of all these Cantonese people and in front of Mary!

Nothing left to do but go for broke. I signal the waiter by raising my hand and saying "*Foh guy*. . .*Foh guy*! The waiter comes around laughing (as are some of the people in other tables). He explains to me in English that the term for waiter is *foh gay* and that *foh guy* means turkey.

The waiter is having a field day at my expense. And now Mary is starting to laugh, and I'm starting to cringe under the table in total embarrassment.

In spite of it all, I proceed to order our dinner. The first item is chicken chow mein or *guy see chow mein*, and the second item is garlic fried crab or *soon gee jow hai*. Laughter erupts. Instead of the items I thought I requested, I ordered chicken shit with noodles and garlic fried shoes. My incorrect tones totally changed the meaning. The waiter exclaims in his clipped English, "You funny. . .you born here." Feeling totally defensive and wounded, I told Mary to stop laughing. "It's not that funny!"

I finish ordering the dinner in English. I want to ensure that we are going to have all of my favourite dishes. The food arrives, and the smells, tastes, and colours of dinner eradicate the awkward moment. The chicken chow mien is pan-fried with oyster sauce-infused julienned strips of chicken and *doong goo* mushrooms. The fragrant garlic fried crab is done with a spicy salt to retain moisture in the meat. The more she savours the food, the more Mary becomes impressed! Food saves the day!

Although an embarrassing moment, this Saturday night is an invaluable lesson for me. Through all my assorted faux pas, I manage to put a smile on people's faces and develop a life-long thirst and hunger to learn more about my heritage.

On this Saturday night, the waiter is my teacher, and I appreciate him correcting me. I am willing to learn and experience life and to let others help show me the way.

Ai ya! What amazing powers food has in nourishing the body and soul, and in connecting with other people. As for Mary? Well, that's another story.

Hot Pot Send-Off

It's Saturday, August 18, 1973. This is the weekend that I'm heading off to Honolulu to start my studies at the University of Hawaii. There's fear and excitement knowing that I'm leaving home for my first extended period of time. Earlier this week, Mom asked me what would I like to have for my send-off dinner. The first thing that I could think of was hot pot. I know it's the summertime and this type of meal is supposed to be for a cold winter night, but I have an affinity for this fondue-like meal. I mean, how else can I play with my food and get away with it all at the same time?!

Photograph courtesy of author.

My parents, Bruce and Vera Sung, on Dad's birthday, July 30, 1973.

This morning I'm driving down to Chinatown to pick up the groceries for tonight's dinner. Yuen Fong market for *bok choy sum*, lotus root, cilantro, garlic, ginger, bean sprouts, and cakes of medium-textured tofu. Le Kiu Poultry to pick up chicken breasts and a couple of cans of chicken broth. Man Cheong market for fresh *doong goo* (shiitake) mushrooms, lemongrass, tiger prawn tails, and rock cod fillets. Fong Lee butcher for wafer-thin sliced beef tenderloin. Gim Lee Yuen for sesame oil, oyster sauce, light soy sauce, salted cooking wine, sweet chili sauce, hoisin sauce, vermicelli, and Thai fragrant rice. And finally, B.C. Royal Cafe for *char siu bau*, *siu mai*, and an ice-cold bottle of Avalon Dairy chocolate milk for lunch.

Arriving home, I rush into the kitchen with all the goodies. Mom and my sister Dee Dee are in the kitchen waiting for me, and Dad's in the den snoring away in front of the television (college football is on). My two brothers are living elsewhere and are unable to dine with us. Only four of us! Great—more food to eat!

Dee Dee has already set the kitchen table with the tablecloth, place settings, wire mesh baskets to cook the food, and an electric deep-dish Dutch tureen perfect for hot pot cooking. She fills the tureen with chicken broth, water, cilantro, lotus root, lemongrass, garlic, and ginger, turns on the electric element to get the broth boiling, and places little condiment plates around each place setting, filling them up with the various sauces.

Dad is still snoring away in the den in front of the blaring television. The three of us proceed to cut up and prepare the meat, seafood and vegetables, dice up the tofu into squares, and wash and cook the rice.

Everything is done and ready to go. All this preparation gets the three of us very hungry. My final duty before we eat is to wake my old man up from his late afternoon nap. I go into the den and announce to him that we're all ready to *sic faun*. His mouth is gaping wide open with a sound of a moose in heat coming out of it. After three tries, no response. Finally, I cup my hands as if they're a megaphone, and yell, "AH BA! LET'S EAT!" Startled, he wakes up, gives me a dirty look, and yells back, "WHAT THE HELL DID YOU SCARE ME FOR! WHAT THE HELL'S WRONG WITH YOU!"

Wonderful! That's all I need—my father mad at me before I leave for school. He sulks for all of five minutes. Finally, the four of us are at the table enjoying this Chinese fondue.

With no *king guy* or talking happening, I can tell that we're totally focusing on the food. The beef is thin and tender, the chicken are juicy little nuggets, the tiger prawns plump and pink, and the *bok choy sum* has a natural leafy sweetness to it. The various dipping sauces enhance the meal, as does fragrant Thai white rice (of which I've eaten four bowls). After the rice, Mom ladles the soup into our bowls. It's twenty-five degrees Celsius today, so after drinking the soup, we're all sweating.

We finally break out into conversation. Dad does his monosyllabic grunts, while the rest of us are talking up a storm. "Who's going to miss me?" Mom says she'll miss me a little bit. Dee Dee says no way is she going to miss me. Dad lets out his samurai grunt, "Uhhhhhhhhhh."

At the end of the meal, Dad and I engage in a male Sung tradition that makes my mother cringe. We start belching.

"Mom, in some cultures it's considered a compliment to belch after a tasty meal."

Mom says, "Do I look that that stupid to even believe your comment?"

Dad says nothing and goes back to the den to turn on the television to continue his nap.

After helping clean up the table and the kitchen with Mom and Dee Dee, I go to the den and watch T.V. with Dad. He's in his chair and ottoman, actually watching the tube and not sleeping.

It's around the 11:00 P.M., late evening news time when I come into the den. Totally out of character, Dad turns off the television and tells me to sit down. He proceeds to tell me that he is very proud of me and that he loves me and will miss me being away from home. This is not his style to be demonstrative. Pleasantly surprised, I shake his hand and impulsively give him a hug. It is more than my stomach that is full and content tonight.

◈ ◈ ◈

Photograph courtesy of author.

Bobby Hot Pot.

It's Saturday, March 3, 2007. Tonight, my company, "Bobby Hot Pot," is doing a Chinese hot pot dinner for clients Roland and Catherine and eight of their friends.

In the late morning I head to my favourite Chinatown stores to pick up the groceries: T&T Supermarket for plump tiger prawn tails, pearl-like digby scallops, and free-range chicken breasts. Superior Tofu for medium-textured tofu cakes. Chinatown Supermarket for *bok choy sum*, lotus root, garlic, lemongrass, bean sprouts, ginger, noodles, basil, iceberg lettuce, oyster sauce, hoisin sauce, chicken stock, and jasmine rice. Wing Tat fishmonger for geoduck clam. San Lee greengrocer for fresh lychee. Ten Ren's tea store for fragrant jasmine and chrysanthemum teas. Dollar Meat store for buttery beef tenderloin sheets.

Mid-afternoon, I go to the clients' home and set the dining table with a crisp white linen tablecloth, linen napkins, cutlery, plates, hot pot tureens, and other hot pot accoutrements. I then don my chef's jacket and proceed to the kitchen to prepare the evening's meal.

Roland arrives home loaded with some German Riesling and B.C. Pinot Noir. He asks, "Do you want to try out the Riesling before we serve it?"

"Better not, Roland. I still need to finish up the food prep."

He nods. "I'll make sure the white wine is chilled before the dinner starts."

7:00 P.M. The guests arrive. I notice that they are all non-Asian. Everyone's gathering in the living room having cocktails.

Image courtesy of author.

A "Bobby Hot Pot" brochure.

I enter carrying an appetizer plate of spicy tofu lettuce wrap. One guest spoons the mixture into the lettuce leaf, then devours it.

"Wow! Goes great with my beer!"

Everyone starts in on the tofu while Catherine introduces me to the guests. I explain to them that not only will they be entertained and fed, but they will also learn some Chinese culture tonight. They chime in unison that this will be their first hot pot experience.

7:45 P.M. Dinner is ready! On the table, the tureens are rapidly boiling with the fragrant broth of chicken stock, water, garlic, ginger, lemongrass, sesame oil, and basil. When everyone is seated, I explain the history of the hot pot, from the nomadic Mongols with their communal pot and freshly killed meat, right up to the various hot pots from the different districts and regions of China.

I go to the kitchen to get the bowls of raw marinated beef, chicken, diced tofu, tiger prawn tails, tilapia, geoduck, scallops, and *bok choy sum*. Now it's hot pot instruction time. I explain how to put a morsel of food into the wire mesh basket and cook it in the boiling stock for about three minutes. Then I tell them how to dip the cooked morsel into the sauce of their choice—and then eat! I look around the table—everyone's amazed by the presentation.

There's silence around the table as they concentrate on the whole experience. I announce, "After you cook your food, you'll be served rice. Then you'll drink the broth that's become flavourful from all the cooking. Pace yourself—or you may need elastic-waist pants!"

The atmosphere becomes livelier as the guests ask questions about how to best experience the meal. "How about some more sweet chili sauce?" "Can I cook the prawns and geoduck together?" "Why aren't you sitting down with us, Bob?" The dinner now has momentum.

Catherine is a accomplished singer, and in the middle of the dinner, she sings Sarah McLachlan's "I Will Remember You." Roland is having a great time, and he expresses his excitement by using his chopsticks and plate as a drum—until I kindly tell him, "Roland, please stop."

I tell everyone, "Drink lots of jasmine tea. It breaks down the oils from the food." Laughing, I also yell, "DO AS YOU'RE TOLD!"

At the end of the dinner, all of the broth is gone. For that matter, all of the food is gone! That's my cue to bring out a bowl of fresh Taiwanese lychee fruit. Everyone grabs a bunch, peels the fruit, de-seeds them, then pops the juicy fruit into their mouths. As they enjoy the fruit, I say, "Eat lots of lychees tonight. The fruit reminds us that we all need a lot of sweetness for a good life."

Author's Note

The "Food and Family Writing Workshop" has been a godsend for me. I've always been a person who is strong in verbally expressing myself, but I'm not strong in putting words to paper. For as long as I can remember, there has always been a major blockage in my writing.

In the fall of 2006, CCHSBC had a presentation at the Vancouver Public Library that featured participants of the first writing workshop, who introduced and discussed a book consisting of their writings from the workshop. When each person spoke, they all had two common goals: developing their writing skills and writing their family stories. I found myself with similar goals.

I enrolled in the January 2007 workshop and have never looked back. Thanks to Brandy for cracking the whip. One technique Brandy has shown me to prevent writer's freeze was to write down words on a "free-flow" basis. Just spurt out the words, and the order and story will sort themselves out eventually.

I have a tourism business in which I conduct a culinary and cultural walking tour of Vancouver's Chinatown; a Chinese hot pot catering business; and a business in which I conduct cooking adventures in China. I feel that through this workshop, I have been able to combine my personal and professional interests, by learning how to express myself more fully, to see the connections among different areas of my life, and to appreciate all the flavours that life has to offer.

Bob Sung

License to Wok: The Drive Behind Sharing Food

Hayne Wai

A Woking Fried Rice (1965)

Gak yea fan—leftover rice—that's what my mother always tells me is the basis for good *chow fan*, or fried rice. The rice should be cooked a day ahead or in the morning to let it harden; otherwise, it will get mushy when you fry it.

Tonight, she's going to teach me how to make fried rice. I've been taking cooking in high school—something new for boys—but all we've learned is Western food—burgers, meatloaf, and potato salad. I'm about to graduate from high school, so I figure it's time I learn how to make some Chinese food.

"Did you wash your hands?" Mom asks.

"Yes, Mother."

"Okay, then break up the clumps of rice. The kernels need to be loose and not stuck together."

She tells me to put some oil in the wok and heat it to medium high. Then I dump the rice in the wok.

"You've got to have a good heat for that fried taste," she says. "And you've got to keep turning over the rice all the time," she lectures me as I work the wok—*clang, clang, clang.*

After I fry and turn the rice for what seems like ages, she tells me to add light soy sauce, a dash of the dark soy, and some oyster sauce. "It's important to colour the rice at this stage and not when all the other ingredients are in the wok, or else everything will get too dark."

She shows me how to mince the *cha siew*—barbecued pork tenderloin—with the Chinese cleaver so I don't end up cutting myself.

"The recipe does not ask for any blood or fingernails," she says quite seriously. The *cha siew* is fried separately to maximize its barbecue flavour before getting tossed into the wok.

We add dried Chinese mushrooms which have been boiled soft and diced, then the green peas.

"Keep on shoveling the rice—don't let it burn," she reminds me, as she adds some shrimp, which she chopped up herself because I was just too slow.

As I prepare to fry the eggs in another pan, Mom says, "Don't burn the eggs—they need to be a fluffy golden yellow." I do not burn the eggs, and they are diced and added to the wok.

The final ingredient is minced green onions, providing a zest to the concoction. The fried rice is almost overflowing, and I spill some onto the stove while turning it over.

"*Ai-ya,*" Mom exclaims, "*lun-jun,*" convinced I'm the clumsiest of all her six children.

After my diligent work, I am beaming. I've made this colourful fried rice without cutting my fingers or burning the meal. While the stove may be messy, my mission is accomplished—I made Chinese food!

"Hey, Mom, do you think I'm ready to make Peking duck?"

She looks at me with a straight face and says, "Tomato and beef—it's a lot easier," and returns to cleaning her stove.

Image courtesy of author.

Then: an image, scanned from my high school annual, of me and a classmate enjoying one of our first cooking lessons. . .

Photograph by Brandy Liên Worrall.

. . .And now: here I'm making fried rice at our CCHSBC writing workshop potluck, held at the Vancouver Museum in February 2007.

A Recipe for Sweating Bullets (1973)

I'm sweating bullets, waiting for the pronouncement by my girlfriend's father on my homemade lasagna. I offered to make dinner for Jenny's parents and three sisters—who are a traditional Hong Kong immigrant family—and was taken to the challenge.

"Make something really yummy," said Jenny's sister Bessie.

Maybe I should have made something Chinese, but I knew they weren't going to be impressed with my fried rice! I wanted to make something different from their usual Chinese cuisine and decided on lasagna, pork chops in mushroom sauce, and garlic bread.

I went all out to impress Jenny's parents, trying to improve their first impressions when I arrived at their door with shoulder-length hair, dressed top to bottom in denim, and speaking in English.

Photograph courtesy of author.

Not only did I teach Jenny how to cook lasagna, but I also taught her how to ride a bicycle (1973).

I grew up on Chinese food and did not taste lasagna until I was in my early twenties. I was immediately transfixed by this heavenly blend of melted cheeses, hearty tomato meat sauce, and earthy spinach nestled in multiple layers of pasta. I had discovered Italy's greatest contribution to civilization since the Coliseum. Birds sang—in Italian—and I could hear the "Triumphant March" from *Aida*. I yearned to learn how to make this incredible dish. My prayers were answered a couple of years later when a friend showed me how to make it from scratch. No, he wasn't Italian, but Japanese American—and he also taught me how to make Mexican food.

The pressure's on—I wanted the meal to be perfect for Jenny's family. Jenny and I started preparing earlier this afternoon. I played chief cook with her as my apprentice. I cooked and drained the fresh pasta that we got from a shop on Commercial Drive. Next came the thick, zesty tomato sauce that I simmered with lean ground beef, garlic, onions, spices, and heaping amounts of fresh mushrooms. Then we prepped the spinach, which we blended with ricotta cheese and egg. There was plenty of mozzarella and fresh parmesan. We layered it all together. Once the lasagna was in the oven, we turned our attention to the centre loin pork chops, which we seared and simmered in a cream of mushroom sauce with onions, mushrooms, garlic, and white wine.

Heavenly aromas from the oven permeated the whole house as we set the dishes on the table. Everyone was staring at the parmesan-crusted pasta and began to salivate. But where was Jenny's father? He was late coming home from golf. Everyone sat wide-eyed and drooling, patiently and hungrily awaiting his return.

Photograph courtesy of author.

This is me and Jenny during less stressful moments (i.e., not cooking for her family).

Finally, he arrived home, washed up, and sat at the table. *Sic fan*—let's eat!

Now, my eyes are fixed on him as he forks his first mouthful of lasagna. Many questions are racing through my mind. What if he doesn't like it? What's my future with Jenny? How could I have bet my future with her on whether or not her father likes my lasagna? I should've asked my parents for a quick lesson on making Peking duck. Now I'm hearing the first few bars of Chopin's "Funeral March."

With his first bite, he nods his head three times with full approval of the mélange of pasta, cheeses, and tomato sauce. *Ho-yeh*—good stuff—he pronounces with a big smile. A sigh of relief. Jenny beams a big smile to me. His next bite is the pork chops in thick savoury mushroom gravy. Another *ho-yeh*. I'm breathing normal again. Then the *pièce de resistance*—garlic bread with an extra shot of fresh garlic and parsley. *Ho-yeh*.

I passed the test—and I'm hearing a gondolier sing "O Solo Mio." I can finally concentrate on my own first bite—except that everyone else has almost finished their first servings and are eyeing seconds!

There hasn't been much conversation at the dinner table tonight, just a lot of *ho-yehs* from everyone and "Pass the garlic bread, please"—in Cantonese.

So I can make Italian. . .but can I do Chinese?

The Green Door, R. I. P. (1998)

Midnight, one more night without sleepin'
Watchin' till the mornin' comes creepin'
Green door, what's that secret you're keepin'?

—"Green Door," sung by Jim Low, words by Marvin Moore, music by Bob Davis

This 1956 hit song about the revelry behind an all-night club was a Billboard Number 1 hit for three weeks. Unbeknownst to the song's authors, the Green Door, a legendary Vancouver Chinatown back alley diner, also had a unique history.

◈ ◈ ◈

He was the manager, waiter, cook, dishwasher, cashier and head of security—a one-man operation. He was the proprietor of the Green Door back alley diner, which closed down in 1999, the end of an era in Chinatown. I remember my conversation with him when our office staff of six went there for lunch a year before it closed. Getting there that day was not a comfortable sight. We traversed the alley between Pender and Hastings Streets, just east of Columbia. Approaching the restaurant known only by its green door—no signage—we were careful not to bother nearby solitary figures awaiting their drug fix in the dark alley.

Once inside, loud music from the oldies radio station greeted us. It was a small diner, rustic, no windows, but clean, and I noticed that we were the only customers. There were about six tables, nothing fancy, which reinforced its diner decor. He was pleased to see the half dozen of us that day. Three members of our office had never been there and were interested in its history.

"The place has known much better times," I explained. "It was originally the kitchen which catered to the gambling club upstairs and ran at all hours of the day and night dating back to the 1940s. Chinatown was different then, a racial enclave defined by state-sanctioned discrimination and racist attitudes. Most of the Chinatown community consisted of adult men, separated from families by head taxes and immigrant exclusion that began in 1923." My colleagues seemed mesmerized by my history lesson.

In the mid 1960s, the Green Door got "discovered." Perhaps it was the hippy counter-culture movement, the legend and mystique of a Chinatown gambling hall kitchen, or the growing appreciation of other cultures and foods, I don't know. But word spread quickly that the Green Door would now offer the public a unique dining experience, eating in a Chinatown gambling hall kitchen! Its reputation as a Vancouver dining destination was promoted in city newspapers and magazines. By the mid-1970s, other gambling hall kitchens also opened to the public and included the Orange and Grey Doors, all within a short distance from each other. They also had no signage, just a painted door to identify themselves. During the summer months, these small kitchen diners were filled to capacity with Chinese and non-Chinese alike, with line-ups outside into the alley.

But that was in the heyday of the 1970s, and by the 1990s most customers had moved on or were too scared to return. The drug scene had grown into Chinatown alleys, and the path to a former well-known city eatery was now strewn with syringes and lonely figures.

We looked over the menu, listening to Bill Haley's *Rock Around the Clock*, Buddy Holly's *Peggy Sue*, and Big Bopper's *Chantilly Lace*—"*Oh, alright baby, you know what I like...*" We ordered sweet and sour pork, beef and *guy-lan*, curry chicken, tofu and barbecued pork, and of course, fried rice.

From our vantage point just a few feet away, we watched him prepare the dishes—washing, chopping, slicing, and woking. He did everything and kept our teapot filled as well. Scintillating aromas of garlic, ginger, scallions, and onions overwhelmed us, accompanied by the sizzling from his wok and the clanging of the steel spatula. Our senses were being tuned for a gourmet feast, and we were not disappointed.

"The curry chicken is real Cantonese-style," said Inder, whose wife is Chinese.

"Great sweet and sour," Shaun said, smacking his lips.

"This is as good as any other Chinese restaurant—and great prices!" Margaret exclaimed in between mouthfuls of fried rice.

"The food is just the way I remembered it," smiled Patsy, who had visited the Green Door going back some twenty years.

I had many questions for the proprietor, which I asked in my limited Cantonese. He had time to talk to us, since we were his only customers throughout the lunch hour. He told me that he had been there for over fifteen years and had many regular customers. But fewer were coming back as the shooting gallery of drug addicts in the alley was scaring them away. He seemed resolved that although he had been broken into several times, he just used stronger locks and hinges after each break in.

"I wanted to quit this place and work elsewhere, but the building owner decreased the lease substantially and asked me to stay for another year," he told me. His long lonely hours took time away from his wife and teenage children. I felt he really appreciated our patronage and conversation.

The following year I read in the newspaper that the Green Door had closed forever. I was saddened and paused to remember our office visit with colleagues. I made phone calls to friends to ask if they had had heard the news, and we reminisced about our years of visiting the diner. It was much like the passing of an old friend, but we realized its demise was inevitable. It was a part of Chinatown history, offering great food at low prices in a unique historic setting. Green Door, rest in peace.

How to Have a Fantasy Office Potluck Lunch (2000)

"Georgie, how about making that incredible upside-down raspberry cake for the office potluck?" I asked, drooling.

"With whipped cream too, Hayne?"

"Yes, please," I said, nodding my head several times, grinning.

I had volunteered to coordinate our provincial government office potluck for our staff of about forty people. I had personal reasons for taking on this task, as the reward would be a gastronomic fantasy come true—a potluck featuring all my favourite dishes. As a staff we gathered a couple of times every year, and these lunches always featured culinary traditions from around the world.

Photograph courtesy of author.

A Halloween office potluck. Even though I came cleverly dressed up as Santa Sushi Chef, I did not win the prize for best costume.

Now that dessert was taken care of, I wanted to focus on getting several different kinds of curries. I asked Dom, a Cantonese colleague, if he could bring a beef brisket or chicken curry—"You know, your mother's recipe?"

"Sure thing," he said.

Then I asked Jan, who was from Fiji, "Could you bring a Fijian curry, please? Any kind, as long as it's Fijian." She nodded yes.

Next on my list was Patsy, who was from Kerala, a state in the middle of India noted for milder and sweeter Indian cooking. I lobbied for a curry from her too. From Phinder, whose heritage is Punjabi, I posed a butter or tandoori chicken. And from Inder, I knew his curry would reflect his wife's Cantonese cooking but perhaps with a Punjabi fusion. *Hmm,* I thought, *too bad there were no staff from Singapore, Thailand, or East Africa.* That would have completed a worldwide curry experience.

Then I turned my attention to nailing down the appetizers. One of my favourites has always been Vietnamese springrolls. I asked Angie for a plate of those. Then I asked two staff members from Chile if they could bring some traditional appetizers. And I could not could not pass by Janine's work station without asking her to make some *tabouli,* a Lebanese parsley salad.

I continued visiting staff along the corridors, and by the time I had walked around the entire floor of offices, I knew it was going to be a great feast.

On the day of the potluck, the large boardroom table quickly filled up with all kinds of foods and smells, including several curries, Vietnamese springrolls, hummus, tzatziki, perogies, devilled eggs, tostadas, bannock, pastas, salads, pies, tarts, sushi, casseroles, noodles and cakes. You name it, it was there, including KFC. As for my contribution—what else but fried rice, as my mother had taught me. I instructed Shaun, my young apprentice at the potluck, on all the particulars of preparing *chow fan.*

While people waited for others to join the gathering, I had one more trick up my sleeve. I commenced passing around the bread, crackers, vegetable sticks, and dips. The strategy was to get people full before the main meal began so I could have more food to myself, but my strategy was noticed.

"What are you trying to do, get us full before the meal starts?" teased Laurie.

I deliberately did not reply but just smiled and continued to pass the carrot sticks.

I was in curry heaven that day, with different blends of chilies, turmeric, cumin, masala, coriander, garlic, onion, habañeras, tamarind, coconut milk, and yogurt. People compared curries and traded recipes.

"You use more cinnamon in yours," Inder said to Patsy. "What else do you use?"

New foods were sampled, and each staff member happily explained their dishes to those who've never experienced them before.

"*Tostadas* are fried tortillas with refried black beans, feta cheese, and hot salsa on top," Angelica said.

Patricio proudly talked about his *empanadas*, which were Chilean meat pies.

"Hey, Hayne and Shaun, your fried rice is much better than the Green Door's!" Patsy said.

During that noon hour, everyone put aside their work to enjoy the culinary creations of colleagues. It was fun, food, and fellowship in their truest meaning. I volunteered to coordinate the next office luncheon but had others bidding for the job as my fantasy potluck strategy had been discovered.

Fried Rice

Colours, textures and tastes complement each other to create a gourmet mosaic dish. Fried rice is versatile, improvised, and can be designed to your taste. The more colours and textures, the better the taste. This recipe serves four as a major side dish, but if Dan Seto is your guest, double the proportions of everything.

6 cups pre-cooked and cooled rice, or leftover rice, clumps broken up into kernels

Vegetable oil for frying

2 tsp light soy sauce

Dash of dark soy sauce

1 tsp oyster sauce

¼ lb Chinese barbecued pork, fried in advance

2 Chinese sausages, steamed in advance

12 cooked medium shrimp

1 carrot, cooked

6 Chinese or Western mushrooms, cooked

½ cup green peas

3 eggs, scrambled and fried

3 greens onions

1 Tbsp fish paste (optional)

Hoisin sauce

Lettuce

Photograph by Brandy Liên Worrall.

Woking Fried Rice.

1.) Add enough vegetable oil to a wok to coat it, and heat the wok on medium high heat. Add rice, which should be broken up into kernels, then add light soy sauce, a dash of dark soy sauce, and oyster sauce. Fish paste can be added to the wok before frying the rice (optional).

2.) Add barbecued pork, Chinese sausage, shrimp, carrots, mushrooms, and peas, minced, one at a time, with the fried egg and green onions last.

3.) Fried rice can be served as a lettuce wrap with hoisin sauce, or with bits of finely shredded lettuce in the fried rice, added just before serving.

Author's Note

I was privileged to participate in my second writing workshop, this time on food and family history. As with the first workshop held in Spring 2006, which produced *Finding Memories, Tracing Routes: Chinese Canadian Family Stories*, it was a very positive learning experience in writing and in sharing family histories.

In 1947, Canada passed its first citizenship act and also repealed the 1923 Chinese Exclusion Act, which had barred Chinese immigration to Canada. Prior to that moment, Chinese Canadians could not become citizens, vote, or enter professions. My mother was born in Victoria in 1917 and married my father, a Hong Kong businessman, in 1939. My brothers, sister, and I were all born in Hong Kong and with our mother's citizenship confirmed, we came to Canada in 1952. Our initial home in Vancouver was with our grandparents in Strathcona, but we moved to the west side of Vancouver, where I grew up and attended school.

In twelfth grade I was fortunate to take an all-boys cooking class, an experimental program at the time, which taught me the basics in Western cooking. But what I really wanted was to learn how to cook Chinese, and so my mother instructed me in the essentials of making fried rice, a memory which I have tried to capture in "A Woking Fried Rice." Mother's cooking lessons helped me survive three years in Ontario as a young man, albeit with regular visits to Vancouver to enjoy my parents' cooking and outings to Chinatown restaurants.

Returning to Vancouver, I sought to use my cooking skills to impress my new girlfriend and her family. "A Recipe for Sweating Bullets" recalls that first encounter in which East meets West. Food definitely made the courtship with my wife go much more smoothly. I think our son and daughter will testify to the Italian, Greek, Japanese, Indian, Chinese, Canadian and other cuisines that we create at home.

What made my years in government enjoyable was the fellowship with colleagues in discussing policy and programs—particularly those discussions over lunch or after work. "The Green Door, R. I. P." represents that spirit of collective learning and dining. As with other Chinatown diners which have since closed, the Green Door was an historic landmark in community history.

My life-long passion for food and culture continues in "How to Have a Fantasy Office Potluck Lunch," in which I describe the cultures and experiences that colleagues brought not only to office gatherings, but also to the workplace and to the publics they so dedicatedly served.

Many thanks to Brandy for her guidance and confidence in our writing. My appreciation also to workshop colleagues, who shared their personal family stories and many exciting recipes.

Happy reading and dining!

Hayne Wai

Jin Doy Joy and Other Pockets of Love

Evelyn Wong

New Year's Dinner Redux

Goon Hing Wong, my father, left Zhongshan, China in 1913 to join his father and brothers in Vancouver. He made seven trips back to China. On one trip in 1920, Goon Hing married Gok See, and following another trip, son Hin Young was born in 1937. After Gok See's death, my father married Poy Ying Louie, my mother. She was twenty-seven years younger than her husband and only eight years older than her stepson. Their daughter Oy Quan (Gwen) was born one day after Chinese New Year in 1949.

Goon Hing brought his wife, son and daughter to Canada in 1952. I was the first to be born in Canada, followed by my sisters Helen, Mary, and Alice. Growing up, we often played with our half-brother Hin Young's three children, Kim, Jim, and Alden. My parents and Hin Young and his wife Brenda took turns hosting joint Christmas and New Year's dinners for our families. Besides the Christmas turkey, my sisters and I looked forward to the annual "Slap" card game tournament with Hin Young's children.

As we children grew into adults and married, the joint holiday dinners became more work for our parents to host, and it was decided to hold separate celebrations. Seven years ago, Hin Young and I thought it was time to revive the New Year's family gathering, but make it a less elaborate dinner. Hin Young provided a prime rib roast, I bought several restaurant dishes, and my mother made a few Chinese dishes. A tradition was reborn.

◆ ◆ ◆

2007

5:30 p.m.—It's cold, dark, and rainy as I arrive home after picking up the sushi tray, barbecued duck, crispy skin chicken, and some other restaurant dishes. I'm almost done setting all the dishes on the table. *Oh, there's the doorbell. I wonder who's arrived?*

"Happy New Year!" I give Kim a hug.

"Look, I brought my Furby!" Six-year-old Griffin proudly shows me his toy.

"Are Kylie and Tabitha here yet?" ten-year-old Perri looks around eagerly for her cousins.

"I brought dessert. Something smells good!" Kim and I walk into the happy chaos.

"Alice is downstairs frying shrimp. Your Dad's upstairs making the *au jus* for the prime rib."

The upstairs kitchen is noisy. Lids clang as my mother, Poy Ying, checks the watercress soup and a pot of Chinese mushrooms. My mother has spent all week preparing her dishes. There were several trips to Chinatown and T&T Market to buy the freshest vegetables and meat. For days, the kitchen counter was filled with bowls of soaking Chinese delicacies, such as dried oysters, *fat choy*, and sea cucumber.

My mother is an excellent cook. I remember asking her if she learned her recipes from my grandmother. To my surprise, she said no, it was a bachelor uncle in Vancouver who taught her most of the dishes we enjoy. This elderly uncle whom we called Li Goong had come to Canada as a young man and worked as a cook.

Hin Young's prime rib is always the centrepiece of the dinner. Hin Young worked for BC Ferries for thirty-four years, retiring as Chief Cook in 1997. He worked on the Queen of the North on the Prince Rupert run and was responsible for overall food preparation, supervising the six cooks and other kitchen staff who served the cafeteria and dining room. Prime rib was served daily in the dining room. When he had been a No. 3 cook, he stood in the dining room and carved slices of the prime rib for customers. He particularly remembered the American tourists enjoying the tender and succulent roast.

For the New Year's dinner, he always orders a big cut to ensure enough leftovers for family to take home. This year, the prime rib is 6.5 kg. Earlier in the day, Hin Young came to the house to season the prime rib and left me with instructions on oven temperature and when to turn the roast over. Then he went home for a few hours to help his wife prepare chow mein. When he returned at 4:30, he brought his personal tools of the trade—meat thermometer, carving knife and fork.

Photograph courtesy of author.

Hin Young carving up his famous delicious prime rib.

I heat oil in the cast-iron skillet to cook the cashew chicken dish. As I start stir-frying, Kim remembers how her brother Jim had once said he liked cashew chicken at a previous New Year's dinner, so every year since, my mother has made sure it was on the dinner menu.

My sister Alice and her children Nathan and Heather came early to help. They spent the afternoon washing and deveining a mountain of icy cold shrimp. Then they used paper towels to pat dry the shrimp before marinating them in a spicy salt mixture. Now Alice comes upstairs with a heaping platter of crisp, golden shrimp.

There's the doorbell again! I run downstairs and open the door for my sister Gwen, her husband Ron, and their sons Eric and Christopher. Eric graduated from Simon Fraser University in the fall, and he's excited about going to Japan to teach English for a year.

"Do you know where you'll be teaching yet?" I ask him as they get settled in.

"I wanted to go to Tokyo because I have a friend there, but I just found out I'm going to Oyama, which is three hours away."

"That's probably better because Tokyo's so expensive," I try reassuring him.

My mother comes to greet them. "Hi, Po Po!" the boys give her big hugs. Her grandchildren like to tease her because she always thinks they're not dressed warmly enough. "Look, I'm wearing my coat, Po Po!" She laughs and gently scolds them in Chinese to wear warmer coats, or they'll catch cold.

The last family to arrive is Hin Young's son Jim and his wife Angeline, with their children Tabitha, Kylie and Evan. This is only Evan's second time attending our traditional dinner. Tabitha and Kylie race upstairs to play Nintendo and Duck Hunt with their cousins.

All the food is ready and waiting on the kitchen table. Hin Young's grandchildren are served first so they can be settled into seats at the kids' table in the playroom. It's fun watching the children of various ages eating their chow mein. Kylie and Tabitha lift a forkful of noodles up high and start eating from the bottom up. Griffin twirls chow mein around his fork. Little Evan finds it easier to eat with his fingers. Perri uses her fork to spear the dark mushrooms and white bean sprouts, and places them into her napkin. She says she likes everything else in the chow mein, even the carrot slivers, although she doesn't normally care for carrots.

I hear laughter coming from the kitchen and hurry back to make sure everyone has something to drink. The adults have surrounded the kitchen table and are helping themselves to the food. Gwen's eyes light up when she sees her favourite dish—dried scallops and Chinese mushrooms. "No one makes this like Mom. This is such a treat!"

Katie looks dubiously at a traditional New Year's meatless dish called *jai* which includes gingko nuts, dried oysters, *fat choy* and red dates. My sister Helen tells her, "Try it Katie, I think you'll like it."

But Katie doesn't feel like being adventurous tonight. "That's okay, Mom, I think I'll pass and just have some barbecued duck."

Jim stands at the counter watching his father skillfully carve a thick juicy slice of prime rib for him. I hand him his drink.

Once I know everyone is enjoying their dinner, I take a sip of my wine and gaze contentedly at the three generations seated in dining room and kitchen. I think of my father and how proud he would have been to see his family coming together, celebrating a tradition all their own.

Photographs courtesy of author.

Wong family gathering for one-month-old Jimmy, 1960. Seated, from left to right—Gwen, Helen, Mary, and me; second row—Hin Young, my father Goon Hing holding Alice, Poy Ying holding Jimmy, and Hin Young's wife Brenda.

2007 New Year's kids' picture. Front row—Heather, Katie, Perri, Griffin, Tabitha, and Kylie; back row— Eric holding Evan, Christopher, Matthew, and Nathan.

Cashew Chicken

8-10 oz boneless, skinless chicken

½ tsp soy sauce

¼ tsp sugar

1 cup chopped carrots

Oil for frying

2 slices ginger, peeled

2 tsp oyster sauce

1 cup chopped celery

½ cup canned water chestnuts, chopped

½ tsp salt

½ cup roasted cashew nuts

1.) Cut the chicken into small cubes.

2.) Place chicken in a bowl and marinate with soy sauce and sugar for thirty minutes.

3.) Parboil the carrots.

4.) Heat oil in a preheated wok. Add ginger.

5.) Add the chicken and stir-fry till almost cooked.

6.) Add oyster sauce and mix well. If mixture is dry, add water.

7.) When cooked, remove chicken with a slotted spoon.

8.) Stir-fry celery in wok until cooked. Add carrots, water chestnuts, salt; mix well. Add chicken.

9.) Remove from heat, and add cashews on top.

Alice's Birthday Dinner, September 1965

For her birthday dinner, eight-year-old Alice chose her favourite dishes—beef tomato and egg foo young. My sister Alice was a picky eater. The youngest in the family, she wouldn't each much meat like duck, chicken or pork, and she especially hated salted duck eggs. Oftentimes, all she would eat was rice with oyster sauce and a little butter. But for some reason, she couldn't get enough beef tomato and egg foo young.

The kitchen was a hive of activity as we prepared for dinner. Mom expertly wielded her cleaver to cut the chunk of raw beef into thin slices, and then marinated the meat in a soy sauce mixture. My sister Helen washed the tomatoes and cut them into wedges. My other sister Mary kept watch on the pot of rice as it boiled.

Mom heated oil in a wok and added ginger and garlic. Soon we could smell the beef sizzling as Mom quickly stir-fried the meat. Popping and crackling noises filled the kitchen. Before the meat was fully cooked, Mom poured thick brown oyster sauce over it and mixed it all up. After scooping the beef out into a dish, Mom cooked the tomatoes in the wok. Tomato juice seeped out to create the sauce Alice loved to pour on her rice.

Meanwhile, I chopped the sticky barbecued pork into small pieces. I caught Alice sneaking a chunk when she thought no one was looking.

Gwen beat the eggs rhythmically with chopsticks. When the whites and yolks became frothy, she measured some soy sauce into a spoon and poured it in. Then she added the barbecued pork and cooked shrimp. After stirring the mixture, she brought the bowl to the stove. The oil sputtered as the eggs hit the hot pan.

Finally, everything was ready, and we sat down to dinner. Alice bit into the egg foo young and smiled as she savoured the combined flavours of shrimp, barbecued pork and eggs. It was cooked the way she liked, with the egg slightly runny. The beef tomato was also good. The beef was tender, and the soy sauce and oyster sauce contrasted with the sweet yet slightly sour tomato. The best part was the tomato sauce on her rice.

Alice said, "When I grow up, I'm going to make beef tomato and egg foo young all the time." We thought it was an admirable goal in life.

Beef Tomato

½ lb flank steak, thinly sliced

1 Tbsp soy sauce

1 Tbsp Scotch whiskey

1 ½ tsp sugar

1 Tbsp oil

2 slices ginger

2 cloves garlic, peeled and crushed

1 Tbsp oyster sauce

1 lb fresh tomatoes cut in wedges

1 ½ tsp cornstarch

1.) Marinate the beef in soy sauce, Scotch whiskey, and ½ teaspoon sugar for 20 minutes. Save the rest of the sugar for the tomatoes.

2.) Heat oil in a pan over medium heat. Add ginger and 1 clove of garlic. Save the other clove for the tomatoes.

3.) When ginger and garlic are golden brown, add beef and fry for about one minute. Add oyster sauce. Remove from pan.

4.) Add tomatoes, garlic, and sugar to the pan. Cook for one minute.

5.) If tomato sauce is too runny, add a little cornstarch paste (cornstarch and water).

6.) Transfer tomatoes to dish, and top with beef. Stir.

Poy Ying's *Jin Doy*, 1970

Chinese New Year was only one day away. For the past two weeks my mother, Poy Ying, had been busy buying the groceries and preparing ingredients for the many traditional dishes that would bring us good luck, prosperity, and long life.

Photograph courtesy of author.

Poy Ying in 2007 with great-grandson Evan.

One of these dishes was deep-fried sesame balls with bean paste filling, called *jin doy*. She'd already started preparation for the filling by soaking three rectangular slabs of brown sugar in water overnight. Now she was washing a pound of the small plump red beans called *hoong dul* and poured them into a pot with cold water.

As she boiled the beans, Mom kept a careful eye on them so they would be soft but not mushy. Once they were the right consistency, she emptied them into a colander to drain for an hour. From the back of her cupboard, Mom pulled out a rolling pin and large pan. When the *hoong dul* were dry enough, she ground them until their texture resembled fine cornmeal. She fried the flattened beans with a few spoonfuls of the brown sugar syrup until they turned into a thick dark paste.

Mom emptied two bags of glutinous rice flour into a large mixing bowl. With one hand she slowly poured sugar syrup into the bowl while using her other hand to mix the flour to form a dough. The dough had to be not too sticky and not too spongy. Then Mom rolled the dough into twelve-inch long ropes. She cut each rope into twelve chunks, and each chunk was shaped in her hands until it resembled a small snowball.

Using her thumb, she made an indentation in each ball and added a spoonful of red bean paste. Mom sealed in the filling and rolled the ball on a plate of sesame seeds and placed it on a cookie sheet. Soon, the tray filled with even rows of the smooth balls studded with tiny brown seeds.

Mom remembered her mother's constant instruction: the oil must be boiling hot or the *jin doy* will be soggy and greasy. That's why she always inserted a chopstick into the middle of the pot of oil—to see if the translucent oil around the chopstick would bubble, indicating that it's hot enough.

She turned down the heat, gently placing some balls into the oil and letting them fry for a few minutes. It's no good being in a hurry when frying *jin doy*; you have to take your time to do it right.

When one of the balls floated to the top, Mom pressed down on it with a long-handled Chinese strainer. The *jin doy* expanded as it rose again, like a hot air balloon. She patiently repeated the movement several times until the *jin doy* doubled in size and appeared big, golden, and glistening.

Scooping out the balls and placing them into a metal pie pan, Mom called us to help shake the pan so the *jin doy* kept their round shape as they cooled. If the shaking wasn't done properly, the balls would deflate. Shake, shake, shake. Meanwhile, Mom concentrated on frying the rest of the *jin doy*.

When the deep-frying was finished, Mom brought a plate of *jin doy* to the kitchen table and made a pot of Chinese tea. We sat down to eat still-warm Chinese doughnut. Mom would always watch us eat our sesame balls before taking one for herself. One bite into the crispy chewy crust, and our mouths filled with soft sweetness. Homemade *jin doy* do take time and effort, but it's well worth it if they bring good luck to the family in the new year.

Letter to Eric

After he left to teach English in Japan, my nephew Eric sent us emails and photos of his experience living in a foreign country. We were glad to hear that he had made several new friends who shared his passion for exploring this new world. When my sister Gwen told me that Eric had emailed a request for her fried rice recipe, I knew it was a chance to discuss memories and stories of migration and settling into a new place. Gwen and I talked about how it's easier nowadays for people to keep in touch when they're away from their loved ones through emails and digital photos. But for Gwen, she recalled how lonely she was when she had moved to Regina with her husband and son twenty years ago. We also imagined how our mother felt when she left China to start a new life in Canada. The emails and discussions about our family's migration history and experiences are what inspired this epistolary story.

◈ ◈ ◈

Hi Eric,

Did you get the care package we sent? Lipton Sidekicks as requested, plus fruit rollups, granola bars and red licorice. It's surprising what you miss when you're away from home, isn't it?

Your last letter said you bought a rice cooker and wanted my recipe for fried rice. I had to laugh when you said not to spare any step, no matter how simple. I guess I should pretend you're from Mars because you know nothing about cooking!

You said your rice was a little dry. As a general rule, I place my finger on the top of the rice, and from that point on I measure the water to the first joint of my second finger. Don't put your finger to the bottom of the rice, or there will not be enough water.

You really loved fried rice when you were growing up, which was fine by me because it was a quick way for me to use leftover rice. It was when you started working at Home Depot that you really began to appreciate my fried rice. I remember you told me you needed a substantial lunch in order to survive those eight-hour shifts!

Here's my recipe (which I have renamed "Martian Fried Rice" in your honour):

1.) Chop some cooked meat like chicken or ham. Shrimp is good too.

2.) Put the frying pan on the stove at medium heat.

3.) Add a little oil, not too much, just enough to lightly coat the pan.

4.) When the oil is hot, add cooked rice (leftover rice is the best because it's a little drier, so it will fry better; if using fresh rice, try to wait till it feels cold so it doesn't clump together when frying).

5.) Stir quickly so the rice doesn't stick to the pan.

6.) Add a beaten egg. Mix it about, let it heat up a bit to let the egg cook, then mix it up some more.

7.) Add a little soy sauce and oyster sauce, and mix together.

8.) Add ham and peas (peas are easy, but you can also use cooked chopped beans, celery or whatever).

Photograph courtesy of Eric Neumeyer.

Eric in front of a temple in Japan.

Ta da. . .fried rice! Hope this helps.

With you in Japan now, and Christopher in Vancouver, I found a lot of food in the pantry and freezer that Dad and I won't eat, like pizza pops, ravioli, and Pepsi. Oh, and all those Kraft dinners you left behind! I have to call your brother and tell him we've got some groceries for him.

Thinking about you living away from home reminds me of how I felt when we moved to Regina. You were just a year old. In order for Dad to move up in the Federal Government, he needed to take this position in Regina. Of course, it was a joint decision. We both were naïve about the move and thought it would be easy to adapt. But when I arrived, I suddenly felt isolated without friends and family. Funny how you take things like that for granted.

It was really hard on Christmas and birthdays. I felt so guilty that you boys couldn't share your birthdays and other special events with Po Po and your aunties and cousins. After five years in Regina, we moved to Halifax and lived there for five years. By the time we moved back to Vancouver, you were eleven, and Christopher was eight.

Photograph courtesy of author.

The Neumeyer family: Eric, his girlfriend Barbara, my sister Gwen, Ron, Christopher.

Of course, your experience is quite different in a country where English is a foreign language and the culture is so different from Canada. Remember when you went to a supermarket and had no idea what anything was because all the signs and packaging were in Japanese? Although not many people in Oyama speak English, you're still lucky because everyone you work with speaks English. Think of how your Po Po must have felt when she came to Canada! Not only did she not understand a word of English, but she had a hard time dealing with things like running water and electricity since she had none of that where she grew up in rural China. Life in Vancouver would have seemed like a huge leap from her life in China, and I cannot imagine the loneliness she had to endure. But she and your grandfather, Goong Goong, were willing to make the sacrifices necessary to live in Canada so that all of us could succeed and prosper.

From photos you sent, Dad and I can see that you and your friends are having fun exploring Oyama and Tokyo. The picture with you in front of a temple is one of my favourites because to me, it marks the beginning of your travels. Not just in terms of geography, but your life experiences. It's the beginning of your independence.

Moves like ours to Regina and Halifax, and yours to Japan, are valuable because they increase our understanding and compassion for the rest of the world. Your life is enriched as you learn how people in a country like Japan live and think. Make the most of it!

I can't go without extending some motherly advice: stay safe, get enough sleep and make sure you eat vegetables (NOT JUST SUSHI!). We miss you.

Love,
Mom

Author's Note

My mother, half brother, and older sister came from China to join my father in Canada in the 1950s. My younger sisters and I were born in Vancouver, but we were all raised with the values and traditions of my parents' Shun Tong village.

It was not common for my parents to show affection to us as children, but their love was expressed through preparation of fresh, tasty food and special Chinese dishes. There were few fast food takeouts and frozen ready-to-eat dishes available back then. My family would wrap wonton, steam radish cakes, fill *gok jay* dumplings, and make other Chinese delicacies from scratch. My four sisters and I took for granted the Chinese delicacies that my parents and relatives prepared for us—abalone, bird's nest, dried scallops. Our immature tastes and desire to eat "Canadian" food led us to prefer pizza and hamburgers. Now my mother's nine grandchildren all know that when Po Po cooks a dish for them, it will be superior to any Chinese restaurant dish.

I wanted to record my mother's recipes since they were never written down. Getting specific measurements for her recipes is a challenge as she doesn't cook using teaspoons or measuring cups! Along with the recipes, I wanted to write family memories surrounding the dishes and traditions.

Creative writing doesn't come easily to me, and I appreciated reading my classmates' stories and learning from them. I enjoyed our lively discussions, which were always punctuated with lots of laughter, as we shared personal and often similar experiences. Thanks to Brandy for creating such a warm, comfortable environment, and for her guiding hand and encouragement.

Special thanks to my family for helping me with my stories. Our memories of the food we grew up with can differ, but it's always exciting to discover a story that had been forgotten. I hope these memories and recipes will help the next generation to appreciate the experiences of their parents, grandparents, and great-grandparents.

Evelyn Wong

The Village of Chinatown

Larry Wong

A Special Chinese New Year's Treat (1943)

Every Chinese New Year, Wong Quon Ho shooed his children out of the store. Once they were out of sight, he'd become busy in the tiny kitchen of their living quarters at the back of his tailor shop in Chinatown.

His three children, Wah, Jennie and Larry, left without question. Wah, seventeen, went straight to his friend's house to discuss their upcoming school finals.

Jennie, age twelve, took Larry, who was five years old, to the public library across the street.

"How come Pop doesn't want us in the house?" whispered Larry as they sat a table.

"He does that every year. Remember last year, he made those *jin dui?*"

"Oh, yeah. Those round balls. Those were good."

"For some reason, he doesn't want us in the house while he's cooking," said Jennie.

Their father knew what the children did not. *Jin dui* was a difficult recipe, which required deep-frying. It was dangerous to cook things in large pot of hot oil in such a small space. The kitchen was really a galley. If he wasn't careful he could easily set the kitchen on fire.

Wong had a woodstove and two hotplates. His cooking utensils were a frying pan, several sizes of saucepans, and one Dutch oven. Wong opened the back door to allow ventilation. Now he was ready.

He checked the ingredients on the counter: cooking oil, rice flour, slabs of brown sugar, sesame seeds, and black bean paste. He reached into the cupboard for a large bowl and started baking.

Wong already made the dough from the flour and sugar. He pinched a piece off the dough and made an indentation with his thumb to insert a tablespoonful of black bean paste. He smoothed the dough over the paste and shaped the dough into a ball. He dipped the ball in water and rolled it in a dish of sesame seeds. He repeated the process until a dozen balls were made.

He heated the large saucepan hot enough to deep-fry. The oil gurgled as bubbles rose to the top. He dropped in one ball. It sizzled, turning a light brown. With the ladle, he gently pushed the ball to the side

Photograph courtesy of author.

Pop preparing a meal, at the age of 75.

of the pot as it ballooned. Smiling to himself, he lifted the cooked ball onto a cookie sheet covered in paper towels and turned his attention to the others.

By the middle of the afternoon, his children returned to the shop. They knew his cooking was over by the smell of deep-fried oil in the air.

"They're ready," he told them, as they eyed the puffed sesame seed balls sitting on plates at the table. The children scrambled to their chairs as Wong cautioned, "Careful now, they're still really hot."

Larry grabbed one *jin dui* with his fingers, not paying heed to his father's words. "Ouch!"

"Use your chopsticks," said his father.

Larry picked up one chopstick and was ready to spear the ball when Wong grabbed his wrist and pulled the chopstick away.

"Never use a chopstick alone! It's bad luck. Always use your chopsticks as a pair."

Larry nodded and flattened the ball with his pair of chopsticks. A little oil oozed out. The *jin dui* was flat enough so that he could pick it up and eat it with his hand. His first bite went through the crispy thin skin and into the chewy soft sweet dough. His tongue searched a tooth's cavity to pick at the toasty sesame seeds stuck there. As he chewed, the smooth black bean paste melted in his mouth, and all he could say was, "Mmm."

Jin Dui

½ cup brown sugar

⅔ cup boiling water

½ lb glutinous rice flour

Black bean, sweet red bean, or lotus seed paste

Sesame seeds

1 quart peanut oil (you can substitute in vegetable oil, but peanut oil has the best flavour)

1.) Melt brown sugar in boiling water.

2.) Stir in glutinous rice flour and mix well.

3.) Form dough into 12 balls. Form each ball into a cup and place a teaspoon of paste inside the dent. Pinch to close.

4.) Brush each ball with water, and roll it in sesame seeds.

5.) Heat oil in a large pot. When the oil slightly bubbles, it's ready for deep-frying.

6.) Deep-fry balls until golden brown. To make the balls puff up, use the back of a spatula to press the balls lightly against the sides or bottom of the pot a few times while frying.

Sharing a Snack with My Sister (1946)

I am eight years old. My home is at the back of my father's tailor shop on Main Street. Pop just closed up shop, made dinner, and went off to help his best friend, George Lee, at his confectionery store on Hastings Street. My sister Jennie and I are left alone. She doesn't mind babysitting me. She always has something to do, like tonight she is washing her hair and doing a perm with smelly stuff and setting her hair with curlers. She also talks a lot on the phone. About halfway through the evening, she hangs up and asks me, "Hungry?"

I look at her, trying to swallow a laugh. She looks funny with the metal curlers all over her head.

I nod, "Oh, yeah."

"Okay. You wait here, and I'll get us some *Gon Pi Quat*."

Wow! Dry garlic spareribs. It is a snack I always hunger for, even after a full meal.

Jennie pulls a shawl over her head and walks up to the corner of Pender Street. I picture her crossing the street and going past G. High Stationery to the K.H. Chop Suey House next to the alleyway. The waiter at the restaurant always recognizes her because we go there so often.

As soon as she returns, she puts the take-out carton on the table and quickly separates the wire handles and flips up the lids. The smell of the deep-fried garlic fills the air. My heart is pounding. The spareribs are bite-sized. There's a golden crust with tender meat beneath. There's no fat on the riblets—all meat, marinated in soya sauce, minced garlic, lemon juice, salt, pepper, vinegar, flour and cornstarch.

Jennie hands me a rib. It is hot but easy to hold. I taste the garlicky coating and the soft pork. My teeth push away the meat, and I spit out the bone.

My sister and I dig through the carton, laughing as we struggle for the same piece. There are no more left. Bones the size of fingernails lay completely naked on a plate.

Photograph courtesy of author.

Pop, Jennie, and me in front of Pop's tailor shop.

We wet our fingertips and try to pick up the small crumbs left coating the inside of the carton. When we've managed to scrape up every single miniscule morsel, we smack our lips.

"Heaven," Jennie says.

It is a school night, so we go to bed around ten o'clock. Pop, in his usual custom, works at the confectionery store helping his friend until midnight. Sometimes on his way home, he drops into one of the many social clubs on Pender Street. If he is lucky and wins, he stops at the New Chungking restaurant, which is open until 2:00 A.M. There, he orders chow mein take-out. When he comes home, he rouses Jennie and me from our sleep to join him for *siu yeh*, another snack for the family to share.

Eating with Pop (1949)

I am eleven years old. Pop is pouring hot water from a kettle into a Chinese porcelain teapot sitting in a padded basket. This is his morning ritual. The teapot in its own cosy basket keeps the tea warm for most of the day. He plunks a cup of tea in front of me. Pop moves back to the kitchen to stir a mixture of boiled Quaker Oats and water over a hot plate.

I make a face as he spoons the porridge into my bowl. It looks and smells like the papier-mâché that I made in art class. It feels like glue.

"Eat. It's cold outside. The porridge will warm you up on your way to school."

I make another face and say nothing.

I like breakfast better when the weather is bright and warm. Then he makes French toast, one of his rare ventures of *lo-fan* dishes. I imagine the aroma of fried eggs and butter . . .

But it is winter. So I pour milk onto the mush and sprinkle sugar on top. Lots of sugar.

While I'm eating breakfast, Pop takes out a couple slices of McGavin's bread and opens up a vacuumed-sealed packet of mock chicken loaf to make me a sandwich for my lunch at school. The loaf is a mixture of pork, beef, and chicken. I don't mind the sandwich. It's mostly chicken, and I like chicken.

He wraps the sandwich with waxed paper before putting it in a paper bag. I'm off to school. I walk out of our living quarters, past Pop's sewing machine and worktable, and through the display of custom-made shirts all neatly lined up in a row behind glass.

In a few minutes, he will open the store and begin his day as a tailor.

My day at Strathcona School ends at three. I go home, say hi to Pop who's busy behind his sewing machine, grab my other school bag, and walk one block to Chinese language school.

School is over by six, and when I return home, Pop has dinner ready. Pop covers the table with newspaper. We have a bright red vinyl tablecloth, but Pop is practical. During dinner, we discard the bones from the fish, beef, or pork and perhaps a melon rind and other bits of food we deem as waste right onto the newspaper-covered table.

After we drink our tea, Pop collects the dishes, bowls, and chopsticks and asks me to roll up the newspaper. I smile and remember how Jennie used to sit next to me during dinner, reading the comic section. Upside down. I roll the newspaper up into a neat bundle and shove it in our woodstove. Pop's idea of instant disposable garbage.

Photograph courtesy of author.

Pop hard at work on his sewing machine. I took this photograph of him when I was a member of the UBC Camera Club in 1959.

Every night, after dinner, an old family friend drops by to look after me as Pop walks down Hastings Street to help his friend at his store.

Photograph courtesy of author.

Me and Pop, circa 1944, in front of the East Hotel on Gore Avenue.

By ten o' clock, I'm in bed, fast asleep. It seems like only moments later when I hear my name. Pop has returned, and I smell food. My eyes are half-open as Pop shakes me.

"Wake up. *Siu yeh*," he says in a sharp voice.

I'm drowsy but make an effort to get out of bed. Pop is in the kitchen, opening the take-out carton and pulling out the chow mein with a pair of chopsticks onto two plates.

I sit down at the table.

"Eat."

I open my mouth and yawn. Oh, I'm so tired. I take my chopsticks and dig into the noodles. There is a smell of fried noodles in peanut oil mixed with the mushrooms, onions, and dark soya sauce. The noodles are covered with egg shreds, and the bean sprouts gleam amidst the layers of green celery and red slices of barbecued pork.

I munch on my noodles. Pop tells me how at midnight, he helped his friend George close up the store and on his way home, decided to drop in at the social club.

"I was feeling lucky," he says. "I played a few rounds of Fan Tan, and I won every one of them!"

I finish eating and start to feel drowsy.

"I got the chow mein from the New Chungking. I felt like *siu yeh* after winning."

My head is nodding, and I fall into a deep sleep.

I awake the next morning, but I don't remember much of last night. Pop pushes a bowl of mush in front of me.

"Aw, Pop, I don't know why, but I'm not hungry."

Guess Who's Coming to Dinner? (1952)

Pop hummed as he made two swift chops with his cleaver to halve the chicken. In a mixing bowl, he poured soya sauce followed by a sprinkle of pepper and salt before marinating the chicken.

"What are you making, Pop?"

"*Whut guy*."

Wow! Pot roast chicken. Chicken first browned, then cooked on medium heat with Chinese mushrooms, wine and garlic. Like the Chinese of his generation, whenever there were guests, Pop always made a chicken dish. He must've had dozens of recipes for chicken in his head. He could make boiled chicken, breaded chicken, braised chicken, fried chicken, anything and everything chicken. And all he had in our tiny kitchen were two hotplates with two elements each and a woodstove.

Our guest that day was Garry, my brother-in-law. My *new* brother-in-law, whom Pop and I never met.

Jennie left home in 1948 when she was seventeen. She wanted to see the world beyond Chinatown. Chinatown was an insular village back then. Everyone knew one another and was happy to stay, but some of the younger generation wanted to go beyond Pender Street.

My older brother, Wah, left home to go to the University of Washington and never returned except for an occasional visit, and now Jennie was returning home, if only just for a little while.

Jennie always missed Mom. Mom died when Jennie was nine, leaving her with Pop, two older brothers and me, the baby of the family. It was a lot for Jennie to grow into her teen years in such a male-dominated family. As much as Pop tried, it was a challenge to be both a mother and a father. Shortly after Mom's death, my eldest brother, Git, died at the age of twenty-one from tuberculosis, a disease common at the time in Chinatown.

The day after Jennie left home, Pop ranted and raved for hours. His voice bounced off the four walls with rage. He usually had a bad temper but that day, he outdid himself. He disowned his daughter and told all his friends about it. Every time he spoke about it, the veins on his neck and forehead visibly pulsed.

At first when Jennie left, I missed my siblings. But I quickly realized that Pop had changed his attitude toward me. He was more attentive. I complained one day while playing Cowboys and Indians that I didn't have a holster for my cap gun. The next day, he made a gun belt and a holster out of some leatherette material. He also measured me and made my shirts.

In the time spent with my father, I learned that he and my mother were in Chinese opera. Before the revolution of 1911, women were forbidden from the stage, so men played the female roles. When China became a republic, the men-only tradition was lifted, and Mom, who by then was in her twenties, eagerly tried out for Chinese opera and was accepted. With the local Chinese opera troupe, my parents were active on stage but in reverse gender roles. My mother played a general, and my father, a fair maiden.

There were times at night when I could hear Pop singing in bed. I ignored it, but later on, I found out his songs were love songs from the Chinese operas. I think he sang them to remember my mother and keep memories of her alive.

The first few years of Jennie being gone, she wrote to me regularly from a town in northern Ontario. With each letter she included a list of Chinese groceries for me to buy for her. She also included a cheque; it was more than enough, as I always had leftover change. The list included bottles of soya sauce, pounds of Chinese mushrooms and sausages, bags of dried Farkay noodles, tins of abalone and canned vegetables and even the smelly salted fish. I shipped off the care packages. I thought nothing of it other than, well, she missed Chinese food, and obviously in a small mining town, Chinese groceries barely existed. Her letters and lists were also a way of keeping in touch with us, even if Pop had disowned her.

When Jennie announced in 1950 that she got married and worse yet, for my father, to a white person, Pop immediately jumped up and down and disowned her again. He was furious. How dare his daughter married outside of our race? What was she thinking? Unacceptable! His voice rose and stayed at an anger-level all week long.

Now, two years later, she was returning home. Pop calmed down, though occasionally he'd gnash his teeth at the mention of her name.

Now, he hummed as he moved about in the kitchen. He was steaming pork pie, or *gee yook bueng*, with a duck egg yolk. The pickled Swiss chard with beef was already cooked in the frying pan, and the steamed salted fish was also ready. The air filled with the smell of garlic and vinegar.

Just then, the front door opened, and in walked Jennie with her husband.

"Pop! I missed you." Tears ran down her face.

"*Mo hamm*," he said. No need to cry.

He stepped forward, his eyes happy to see his daughter, but when he shifted to the tall, blond man, his new son-in-law, Garry, he sighed. His body sagged, but he extended his hand. His eyes were wet.

Jennie raised her arms to give Pop a hug, but he stood with his arms at his sides. She hugged him awkwardly.

"*Sik chan*," were the only words he could say. Let's eat.

We all sat around the dinner table. Jennie laughed when she saw the newspaper tablecloth. Garry sat next to Pop, and I next to Jennie.

"I can still read the comics upside down," she said. I laughed and smiled at Garry.

Pop had already set the food on the table. "Oh wow," said Jennie. "My favourites."

Mine too, I thought. But what about poor Garry? I couldn't imagine that any of this village food would appeal to a white person.

"What do you do for a living?" Pop asked Garry.

"I'm a butcher."

"A butcher?" said Pop, his eyes widening. "That's good. People have to eat so you'll never be out of a job."

He offered Garry some Johnny Walker, and they toasted to the occasion.

"I have a job waiting for me here so we'll be staying in Vancouver," Garry told Pop.

Pop nodded and pointed to the food on the table, "Eat."

To my amazement and more so for Pop, Garry started on the salted fish and ate it with gusto. My eyebrows went up. He was using the chopsticks as if he had been using them all his life. He was eating up all the village food, the peasant stuff. One was the dish of the dark green pickled Swiss chard with its sour taste, accompanied with the fine slices of fried beef. Next to that was the pork pie, with a bright orange salted duck yolk sitting in the middle. Another dish was the pot roast chicken, with sizzling garlic and Chinese mushrooms.

These were dishes you don't normally order in a Chinese restaurant. Pop raised his eyebrows. He'd hoped to discourage this young man, but Garry passed the test. How could a *lo-fan* eat this village fare?

When dinner was over, there were some traces of sauce remaining on the plates. We all sat back, our bellies full and satisfied. Pop pulled out a pack of cigarettes and offered one to Garry.

Pop reached for the bottle, "Whiskey?"

Years later, Garry still has a healthy appetite for Chinese food. But I had to ask Jennie.

"How did you get a prairie boy from Saskatchewan whose parents were from Great Britain and brought up on meat and potatoes to finish that dinner Pop made?"

"Remember those care packages you sent me?"

"Yeah, I remember those."

"When I was living at home, I used to watch Pop in the kitchen. I missed Pop's cooking when I moved to Ontario. So I ordered whatever groceries I could and practiced cooking from memory."

"Just from watching Pop?"

"Yeah. And of course, with Garry, he was tired of meat and potatoes, so I cooked Chinese for him."

She paused. "I knew I had to eventually introduce him to Pop." She shrugged with her palms facing up.

Pop and Garry got along famously. He never complained about Garry or mixed marriage in his family again. In another year or two, Garry's parents came to visit us from Sintaluta, Saskatchewan. Charlie and Vera Diment went to Pop's tailor shop. Pop made English tea for them by boiling water in a saucepan and letting the tea bag steep for a minute before stirring in spoonfuls of sugar and gobs of condensed milk. The Diments politely drank it all up.

In June 2000, Jennie and Garry celebrated their fiftieth wedding anniversary.

Pop died in 1966, and we buried him at Ocean View Cemetery. When Ching Ming time comes around, I place my bouquet and food offerings at his bronze gravestone and bow three times before him. I think back to the memories of Pop, running them through my mind like a movie and pausing at the happy moments. Of them all, that one of the dinner that changed the family forever.

Photograph courtesy of author.

Jennie and Garry in Edmonton in 2001.
This was taken in their 51st year of marriage.

The sun warms my face. I close my eyes and see coloured patterns dance before me. I take a deep breath. I can smell the freshly cut grass and feel the gentle breeze. I open my eyes and look into the blue skies.

If I listen carefully, I can hear Pop singing in his bed—love songs he sang to my mother.

Author's Note

When I read the stories in *Finding Memories, Tracing Routes*, a result of the CCHSBC family history workshop conducted by Brandy, I kicked myself. I would have really enjoyed writing my family history had I bothered to sign up.

As it happened, Brandy planned another workshop, this time on my favourite subject: food. In my family, my father and siblings loved to cook and eat, though not necessarily in that order. My father was a great cook. It wasn't until I visited the home village in China that I found out he'd come from a long line of cooks in the clan.

What I got out of the workshop was not only the enjoyment of camaraderie among fellow participants but also a sense of achievement. Brandy demanded, in an encouraging way, that we turn in our drafts on time. Discipline, as we all found out, drives writing. And writing requires rewriting and more rewriting.

I was able to write about growing up in Chinatown, all centred on the delights of food and eating. My father was a widower who earned his living as a tailor. We lived in the back of the store on Main Street. I enjoyed my father's cooking; it set the standard for all my future enjoyment of eating. To revisit those moments of my childhood was to relive the pleasure of simpler times through the four senses. We live only once, but to journey back to the past is to find the essence of ourselves.

I am reminded of a quote from T.S. Elliot's "Little Gidding":

> We shall not cease from exploration
> And the end of all our exploring
> Will be to arrive where we started
> And know the place for the first time.

Larry Wong

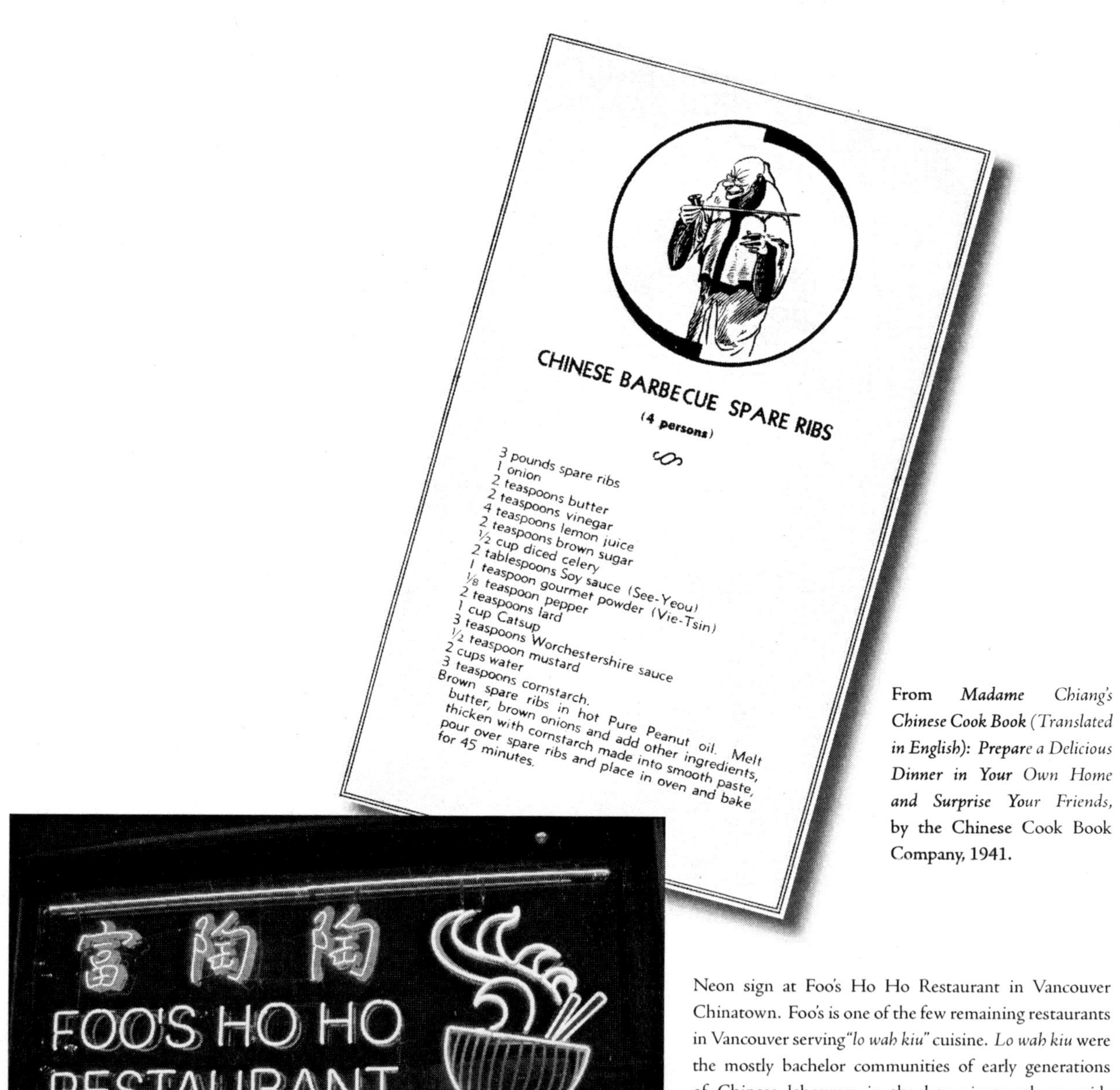

CHINESE BARBECUE SPARE RIBS

(4 persons)

3 pounds spare ribs
1 onion
2 teaspoons butter
2 teaspoons vinegar
4 teaspoons lemon juice
2 teaspoons brown sugar
½ cup diced celery
2 tablespoons Soy sauce (See-Yeou)
1 teaspoon gourmet powder (Vie-Tsin)
⅛ teaspoon pepper
2 teaspoons lard
1 cup Catsup
3 teaspoons Worchestershire sauce
½ teaspoon mustard
2 cups water
3 teaspoons cornstarch.

Brown spare ribs in hot Pure Peanut oil. Melt butter, brown onions and add other ingredients, thicken with cornstarch made into smooth paste, pour over spare ribs and place in oven and bake for 45 minutes.

From *Madame Chiang's Chinese Cook Book (Translated in English): Prepare a Delicious Dinner in Your Own Home and Surprise Your Friends,* by the Chinese Cook Book Company, 1941.

Neon sign at Foo's Ho Ho Restaurant in Vancouver Chinatown. Foo's is one of the few remaining restaurants in Vancouver serving "*lo wah kiu*" cuisine. *Lo wah kiu* were the mostly bachelor communities of early generations of Chinese labourers in the late nineteenth to mid-twentieth centuries. *Lo wah kiu* cuisine can be thought of as part Chinese village homestyle cooking and part early fusion—a mixture of Chinese and Western Canadian tastes. Photograph by Janice Wong.

Generation Fusion: a picture story

Todd Wong

Memories in My Cup

I'm at the White Heather, a Scottish teahouse in Victoria. While sitting here, I'm overwhelmed by a flood of memories about having tea and sandwiches at my grandmother's home. My Canadian-born Chinese grandmother, Mabel Mar, grew up during the last years of Victorian culture in British Columbia.

My girlfriend Deb, Poh Poh, and me celebrating Mother's Day in 2007 with a Bon Ton diplomat cake.

High tea at the White Heather.

At Poh Poh's house we always had "English tea"—black tea with milk and sugar served in English teacups. Poh Poh would slice the crusts off the sandwiches, and then cut the sandwiches into quarters. She presented the finger sandwiches on three-tiered serving trays. As I enjoy my treats and tea at the White Heather, it dawns on me just how English my grandmother and maternal family had been—and how tea has been the bridge between Chinese and British cultures.

All photographs courtesy of author.

A Wong on the Loose

Here, I am sixteen years old. Dad had a seventeen-foot boat he named A.W.O.L.—which, as he proudly told people, stood for "A Wong On the Loose." We used to go fishing at Pender Harbour, Howe Sound, and Georgia Straight. Mom's favourite way of cooking fish was steamed. She would pour hot oil over the fish with ginger and green onions. I would later adapt the recipe to use sesame oil. Today, I go down to the docks, buy fresh salmon, and clean and cook them right away.

The big ones that didn't get away.

Here I am, celebrating Robbie Burns Day Chinese New Year for the first time. Photograph by *Vancouver Province*.

Of Kilts and Pomelos

Robbie Burns Day is celebrated on January 25th, and in 1993, Chinese New Year was a mere two days away from this Scottish celebration. At the time I was asked to participate in Simon Fraser University's annual Robbie Burns Day festivities. I initially passed on the opportunity—after all, it wasn't cool to wear a kilt back then, especially if one were Chinese Canadian. But since no one stepped up to the task, I agreed and quickly realized that with the synchronicity between Chinese New Year and Robbie Burns Day, there could be a wonderful chance to make a multicultural statement.

It was a fun way for a multigenerational Canadian to flip cultural stereotypes. For this picture, which was taken for a *Vancouver Province* article about my celebration fusion, I grabbed a traditional Chinese New Year offering of pomelo, surrounded by mandarin oranges and *li-see* (Chinese red envelopes containing "lucky money"), while donning my kilt.

Gung Haggis Fat Choy!

What is Gung Haggis Fat Choy? It is a Robbie Burns Day Chinese New Year Dinner. It is the intersection of Chinese and Scottish cultures. It is the recognition of pioneer Scots and Chinese in British Columbia. It is a celebration of Asian Canadian arts and culture. And it is a good excuse for a fun party, filled with music, poetry, and food.

In 1998 the first Gung Haggis Fat Choy dinner started with sixteen people in a living room. The following year, I decided to move the dinner to a restaurant so I wouldn't be stuck in the kitchen so much. By 2005, the dinner had grown into a huge event with 570 people in attendance.

Photograph courtesy of Becca Fong.

Becca Fong and Rory Denovan of Seattle, Washington came to the first international Gung Haggis Fat Choy dinner in Seattle on February 18, 2007.

Mayor Larry Campbell, me, and Dr. Enid Campbell at the 2005 Gung Haggis dinner. Photograph by Ray Shum.

During the banquet dinner, we have readings of Robbie Burns's poetry as well as readings by Asian Canadian poets. We sing songs like "When Asian Eyes Are Smiling" and "Haggis Night in Chinatown." We serve haggis wonton, haggis lettuce wrap, and a plate of traditional haggis.

Gung Haggis Wonton

I was invited to present a gift to Shelagh Rogers, whose "Sounds Like Canada" CBC radio show was moving from Toronto to Vancouver. I could think of no better gift than food. I also wanted to recognize my Chinese heritage and my family's seven-generations history in Vancouver. So I brought *lo bok goh*, a turnip cake that my great-grandmother Kate Lee would make for me when I was a child; apple tarts from Chinatown, like the ones my father used to bring home as treats; and the very first haggis wontons, to represent the fifth, sixth, and seventh generations of our family that are born of Chinese and Caucasian heritages. After tasting the wonton, Shelagh said, "Your haggis wonton and plum sauce go together like Bogart and Bacall—a wonderful marriage of cultures!"

Gung Haggis Wonton.

The making of the haggis wonton…

…and the eating of the haggis in an eating contesst (with contender Dan Seto)!

Deep-Fried Gung Haggis Wonton

40 wonton wrappers
4 oz haggis
2 oz water chestnuts, finely chopped
1 oz shredded bamboo shoots, finely chopped
1 oz of celery, finely chopped
½ oz Chinese parsley
½ oz green onion, chopped
½ tsp salt
½ tsp sugar
½ tsp sesame oil
½ tsp tapioca flour
Pinch of white pepper
½ tsp scrambled egg
Oil for deep-frying

Haggis wontons and spring rolls, created by Floata Seafood Restaurant. The original recipe for haggis wonton was developed by Joseph Lee of Flamingo Restaurant and was later modified.

Dipping Sauce

1 Tbsp mustard, plum, or sweet and sour sauce
1 Tbsp maple syrup
* Mix ingredients together.

1.) Mix together haggis, water chestnuts, bamboo shoots, celery, Chinese parsley, green onion, salt, sugar, sesame oil, tapioca flour, and white pepper.

2.) Place 1 teaspoonful of the mixture onto the centre of the wrapper. Moisten the wrapper with the egg to hold corners together and fold.

3.) Heat oil in a deep fryer or wok. When the oil is hot enough, carefully place the wrapped wontons into the deep fryer or wok, and cook until they turn golden brown. Serve with dipping sauce.

Author's Note

I wanted to join the CCHSBC writing workshop because I knew I wanted to be part of something very exciting. I was sorry that I had missed the first workshop, which focused on family stories, so I didn't want to miss this second workshop.

As we discussed our memories and writings during workshop, I realized that for a lot of people, creative cooking involves improvising with different ingredients. Fusion cooking has really taken off! My Toddish McWong persona revolves around food, culture, history, and writing. What do you do with the haggis? Cook it Chinese Canadian style! Mix in water chestnuts. Add maple syrup to plum sauce or sweet and sour sauce. Haggis lettuce wrap! Haggis spring roll! Haggis dim sum!

I'm currently working on a children's story about the origins of Gung Haggis Fat Choy. I have very personal intentions for this story—it is meant for the future generations of our family descended from the Reverend Chan Yu Tan. All my cousins have married non-Chinese. The seventh generation is only one-quarter ethnic Chinese. We also have a branch that is part First Nations, in which the sixth generation is one-eighth Chinese.

I continue writing on my blog, **http://www.gunghaggisfatchoy.com**—a little bit of history, arts, culture, dragon boats, and the occasional food review.

It was really good to be pushed through the writing process by Brandy. When we writers would fall into stereotypes and clichés, Brandy offered fresh perspectives. Sometimes things had to be deconstructed before they could be rebuilt with more solid foundations, stronger characterizations, and deeper personal meaning.

When I fell ill during the workshop and hit some writing blocks, Brandy and the participants encouraged me and still made me feel included. I am thankful that Brandy suggested using my photographs as an alternative medium to share my stories.

Todd Wong (a.k.a Toddish McWong)

Irish Smoke Signals, Going Native, & Just Desserts

Harley A. Wylie

Going Native

My father, Ralph Wylie, Sr., was of Irish ancestry, although at the time, to me he was, well, just Dad. He worked in Seattle, Washington as a mechanic for Safeway. Mom was an Indian, but I still had not completely sorted this out in my young mind. Although I had begun noticing some differences in people's skin colour, there was no "us" or "them" concept in my outlook back then. People were still just people to me.

Mom looked after the house, did the laundry and cooking, and looked after Dad, my baby brother Ralph Jr., and me. My baby brother Ralph was just that—a baby. He was cute, and I really did like him, but he didn't do much besides eat, sleep, and fill his diapers up with poop—not much of an act for a big brother that wanted a buddy to play with. My imagination worked overtime, and I found ways to entertain myself and have fun, but I yearned to play with other kids. Fortunately, we all found more fun on some weekend trips.

On a Saturday or a Sunday, we'd go for a drive, perhaps to a beach or an airport because Dad loved watching airplanes. But when I heard the word "Tulalip" in the conversation, I began anticipating a nice drive, playing with friends, and eating great food. When we left for the Tulalip Indian Reservation, we usually took off sometime in the late morning or around noon. Even the anticipation of the trip was a pleasure—thoughts of whom we would see, what we would do, and most importantly, what we would be having for dinner.

We'd leave the dead-end street in our neighbourhood, drive down the hill, turn left onto Highway 99, drive north, go through Everett, pass the Rip Van Winkle Hotel, go across town, pass the smelly old Weyerhaeuser Pulp Mill, go on the long steel bridges over the Snohomish River and other bridges over rivers like Steamboat Slough, into Marysville, left off of Highway 99, pass the Cascade Drive-In on the right, pass the little grocery store also on the right (if it was a good day, we'd stop at the store, where I might've scored some pop, candies and a comic book!), drive through the country, turn left to go to the reserve, drive past the cemetery with the two tall totem poles on each side of the entrance, drive further down the gravel road, and finally (!) we would arrive at the Tulalip Indian Reservation—a mere one-hour drive from our house.

As we drove down the gravel road, people recognized our car and waved and yelled hello to Mom and Dad. As soon as we got out of the car, folks smiled and chatted and joked around with us. In the middle of the field, an open fire was burning and usually had one or two men watching over it to make sure fresh logs were added

Mom and Ralph, Jr., a.k.a."Bimbo," at Tulalip Indian Reservation, c. 1953.

and put in the proper position so the fire burned steadily. People stood around the fire, sat on logs or on the grass, drinking beer, wine or pop, and enjoying each other's company.

These were spring or summer days with warm sunshine, a gentle breeze with salty ocean air, and smoke from the open fire. Fishing boats were lined up along the beach, going back toward Coy's dock near the main beach area of the reservation. They were small wooden gillnet boats, twenty to twenty-five feet long, each painted different colours. Each boat had a small plain box-type cabin, usually painted white and with no windows. The rear of the boats had a round wooden drum for the gillnet with its cork floats on top and lead weights on the bottom. Just behind the drum at the stern were two tall, thin, upright rollers on each side to guide the gillnet when it was being released or pulled back onto the boat. The fishing boats weren't high-tech or pretty, but they were very good at what they were built to do—they caught fish.

When it was time to fish, all the boats left shore at the same time. At least two boats beside each other would leave their nets attached to a drum, or a large spool, on the shore, and left shore at the same time, going straight out into the bay. As they neared the end of their nets, they would both turn in toward each other and meet beside one another, and the operators tied both nets together. Once this was done, the people on the shore at the drums took over.

On each side of the drums was a large X-shaped handle that one or two men on each side used to turn the drum manually and pull the net slowly into shore. As the net got closer, the water started to come alive with trapped salmon jumping and splashing, frantically trying to escape. The excitement level grew for everyone, young and old alike. Some people would wade into the water to grab the salmon right out of the water, while others stayed beside the drums to help pull salmon off the gillnet. Either way, everyone was excited about the wiggling and jumping mound of fish because we knew what they were to us. They were our dinner!

Once the fish were gathered up on shore, some people would be ready to clean and gut them right on the beach. Then the salmon would be taken up to the field near the fire, and someone would cut off the heads and fins. Another person would gather up the remains and take them away, to be used later or given to someone. The salmon would be filleted, with two cedar wood stakes piercing each side of the fillets. Then we would stick the fillets in the ground in a circle around the fire to be barbecued open-pit style.

The fire took on a new dimension and aura as the salmon started to cook. With salmon juices dripping off and around the fire, an aroma of burning wood blowing around with the salty ocean air filled our nostrils.

Waiting for the salmon to cook was part of the joy of these outings. We kids would run around and chase each other in the field, play on the beach, wander around looking at boats, people or fish, venture into the old small sawmill on the beach, and climb in crabapple trees in the field. If apples were in season and filled the trees, that was a bonus.

Photograph courtesy of author.

Me, Ralph Jr., Mom, and my older half-brother Jesse, and dog Cubby in the background, at Tulalip.

When we got hungry, we found our way back to the grown-ups sitting by the fire. As we neared the pit, our stomachs rumbled at the delicious scent of barbecued salmon drifting everywhere in the summer air.

We joined the adults and ate salmon, potatoes, rice, and salads. There was no dinner table, no having to be neat and "not make a mess." We could dig in with our fingers if we wanted. The salmon brought each taste bud to life, the flesh melting in my mouth. And the crunchy salmon skin. . .

It didn't matter to any of us kids or parents that we had salmon juice dripping out of the sides of our mouths or that some pieces fell onto our clothing. We were all enjoying the community event of catching fresh fish, preparing it, and sharing a wonderful meal with family and friends. This stuff was finger-lickin' good long before "The Colonel" ever came up with the phrase.

Eventually, evening would be upon us, and people slowly began returning to their homes on Tulalip, or like our family, loading up for the trek back to town. These were good times and good memories with different cultures that fought each other in past—but not this generation. There was no time I can ever recall that the adults or children had any arguments, and I can't remember ever hearing a racist comment by anyone.

Oh yes, I cannot forget my baby brother Ralph Jr. I am certain he had fun eating, sleeping, and filling up his diaper at the Tulalip Indian Reservation's community salmon fishing and barbecue. Yeah, I'm sure of it.

I have not been to the Tulalip Indian Reservation since 1962, but I remember social gatherings like these like they were just yesterday. And I didn't see my dad as a white guy among the Indians or see my mom and the others as Indians; they were all just people to me and the other kids. As time went by, I would learn of and hear too many negative and racist Hollywood movie sayings about Indians. But for me great memories like these with Indians welcoming white friends, catching salmon, sharing a meal, and celebrating life together are really what it means to "Go Native."

No Ketchup Required

Thank god for the genius that invented ketchup. My father didn't cook very often, and when he did, the rest of us were pretty thankful for whoever invented ketchup. Dad was a great mechanic and could repair cars, trucks, tractors, boats and pretty much anything mechanical—but he was not that great a cook. Actually, he sucked at it; most of his cooking tasted like crap. Worse yet, he didn't care. To sum it up honestly, he seemed to put about as much effort into it as he did when he fed the dogs. But there was one dish that he was quite good at that he cooked in a very unconventional way. He cooked a mean steak.

Photograph courtesy of author.

My father, Ralph, Sr., a WWII naval aviator in front of a F6F Hellcat, c. 1945.

When he cooked steaks for dinner, he'd never cheap out on the cut or quality—it was usually a T-bone or some other high-quality cut. When we were at the supermarket or butcher and Dad went into the store with Mom, we knew we were going to have a steak dinner. He made sure he got a fresh red colour and the right thickness—cost was never an issue.

When we returned home with the steaks, it was pretty much, "Let the games begin!" Either Mom or I would set the table. Ralph—or Bimbo, as we called him—and I were allowed to provide minimal assistance by removing the steaks from their wrappers. Once we got the tape undone and the wrappers off, we put the steaks on a plate or the counter. Our little hands felt the squishy texture of thick, fresh beef that still had a little bit of blood leaking out of it. It didn't look gross to us little carnivores. To us kids, the steaks were huge, gooey, bloody pieces of beef that were going to be a better dinner experience for us than our usual fare of hamburgers, wieners, bologna, or other economical family meals.

Once we unwrapped the steaks, we knew it was time for us to leave the small cooking area of our trailer. Mom prepared the salad and had the potatoes cooking in the oven, and knew that she would be sitting out the meat-cooking part. She appeared to be fine with sitting and watching Dad prepare dinner.

When Dad put the cast-iron fry pans on the stove and heated them to the highest setting, we went to work. We opened the kitchen door and living room windows on our trailer. Dad sprinkled generous amounts of pepper on the steaks and then in the pans. As the pepper hit the hot fry pans, there were soft, muffled sounds—the pepper began to puff up and pop. The cooking was ready to begin.

The kitchen came to life. The steaks were plopped onto the pans, turning each of the fry pans into miniature volcanic eruptions with a loud sizzling medley of meat getting cooked in searing heat, juice, blood and fat splattering! Pepper-scented smoke drifted to every part of our trailer, floating out the kitchen door and living room windows. The scene looked like a controlled smoke fire, which was actually what it was.

Photograph courtesy of author.

Our last home on 2505 Cooper Road in Everett, Washington.

We stood watching Dad's kitchen performance, while the smoke mildly irritated our eyes, mouths, nostrils, and lungs. But we knew it was worth it. Each side of the steaks was cooked at high heat for two to three minutes. When Dad began turning the steaks over one by one, Mom would begin putting the potatoes on our plates and placing the salad in the middle of the table. When the steaks were all cooked, Dad would put them on a large platter and bring them to Mom. Bimbo, Flossie, Jean, June and I obediently and patiently sat at the kitchen table.

Did we hear the loud noises from the steaks in the searing heat of the fry pans, and did we have to breathe in the smoke that bombarded all of our senses? Hell yeah. Did we care? Hell no! The open door and windows let out the smoke, and our time and attention was spent on enjoying a family treat of T-bone steaks for dinner. Mom also appreciated a break from her regular kitchen duties and being served a dinner that Dad, Bimbo, and I made. She got to enjoy all of us sitting and sharing a meal that Dad helped cook.

In spite of what the method of cooking might sound like, the quality of Dad's steak dinner and dining experience was exceptional. No ketchup required.

And how do you think I cook my steaks now? There is one thing that my son does that we didn't do back then. He unplugs our smoke detector!

Comfort Cooking

I don't recall having a comfort food as I grew up, as I lost both my parents before my teen years. However, one memory of the closest thing to a comfort food comes from when Mom made apple pies in our humble home. In our yard and the open field behind our house, we had apple trees, huckleberry and blackberry bushes, and other plants for our adventures in the woods. All of this was available to play in when the weather was good.

At a time before Bimbo and I went to school, we'd join Mom in the kitchen and help get out the apples, flour, sugar, and other ingredients needed to make apple pie. After Mom added more wood to the stove so it would slowly but steadily begin to heat up the oven, we'd help peel the apples and set aside the apple skins and

My mother, Evangeline (Eva) Mildred Thomas, c. 1940s.

cores in separate piles. Mom would take charge of cutting the apples into slices, and we'd help with the preparation of the pie crust. Bimbo and I stirred the mix for the crust. We liked the feeling of the flour, sugar, salt, and other ingredients sifting through our fingers as we mixed it all up in the big ceramic bowl before the water was added. One of the things I enjoyed was that no one got mad if we made a mess and spilled flour or anything else on the table or floor. Actually, if we didn't make a bit of a mess, we weren't working properly.

After we had spent what seemed like a long time mixing, Mom added water to the bowl while we kept mixing. The dough slowly took on various degrees of gooeyness as we kept mixing and squishing it between our little fingers.

After Mom finished slicing the apples, she'd take out her pie pans and grease them with lard so the crusts wouldn't stick. Then she'd help us finish getting just the right amount of texture for the dough.

Mom took the dough out of the bowl and began flattening it out on the table top with the palm of her hands. Once a large piece was flattened out, she began flattening it further with her rolling pin. She'd let us grab some handfuls of dough to put on the table to be added to the dough getting squished by the rolling pin.

Mom placed the dough into a pie pan and squeezed everything into place with her fingers. She pinched off the extra dough around the pan. She added the apple slices and sprinkled sugar on top, maybe some cinnamon. Finally, she covered the pie with another sheet of dough, cutting around the outside edge of the pan. Bimbo and I were allowed to squish the upper and lower pie crusts together. Then Mom poked and cut holes and slits in the top of the crust. The pies were ready for the oven, which by now was really heating up the joint!

But that's not the end of it. Mom would sprinkle sugar onto a pile of leftover apple peelings and slices, and we got to eat them as a snack before we went to play outside. But before we went outside, Mom would let us take the extra dough and flatten it with our hands. We got to use the rolling pin to flatten the dough for an extra special treat—sugar cookies for my brother and me!

We cut the dough and formed it into cute or odd shapes. Then we sprinkled sugar and cinnamon on them too. We placed them in a pie pan or a baking pan, and Mom put the pans in the oven after the pies were done. Apple pies and cookies! Sweet!

Our work in the kitchen being done, we went outside to play and have fun! Some time later, we'd finish the important duties of serious childhood play, burning off our energy with adventures. We would go inside the house—tired, thirsty, and hungry. By then the pies were cooked, and the hot kitchen smelled like a wonderful wood-burning bakery with the scent of cooked sweet apple pies and sugar cookies in the air. Our cookies were very simple, but eating warm, crunchy, golden brown, sweet desserts that we actually helped bake was a wonderful experience.

Photograph courtesy of author.

My grandmother Millie, Mom, and me in Washington.

Those homemade cookies were our comfort food, made together in a humble home with the love of our mother being the best ingredient a child could hope for. Oh yeah—the apple pies were pretty good too!

A First Nation Recipe

By Harley A. Wylie, Nuu-chah-nulth–Huu-ay-aht (Bamfield) and TseShaht (Port Alberni) ancestry

1.) Catch a salmon.

2.) Cook the salmon.

3.) Eat the salmon with friends and family.

4.) If you are a kid, then play with your buddies and have fun. If you are an adult, then visit with your friends and family and relax.

5.) Repeat as often as possible!

Author's Note

I was born in Edmonds, Washington, in a little wooden hospital that no longer exists. My father, Ralph Ingram Wylie, Sr., was an American WWII naval aviator, and from what I recall, was of Irish ancestry. My mother, Evangeline Mildred Thomas, was a Canadian First Nation, of Nuu-chah-nulth (Tse-Shaht) ancestry. My parents met after the war when my father was a member of a big band in Seattle, playing trumpet. My parents' early years were a financial struggle, but they were both hard-working people. My earliest memories are of the different berry camps and fruit orchards where they worked. We survived and eventually owned a small piece of land (it was given by my dad's older sister, Florence Wayman), and our family grew as years went by.

I have been writing a difficult autobiography for years now, and the writings presented in this collection cover parts of it—some of the nicer and more memorable parts. Professionally, the best part of this workshop was to reaffirm similar historical, legislative, social, and other experiences between the Chinese and First Nation cultures. Personally, it was refreshing and heartwarming to see my two brothers read, contribute to, and comment on my written pieces. Most importantly, it has given us an opportunity to talk about a family and childhood that we lost abruptly over forty years ago when we lost our parents tragically in a murder/suicide. The assignments prompted many memories I hadn't expected, allowing me to think of details that in past had been mundane or blasé and that I now appreciate having experienced.

Family reminiscence is not something my family has done much of. Surviving and moving forward, rather than looking at the past, has been a common practice for most of us. I am thankful to family and relatives on both sides of my family for the memories, discussions, or in some cases no discussions (to avoid the past), which prompted me to hang onto memories even more.

If Shirley Chan had not invited me to the October 2006 launch for *Finding Memories, Tracing Routes*, I would not have met the writers of that collection, CCHSBC President Hayne Wai, workshop facilitator Brandy Liên Worrall, and all the members of our writing group. Thanks to Shirley, Hayne, Brandy, and everyone I met and worked with during the workshop. My final thanks to Ray Parks and Denis Johnston at the Provincial Capital Commission for sponsoring Jacquie Adams, of Ahousaht First Nation, and me, of Huu-ay-aht/TseShaht ancestry, to participate as writers for this book.

This is the first joint writing effort with Chinese, Vietnamese, First Nation and Métis writers collaborating together, and I am honoured to be part of it.

Harley A. Wylie

Letting It Simmer: Soups for All Seasons

May Yan-Mountain

Mother thinks soup is the heart and soul of every meal—the key to a healthy body and longevity. "Everything starts with prevention," she often stresses. "You need to be ready because it will take time to rebuild your defence against any diseases once the immune system is down." We grew up with her teaching us the good sense of prevention and of the wondrous harmony and blend of elements in soups created to aid in prevention. This is the family tradition she has passed onto us.

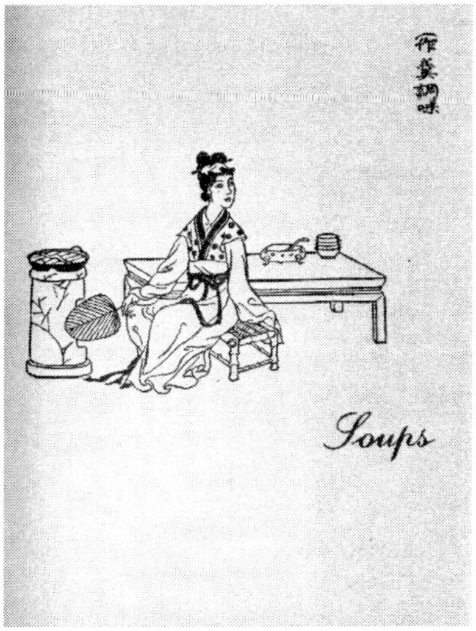

A page from the *House of Chan Cookbook* by Sou Chan, 1952. Drawing by Siu Lan Loh.

Chicken Soup

One day, when we were still living in Hong Kong in the 1970s, Mother, for some unknown reason, had decided that we three youngest kids were ready for the real world of soup making. Maybe she thought that we reached the age at which we needed to learn certain life skills, with my older brother Peter being in his teenage years, myself just barely a teenager, and my younger sister Sarah ten years old.

As usual, we followed her to the local market where poultry was purchased. Once we arrived, she asked the chicken supplier to pick out a live chicken from the big wicket coop—a cage with holes for circulation and display purposes. The use of this type of cage was a common practice to assure the customers that the birds were still alive and moving about. Freshness was very crucial.

"Just put it in this basket, I will take it with me," Mother instructed, much to the surprise of the supplier.

In Hong Kong the procedure of cleaning a bird was open to public viewing. One chicken supplier we often went to demonstrated how to kill and clean a chicken, like a show-and-tell for his young audience.

First, the supplier tied a numbered wooden clip to the selected chicken's leg so he knew which customer the chicken belonged to after it was cleaned. The bird's throat was slit, and it was placed in a rubber container for the blood to drain.

Photograph courtesy of author.

From left to right—me, Mother, Peter, and Sarah.

After a few minutes, the supplier poked the chicken a few times to make sure it was dead before throwing it into a wide metal cylinder with a pipe attached to the side and a tiny hole on top of the lid. As soon as the supplier turned on the machine, the chicken (or chickens, as it was more cost-effective and energy-saving if several were cleaned at the same time) started churning inside, with pressurized hot water running through the metal pipe. The combined motion of water spraying and spinning caused the feathers to fall from the body.

After twenty minutes, the churning subsided, the steam stopped hissing, and the chicken supplier opened the lid and took out the cleaned hot chicken.

This is how the process of buying a live chicken usually went. But this time, when Mother asked for the live chicken to remain as such, so that she could take care of the deed, the chicken supplier had a puzzled look on his face. Without a word, he gave her the basket with the live chicken.

Mother carefully handed over the basket to Peter, who was standing next to her. We were silent for the entire walk home. While I continued to stare at Peter and the chicken up and down, Sarah tightly held our quiet mother's hand.

When we got home, Mother tied the chicken to one of the steel bars in the window of the washroom. Before heading out the door, she announced that she'd be gone for an hour and during that time, the three of us were to prepare the chicken. After she left, we gathered in the living room to figure out what to do next.

"Peter should do it, he's the oldest," Sarah suggested.

"Why me? You are the bravest," Peter said back to her.

"I am not, I am the youngest, besides, you're a man, aren't you?"

"It has nothing to do with whether I am a man or woman. Besides, I don't know how, I've never prepared a chicken before!"

"Well, there's always a first time, isn't there?"

After thirty minutes of their arguing, we decided to go for it. After all, we saw how it was prepared in the market. True, we didn't have a de-feathering machine—but first we had to kill the thing.

Peter approached the frightened chicken with our one and only cleaver in the house.

"Sarah, hang onto the chicken's body while May takes the feet," Peter said authoritatively. Sarah did as she was told, while I stood there frozen, thinking, *How am I supposed to grab the feet when it's still alive?*

"I. . .I . . .can't, I'm afraid!" I stuttered.

"Ah, you chicken!" Sarah teased. "Just watch me. There's nothing to it." She grabbed the feet with the numbered tag still attached and held it up high.

"What now?" I asked.

Peter plucked a few feathers from the chicken's throat, clearing a narrow path to perform the sacrifice, with Sarah holding up the chicken, proud as she'd ever been.

Peter attempted to cut the chicken's throat, but our one and only cleaver was too dull to do the trick. He had to slide the cleaver back and forth across the chicken's throat many times, as if it were a saw. The chicken started flapping its wings, struggling to break free. With horror, we fled from the scene and closed the door behind us, praying the poor soul would not come back as a chicken ghost to haunt us.

Thirty minutes or so passed, and not one word was exchanged. We watched television, pretending nothing had ever happened. Then I whispered, "I think the chicken is dead."

Reluctantly, Peter approached the door, pushing me and Sarah along.

When we opened the door, I nearly fainted while Sarah simply fell to the floor, and Peter leaned on the door, flabbergasted.

Blood everywhere!

The chicken must have had put up a heroic fight before it expired.

"What now?" Peter said in a shaky voice.

"I don't know," I said, unable to ease my queasiness. Fearing I would puke and make more of a mess, I returned to the living room and sat down with my head between my legs.

Luckily, Mother returned at that moment. She immediately regained control of the situation and spent the entire afternoon scrubbing away the blood with us.

My first chicken soup lesson ended in bloodshed. Since then, I've refused to prepare chicken soup unless the main ingredient is bought from the supermarket, cleaned and frozen.

Winter Soup

紅棗、東虫草燉雞

15 g cordyceps sinensis (a fungus you can purchase in a traditional Chinese medicinal herb store, commonly called "caterpillar fungus" or "vegetable worm" in English)

Several jujube (red dates)

2 chicken breasts

1 slice of ginger

Salt to taste

1.) Rinse cordyceps sinensis, and drain well.

2.) Rinse red dates and remove the pits if not already pitted.

3.) Rinse chicken breasts, and pat dry.

4.) Put all the ingredients into a small tureen or ceramic pot with a lid. Pour in boiling water or stock to 80% full. Cover, and place the tureen in the center of a deep pan.

5.) Fill the pan with hot water until the water is about halfway up the side of the tureen. Simmer on low heat for 1½ hours.

6.) Remove from heat and season with salt to taste. Serve hot.

Spring Soup

"You mustn't put in too many south and north apricot seeds," Mother spoke up so her instructions carried over into the living room where I was reading and listening to her during my visit.

"Remember, the ratio is two-thirds south, one-third north," she said. "The portions must be just right because the strength of north apricot seeds is more powerful than south apricot seeds. If measured out appropriately, they will strengthen our respiratory system. But if you don't pay attention, you will have nausea, headache, or even cyanide poisoning." She came out of the kitchen with her hands cupping the seeds she scooped from her herbal container to show me what the correct amount should look like.

Mother has jars upon jars of labelled ingredients neatly lined up in her cupboard. She always says that ingredients must be stored separately before going into the pot. I once asked her why bother if all those uncooked items eventually end up dancing together in the simmering process?

Photograph courtesy of author.

Mother and baby Alex.

"I need to be able to tell them apart before they land in our stomachs."

Mother gave me further instructions on how to make spring soup. "Two things you must do before you add dried mandarin orange skin to the soup: first, soak it in water until it is softened, and second, scrape away the surface on the inside. If you don't scrape it away, it will make the soup taste bitter. Besides, with so many chemicals sprayed on fruit, it's always a good idea to rinse the dried ingredients before adding them to the pot."

Mother stopped and stared at me to make sure I was still paying attention. Satisfied that I was taking it all in, she continued, "Don't mix up *chun bui* with the pearl-like barley you find in English soups. They look a lot alike, but *chun bui* tastes much more bitter when raw or cooked. It has a sharp medicinal smell that barley lacks. Add barley moderately to the soup; it helps relax the lung muscle. Alex will sleep better at night."

My son, Alex, was a premature baby. He was born hypoglycaemic, at four and a half pounds, which made it more difficult to care for him, not to mention his recurring asthma. One spring morning when he was five years old, Mother's words of wisdom came back like thunder: "Prepare your child with soup according to the seasons. Start him off well, and he'll be strong. Let the essence of the ingredients absorb into the blood stream, and his body will do the rest."

I got out my clay pot. It is commonly believed that stainless steel reacts adversely to ingredients in the heating process, so a clay or ceramic pot is more desirable for simmering soup at a low heat. A clay pot also emits a special aroma, making the waiting worthwhile.

Spring Soup

西洋菜、蜜棗、紅蘿白、果皮、南北杏、豬展湯

1 lb watercress (can substitute with dried pakchoi)

1 lb pork shank

1 whole dried mandarin orange skin

6 sweet dates

10 south and 5 north apricot seeds

2 carrots, peeled and chopped

Salt to taste

1.) Wash watercress thoroughly in salted water. Drain well. Cut the watercress in half. (If using dried pakchoi, soak it in water and rinse well.)

2.) Rinse pork. Braise the meat, then drain.

3.) Soak dried mandarin skin in warm water until softened. Scrape the white stuff from the inside surface.

4.) Rinse sweet dates.

5.) Rinse south and north apricot seeds.

6.) Add the south and north apricot seeds to a large pot of boiling water. Then add the pork, sweet dates, carrots and orange skin. Once water comes to a boil again, turn the heat down to low, and simmer for 2 hours.

7.) Add watercress, and continue simmering for 1 hour. Serve hot.

Summer Soup

As the temperature rises in the summer, our appetite decreases. A good soup replenishes the fluid lost over sweating.

Photograph courtesy of author.

Mother tending to the barbecue in Vancouver.

"What's wrong with you modern people?" Mother likes to refer people younger than she in such a way. There is a clear distinction between her generation and mine. She defines women who don't make soup for the family as a "generation of improper."

"But Mom, who has time to make soup when everyone is so busy making a living? Not to mention the fact that the kitchen is hot like hell in summer with all the steam and heat coming off it! I will be cooked instead of cooking!"

"It serves you right if you get dried up in the winter like wrinkled shrimp!"

"Yes, Mother." Not wanting to get into a long debate with her, I relent, as usual. Like all mothers, including myself, she can nag forever when it comes to making sure her children take care of themselves and their families.

"You should add the *bak hap* (lily bulbs) to the soup because they have the ability to reduce internal heat. My mother taught me that before she died." She always invokes people from the past in order to drive home her argument, as they are people whom we can't possibly question.

"But what is internal heat, and how can a petal of lily bulb reduce it?"

"See what happens when you don't pay attention when you should?"

She goes into the kitchen to get a glass of water—a sign that her long lecture is about to begin.

She returns to the living room, clears her throat, and sits in her rocking chair.

"When external pathogenic factors penetrate through the Wei into Qi, you will feel as though you are flaring. Sweating is no longer effective. The movement from the exterior to interior is also an indication of the increasing recurrence of the disease. When you feel feverish, irritable, thirsty, have scanty dark urine and yellow dry coating on the tongue, you will need to add the coolest herbs in your soup to clear excessive heat. The Yin will balance out the Yang. Do you understand?"

It is definitely too complicated for a "modern woman" to grasp. My mind is somewhat off-balance from all those medical terms thrown at me. I usually judge my soup by the effects people have after drinking it: full of energy means I got it right, lethargic and grumpy means I didn't.

Mother continues her lecture, "Just remember this: *bak hap* isn't the coolest herb, but it balances heat in the summer as long as you add a modest amount to the soup." She isn't sure that I'm still listening. She leans in close and reminds me, "Ingredients in each soup recipe have gone through billions and millions of critics before they entered your mouth. I might lack the scientific evidence, but the lifespan of each generation proves what works, what doesn't."

How could I, someone in the twenty-ninth generation of my clan in Guang Dong, ever argue with that?

Summer Soup

花旗參、百合、南棗、無花果、豬展湯

½ lb pork shank

25 g of *bak hap* (lillium brownii—you can purchase this in a traditional Chinese medicinal herb store)

8 jujubes (red dates)

3 figs

10 g ginseng

Salt to taste

1.) Rinse the pork. Braise the meat, then drain.

2.) Rinse *bak hap*, jujubes, and figs.

3.) Add all the ingredients into a large pot of boiling water. Once water comes to a boil again, simmer on low heat for 1½ hours before serving.

Soup for *Sui Lui Bao*

Our soup was served at least ten minutes prior to dinner, not with dinner or after dinner. It was our family tradition. It was also a tradition that I struggled with, as Mother tried to literally force it down my throat.

Photograph courtesy of author.

All grown up: from left to right—me, Peter, Mom, and Sarah.

"*Sui lui bao* (female version for rascal, referring to me), *im tong la, dong tzo mm ho im*." Soup doesn't taste as good when it is cold, was her constant reprimand.

Peter and Sarah always dashed into the kitchen when Mother called, picked up their bowls, gulped down the soup in record time, and wiped their mouths with satisfaction. I, on the other hand, slacked behind with a solemn face as though I was about to face my death sentence. But in fact, most of her soups were light and clear, sometimes even savoury and comforting to the nerves. Nevertheless, I still felt life was coming down hard on me whenever I had to drink the "stuff" I often associated with *raw chives*.

I had several head injuries when I was seven years old. Mother found a recipe that called for consuming raw chives because they supposedly helped to unclog the blood in my brain. It tasted more or less like cyanide (not that I ever had cyanide before). How many seven-year-olds have been forced to eat a dishful of fresh chives every day for an entire week? It was because of this "cure" that I developed a bad taste for Mother's soups.

As a teenager, I knew I had to come up with an idea to have the soup disappear fast. It was quite a plan—I poured the soup into my rice bowl, and the soup bowl was emptied. Voilà—out of sight, out of mind!

It didn't take long for Mother to catch on to the disappearing act. She became suspicious of the way I was suddenly all too ready to accept the soup, all the while making noises as I ate the soup and rice mixture. "*Ai ya, wai wui gar*," her voice became loud and tense.

I countered with, "Most things *do* end up in one place, and that's our stomachs, Mom."

Having failed with my little trick, I squished my face as hard as I could for each slurp of unadulterated soup, whining, "*ho fu ar*," like I did as a kid when I had to drink the herbal teas she made when I got sick.

Shaking her head, "*hi ho ho im*," she'd say as I sipped the soup. Occasionally, she even threw in an English word—"Good"—with her thumbs up to emphasize how delicious the soup was and to encourage me to finish it.

Mother is celebrating her eightieth birthday this year. I am going to make all the soups she taught me, one recipe a week until October. I doubt she will need any reminders that soup is good for her, as she still talks louder and walks faster than any of her children. What's more, she still remembers my tricks.

Autumn Soup

燕窩、川貝母、雪梨燉冰糖

7 g bird's nest

1 Ya pear

15 g *chun bui* (Fritillaria cirrhosa—you can purchase this in a traditional Chinese medicinal herb store)

2 lumps rock sugar

4-5 drops of ginger extract

Salt to taste

1.) Soak the bird's nest in lukewarm water, and rinse out the impurities.

2.) Peel and pit the Ya pear. Cut into bite-sized chunks.

3.) Ground *chun bui.*

4.) Pour all ingredients into a tureen. Add 1½ bowls of boiled water and cover with lid. Place the tureen in the center of a deep pan, then fill the pan with hot water until the water is halfway up the side of the tureen.

5.) Simmer on low heat for 1½ hours before removing it from heat. This soup can be served hot, or cold as a dessert.

Author's Note

When my father helped write our clan history (**http://www.yanfamily.ca**), he provided a means for his children to recognize the significance of what a lineage is about: 薪火相傳 (the passing on of values, identities, responsibilities, and dreams from one generation to the next). From this genealogical record, I've learned who I am, what my origins are, and why and how I should appreciate the legacy of my ancestors.

My mother's soup recipes are a vital part of our family traditions. Her philosophy of soup making reflects a mother's love, care and moral and holistic teachings to the family, especially to her children.

As a daughter born into a Chinese family, I hope the insight gained from recounting these events from my childhood helps my son Alex and his future family, as well as my Canadian husband Rod, understand more about the history of Chinese home cooking and what role it plays in taking care of one's family. My sincere thanks go to my siblings, particularly Sarah and Peter, for their support and encouragement. Most of all, I owe my deepest gratitude to my parents, for shaping me into a historian and a storyteller.

May Yan-Mountain

Fried Rice (Magazine)

2 T salad oil
1/2 cup chopped onion or scallions
2 celery stalks, chopped
2 cups roasted pork, chicken or beef, cut into thin strips.
1/2 tsp garlic salt
1/4 tsp ginger
2 cups cooked rice
3 T soy sauce
1 cup cooked or canned peas
3/4 cup bean sprouts
1 can (3 oz) sliced mushrooms, drained
over for method

CHINESE COOKING CAPTURES AMERICA

INTRODUCTORY

For several years I have been interested in Chinese cookery, and have served in the capacity of a Chinese chef in America and have prepared a number of Chinese seven-course dinners in the best clubs in this country.

The art of Chinese cookery has always been surrounded with a sort of a mystery to the American public.

Always use Pure Peanut oil in preparing Chinese Food, any other composition, such as Lard, olive oil or highly advertised greases, deteriorates the delicious flavor of Chinese Food.

Hundreds of American housewives have often expressed the desire to receive the authentic recipes of Chinese dishes, which consist principally of vegetables and are easily digestible but contain the nutrition attested by leading dieticians.

All grocery stores carry a stock of Chinese Sauces and Groceries.

As a beverage BEER is always used as an appitizer in serving a Chinese dinner, and Chinese Oolong Tea is served as an after-dinner beverage.

Translated by
FRANK YEP

Heat oil in a large skillet. Add onion, celery, meat, garlic salt & ginger. Mix well. Fry for 2-3 min. Add remaining ingredients, mix well. Cook for 5-8 min. or until heated through.

FRIED RICE

3 cups raw long-grain white rice (12 cups cooked)
¾ cup salad or peanut oil
¾ cup chopped green onion
⅓ cup soy sauce
Salt
Pepper
6 eggs

1. Cook rice, following package-label directions for cooking firm rice. Refrigerate, covered, overnight.
2. Heat oil in 12-inch skillet. Add rice, and cook, turning frequently with spatula to separate grains and coat with oil, until heated through.
3. Add green onion, soy sauce, 1½ teaspoons salt, and dash pepper; mix lightly until well blended. Keep warm over low heat.
4. In small bowl, with fork, beat eggs with 2 tablespoons water, ½ teaspoon salt, and dash pepper.
5. Push rice to side of skillet, to make a circular space 6 inches in diameter. Pour egg mixture into center; cook, stirring egg mixture, until it is set but soft. Toss lightly with rice, and serve immediately.
Makes 12 servings.

From *Madame Chiang's Chinese Cook Book (Translated in English): Prepare a Delicious Dinner in Your Own Home and Surprise Your Friends,* by the Chinese Cook Book Company, 1941.

What Mary Cooked

Candace Yip

Food and Order

In our house there were two separate yet equally important cuisines—Cantonese, which included everything with its back to heaven, and *lo faan* (foreign), limited to steak, roast beef, and fried chicken. Growing up in Vancouver in a food-focused family has taken me from two distinct food cultures that co-existed but did not cross over each others' boundaries during my childhood, to today's multicultural mosaic of ethnic and fusion dishes. These are my stories.

Lunch at elementary school was my first encounter with *lo faan* cuisine outside the home. The cafeteria had a weekly revolving menu: Monday, meatballs and mashed potatoes with gravy; Tuesday, pork and beans with homemade bread; Wednesday, hamburgers and chicken noodle soup; Thursday, shepherd's pie; and Friday, hotdogs. I meekly waited in a long line that snaked down the dim corridor leading to the cafeteria to place my order: "main dish and cocoa," or "main dish and soup" was the usual mantra I whispered, as I traded my nickel and dime for the small brown plastic tokens marked *M, S* or *C.*

I distinguished myself from the rest of my classmates not so much by what I ate but by what I refused to eat. Tuesdays and Fridays were everyone's favourite lunch days. Who could resist pork and beans and hotdogs? Those were the days I insisted that my mother pack me a lunch. She knew enough about the cruelty of children not to stick stinky leftover *haahm yu yuhk beng* (salt fish pork hash) in my lunch box. Instead there would be a *chasiu* (barbecued pork) sandwich, an apple, and a thermos of soup or cocoa.

Because I was a glacially slow eater, eating my lunch was a race against time. Every Tuesday and Friday, I'd take my lunchbox with me down to the girls' basement at recess, sit down on a wooden bench in the corner, and get a head start on my lunch while everyone else was playing. That way, I would have a chance of finishing it by the end of the lunch hour.

It was on one of those first Tuesdays in first grade that a tall, ungainly tomboy barged her way onto the bench beside me. "What's the matter? Can't open your thermos? Let me do it!" Before I could answer she grabbed my thermos, and with the tip of her tongue curled up against her top lip in concentration, twisted the top off. "There! What's this gooey stuff? How come you're eating lunch now? Don't you wanna play? I'm

Jo-Anne. What's your name?" Under the barrage of questions, I shyly squeaked out my name and continued ever so slowly to eat my congee, grateful to Jo-Anne for opening my thermos.

That wasn't all that she opened up. Jo-Anne was my first non-Chinese friend. We became, and to this day remain, best friends. She was my entrée into the Wasp world of Sunday school, C.G.I.T. (Canadian Girls in Training), choir, rollerskating, bicycling, building forts in the park, swimming, skiing, secret clubs, and clandestine readings of *Lady Chatterley's Lover* at pajama parties. It was at one of Jo-Anne's pajama parties that I had my first casserole—"Tuna Casserole Supreme."

"Jo-Anne! Here comes your mom!" I hissed as I heard the basement steps creaking. Jo-Anne quickly shelved D. H. Lawrence under a pile of Nancy Drew's. In came Mrs. Bentley carrying a tray of two Corningware casseroles dishes. "All that reading must make you girls hungry," she said as she served us our midnight snack.

It was love at first bite. I never knew that you could combine so many different things from cans in a big dish, throw it in the oven, and come out with such a creamy, gooey, satisfying concoction. My mother never cooked like that.

Photograph courtesy of author.

Me, Jo-Anne, and my cousin at my birthday party.

Mrs. Bentley's Tuna Casserole Supreme

3 cans cream of chicken soup, undiluted

2 cans cream of mushroom soup, undiluted

1 cup milk

½ cup water

1 lb thin spaghetti noodles

3 tsp curry powder mixed with a little hot water to make a paste

1 Tbsp grated onion

1 tsp dried thyme

½ tsp dried basil

½ tsp dried oregano

3 cans solid tuna

1 cup grated cheddar cheese

1 cup bread crumbs

1.) Combine undiluted cream of chicken soup, undiluted cream of mushroom soup, milk and water in a saucepan or pot. Simmer for 10 minutes.

2.) Cook the spaghetti according to the directions on the package. Drain the spaghetti and add it to the soup mixture. Stir.

3.) Add curry paste, grated onion, thyme, basil, oregano, and tuna to the mixture. Stir. Simmer for 10 minutes.

4.) Place in a large casserole dish, and sprinkle with grated cheddar cheese and bread crumbs.

5.) Bake at 325 degrees until the cheese bubbles and the bread crumbs brown to a golden colour.

Serves 10 to 12.

How Did She Do It?

For as long as I can remember, my mother worked outside the home. Yet for every one of my birthdays from age six to twelve, she sewed me a party dress from a pattern of my choice from *Butterick* or *McCall's*, served a sit-down lunch complete with chow mein, honey garlic spareribs and deep-fried wontons, and entertained me and my guests with games like pin the tail on the donkey, musical chairs, charades, and pick-up sticks. The centerpiece of the celebration was a homemade lemon chiffon cake, dressed in creamy white butter icing with clusters of delicate pink rosettes framing the beautifully handwritten letters of my name, and a row of lime green leaves encircling the foot of the cake like the frilly hem of a ball gown.

Photograph courtesy of author.

Mum in a pastry-making class, standing next to the instructor, in the late 1950s.

I can remember closing my eyes tightly as I made a wish before blowing out the candles with more spray than breath. Then the beautiful cake would be deconstructed and divided among the guests, each piece adorned with a pink multi-petaled rose. Mum had learned at night school to make everything from petit fours to three-tiered wedding cakes.

Most of my friends' birthday parties paled in comparison—hotdogs, store-bought cakes, a game of tag on the front lawn. A scant generation later, the production of my own children's birthday parties was often delegated to pitchmen of the fast food industry like Ronald McDonald or Chuck E. Cheese, in the business of entertaining children while parents look on, appreciative of not having to put much effort into the celebration and not having to mess up their own houses. Why did my mother go to so much trouble for my birthday? Perhaps simply because she could. She was a woman of many talents, never wasting any of them.

Mary's Honey Garlic Spareribs

Vegetable oil for deep-frying

1 lb pork side spareribs

4 garlic cloves, finely minced

2-3 Tbsp honey

1-2 Tbsp light soy sauce

1 tsp cornstarch mixed with 2 tsp water

1.) Deep-fry spareribs in medium hot oil until brown. Set aside.

2.) Add a tablespoon of oil to a pre-heated wok. Add minced garlic, stir-fry a minute, add honey and soy sauce, then stir in cornstarch mixed with water.

3.) Add spareribs to wok, and toss to coat them with the sauce.

Maryvale

My father named his new enterprise after my mother. Maryvale was our Chinese-Canadian delicatessen located on Robson Street, or rather, "Robson Strasse," as it was known in the fifties and sixties. In the predominantly German neighbourhood of shops, our deli stuck out like a sore thumb, just like our family did, living in the Oakridge area of Vancouver. Maryvale opened with great fanfare—free samples of cubed cold cuts and cheese skewered on toothpicks, and tiny purple orchids given out to prospective customers, only to close a year later due to our anomalous offerings of chicken chow mein and honey garlic spareribs sitting cheek by jowl with potato salad, bratwurst, and sauerkraut. It was sold to Adolf Prinz, whose legendary sausage-making made Prinz's Delicatessan hugely successful.

For our family the year was marked by losses—financial and otherwise. My mother, who started off each day making a hundred pounds of potato salad, would later say that she lost ten years of her life in that one year, together with her taste for potato salad. That mountain of creamy white salad was slowly eroded away each day as the little old ladies who lived in the nearby apartments and hotels came in to buy twenty-five cents worth at a time. One of those blue-rinsed, pillboxed, white-gloved ladies, Mrs. Hillman, became a fixture at the deli on both sides of the counter.

"How's my adopted godson today? Oh, it's busy in here. Let me help you, Andy."

"Okay, Kai Mah" (Cantonese for godmother), my dad would say while handing her an apron to protect her herringbone tweed suit.

Mum and Dad suspected she was lonely and probably preferred waiting on customers to sitting alone in what they imagined was her sumptuous apartment in the Georgia Hotel.

For my brother and me it was a year of learning to be self-reliant while our parents worked. Our first attempt at taking the #15 bus downtown to Robson Street by ourselves ended badly with neighbours and police recruited to find us. I remember standing beside my brother on the crowded bus, neither of us tall enough to see the stops as the bus lurched downtown. At the end of the line, the bus driver stopped the bus, got out of his seat, and walked down the empty aisle to our seats in the back. "Where the heck are you kids going?" He made sure he called out our stop on the long trip back.

After that debacle we stuck close to home. I played with my friends in Queen Elizabeth Park after school until everyone was summoned home by his or her mother with the blowing of a distinctive whistle. "Tweeeeeeeeeet, tweeeeeeeeeet, tweet!" meant it was time for Jo-Anne to leave me and head home.

At the ages of nine and six, my brother and I were the only latchkey kids in the neighbourhood. I came home to an empty house, often after being chased down the back lane by two bounding snow-white Alaskan malamutes, husky dogs bigger than me, affectionately named "Whiskey" and "Soda" by our neighbour, Mrs. Mitchell, after her favourite drink. Dad would arrive home at four o'clock with cold food from the deli for our dinner and then go back to relieve Mum. She'd come home at seven o'clock, while Dad cleaned up and closed the shop. His day would end at eleven and begin all over again at six in the morning, six days a week.

It wasn't all work and no play. My brother and I managed to have fun in the back of the deli on Saturdays. When we finished peeling potatoes, we got to push them into the torpedo-shaped chamber of the fry cutter and, with a cry of "ready, aim, fire!' we'd take turns pulling down on the handle and watch the perfectly formed fries as they spewed from the chamber and landed in a round stainless steel bowl. From there they went into the deep-fry baskets and were submerged in boiling oil with a loud sizzle in a haze of smoke, until they began to turn pale yellow. The basket would be lifted out to let the oil drain for a while, then re-submerged in the oil until the chips turned a golden colour and became crisp on the outside but soft in the centre. They smelled of summers at Locarno Beach where we lined up at the concession stand in our wet, sandy bathing suits for the little cardboard container of chips that we would douse with malt vinegar and generous shakes of salt.

My mother confided to me that the secret to good fish and chips was in the double dose of deep-frying. Years after the demise of Maryvale, she would say, "You know what would have been a good little operation?

A fish and chip shop near the beach, open for lunch only." That idea never came to fruition. Maryvale was my parents' last food venture. From time to time, with a little coaxing, Mum would pull out the electric deep-fryer and make her famous twice-fried fish and chips, just to make sure that she hadn't lost her touch.

Mary's Fish and Chip Batter

1 cup bread flour
1 tsp baking powder
1 tsp baking soda
1 tsp sugar
Pinch of salt
Pinch of garlic powder
Approximately 1 cup ice-cold water to make a thin batter
Fresh halibut or ling cod

Photograph courtesy of author.

Mum and Dad in front of Rose Coffee Shop and Confectionery, 1943.

If You Can Read, You Can Cook

After I left home, my bedroom became the repository of my mother's burgeoning collection of books. Her appetite for reading novels, biographies, histories, business journals, magazines and especially cookbooks, was voracious. She was very fond of saying, "Any dumb ass can cook. If you can read, you can cook." My apprenticeship with her began when I was twelve. She taught me how to clean, measure and cook rice, and make the broth for soup. That way, when she got home from her job as a bank teller, she could prepare a five-course Cantonese meal within a half-hour or so. I can still picture her at the stove, stir-frying with her coat and hat on, not wanting to waste a moment in getting dinner on the table.

My mother must have learned to eat well, and no doubt, quickly, in the house on Ridge Road in Victoria where she grew up with six siblings and ten cousins. "*Yat, yih, saam, sei, ngh, luhk, chat, baat!*" Second Uncle would stand at the head of the table and count the number of dishes laid out before him before anyone was allowed to start. Getting a share must have been a competitive sport with up to twenty pairs of chopsticks poised to pounce on the tasty morsels of meat, fish, shellfish, and vegetables. Mum's little brother, Abie, his rice bowl held up to his mouth, level with the table, would slyly shovel food that he didn't like out of the bowl and let it drop between his knees to the floor. My mother would have to sweep it up before Second Uncle noticed.

I don't really know whether Mum first learned to cook growing up in Victoria, or in Vancouver where, at age seventeen, she moved in with her eldest sister, Victoria, who had married the sixteenth son of Yip Sang. What I do know is that she was the consummate cook. There was nothing she could not create or improve when it came to food.

One of her specialties was lettuce wrap (*saang choi bau*), a lunar new year's dish made with ground pork and the dried oysters (*houh see*) that are a synonym in Cantonese for good things. When I left home and cooked for my non-Chinese friends, I adapted the recipe by substituting canned smoked oysters for the dried oysters. A subsequent kid-friendly version of the dish using ground turkey and leaving out the oysters has made many appearances as a potluck offering at dinner parties and school functions under the multicultural moniker of "Chinese Tacos." Last Chinese New Year's, it underwent a drastic revision, owing to my husband's conversion to a vegan diet for health reasons. Instead of ground pork or turkey, I use Yves's Veggie Ground Round and have had to abandon Chinese sausages and oysters. The dish looks the same, but the texture of the soy protein is mushier and lacks the juicy roughness of either cooked ground pork or turkey. But once you load up your lettuce cup with a mound of filling, slather the mound generously with hoisin sauce, roll it up like a soft taco and feel a rivulet of gravy run down from your hand to your elbow as you take a bite of the crisp lettuce and its juicy contents, you can hardly tell the difference—that is, unless you have been raised on the real thing.

Mary's Lettuce Wrap, *Houh See Sung*

4 Tbsp canola oil

2 garlic cloves, smashed with the flat side of a cleaver, skin removed

2-3 slices of ginger root

1 lb ground or minced raw pork

2 tsp dark soy sauce

10 medium-sized dried oysters, soaked overnight to soften, washed, cleaned and diced

1 onion, diced

½ cup celery, diced

½ cup canned bamboo shoots, diced

2 carrots, diced

6 water chestnuts, peeled, washed and diced

3 Chinese sausages (preferably "Wing Wing" brand), diced

8 dried shiitake mushrooms, soaked 2 hours to soften, washed, cleaned and diced

1-2 Tbsp oyster sauce

1 tsp sesame oil

Salt and pepper to taste

1 Tbsp cornstarch mixed with 1 Tbsp water

Diced green onions for garnish

Iceberg lettuce, cut in half to form lettuce cups, soaked in ice-cold water and drained

1.) Heat oil in a wok over high heat. Add garlic and ginger and stir-fry for a minute. Remove garlic and ginger from pan, if desired.

2.) Add ground pork to wok and stir-fry for 2 minutes. Season with 1 teaspoon of soy sauce, salt and pepper. Turn down heat to medium and cook pork for 5 minutes, stirring occasionally.

3.) Add diced oysters, stir-fry a few times and if a little dry, add some of the water you used to soak the oysters in overnight.

4.) Add onion, celery, bamboo shoots, carrots, water chestnuts, Chinese sausage, and shiitake mushrooms. Cover and cook for about 5 minutes.

5.) Add the oyster sauce, remaining soy sauce, sesame oil, and salt and pepper to taste.

6.) Blend cornstarch with water, add to the wok, and stir in to thicken gravy. Add more water, chicken broth, or sherry if needed to get the right consistency.

7.) Garnish with green onions.

8.) Serve in lettuce cups with a dollop of hoisin sauce.

Food and the New Order

Aunt Lil is standing just inside the event room at the private club. She greets every guest with a smile that flashes like ivory neon, resplendent in a shimmering black lamé dress, her small but erect shoulders draped in an ebony mink coat on the occasion of her ninetieth birthday. I stoop down to receive a hug and a kiss on each cheek. At ninety she is now the matriarch of my late father's family, the eldest of four surviving girls in a family of six sisters and three brothers. I make the rounds of the other three aunties, Jayne, Lorna and Mickey—hug, kiss, kiss, hug, kiss, kiss, hug, kiss, kiss.

This is not the usual venue for our family gatherings. Now that the aunties are all "of a certain age," we congregate at hotel restaurants with all-you-can-eat buffets, heavy on the desserts which no true Yip can resist. Up until a few years ago when the older generation was more mobile, we would meet annually at Stanley Park near the Children's Zoo for a mid-summer potluck picnic and *mah-johng* marathon. Five or six wooden picnic tables would groan under the weight of a hodge-podge of homemade and purchased offerings. Cold Asian noodle salads redolent of pungent black vinegar and sesame oil nestled next to Church's fried chicken in all its crispy, greasy glory, overpowering the delicate aroma of melt-in-your-mouth coconut cake. Here at the club the buffet is attractive but uninspired. There are no innovative fusion dishes, no exotic spices—nothing reminiscent of our diverse potluck picnic fare.

But tonight it is not about the food. My mission, tape-recorder in hand, is to find out more about one of the businesses that my parents operated in the forties in Vancouver—Rose Coffee Shop and Confectionery at the corner of Dunsmuir and Richards. Almost all of my father's siblings worked at the shop, and two of the girls met their future husbands while working behind the counter. I had always thought it unusual that there were two mixed-race marriages in my father's family. Now, as I scan the room, I see my cousins with Caucasian, Filipino, Nisei, Vietnamese, Taiwanese and Chinese Canadian spouses and their offspring, who are all mixed up like the California rolls and Chinese tacos of our fused West Coast-Asian cuisine. Every time we drove down East Hastings Street, my mother would point out the portrait studio of the Japanese family whose son had supposedly been the first Japanese to marry a Chinese girl after the war, like it was a historical landmark on the national registry of infamy.

Tonight I learn from Auntie Lorna that but for the misfortune of the Japanese in Vancouver who were evacuated and interned in the interior of the province during World War II, our family's first foray into the food service industry may never have been made. Dad and his mother bought the Rose Coffee Shop in 1942 from a Mr. Kariya and put the whole family to work there. "I'm not exactly sure about the name, but I think it started with a K," my aunt adds. The other aunts chime in, "We never got paid at all in the first year—just bus fare and a new suit at Christmas made at Dunn's Tailors. We all worked there until we got married." It's no wonder that the shop was always busy—the sisters were bombshells, and the Merchant Marine Hostel was just across Dunsmuir Street.

Rose Coffee Shop.

Photographs courtesy of author.

Dad's sisters: Lorna, Mickey, Jayne, and Lil, 1940s, in front of the Holy Rosary in Vancouver.

"Attention everyone, it's time to sing 'Happy Birthday' and cut the cake!" With that announcement Auntie Jayne heads for the podium and takes the microphone for her solo performance but is joined by one of her nephews in a loud, rousing duet. "Sing it again!" shouts another nephew. She obliges with four encores in her lovely, lilting soprano voice. Everyone laughs. Not because she can't sing, but because she can—anywhere, anytime, *a cappella, ad infinitum.*

As we feast on birthday cake, I pull out and pass around a menu from Rose Coffee Shop and a couple of photos that are interleaved in my mother's old leather-bound journal. In one photo of the shop, you can see

Photograph courtesy of author.

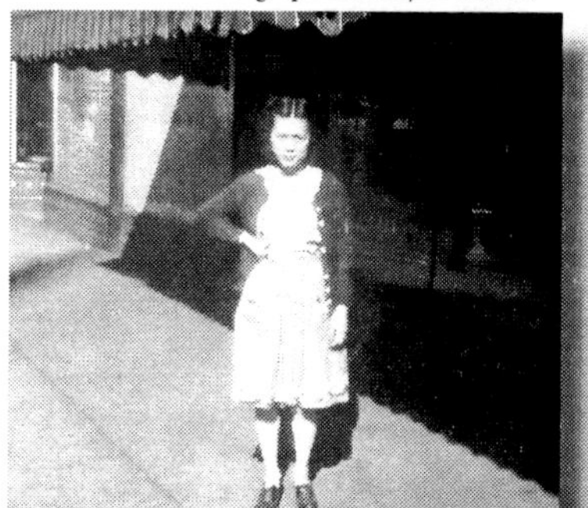

Mum in front of the store.

the sign "CONFECTIONERY" and what look like eight pendulous columns of bananas suspended in bunches above boxes of various fruits displayed in the window. On the menu there is not one item of Chinese food—just the usual sandwiches, salads, soups and desserts, and the unexpected inclusion of Bromo Seltzer and Alka Seltzer for ten cents. In another snapshot my mother, dressed in a frilly apron, cardigan sweater and bobby sox with sensible Cuban-heeled shoes, impatiently waits, hand on hip, to be photographed.

She had met my father when she moved from Victoria to Vancouver at the age of seventeen and, after an eight-year courtship that survived despite his mother's opposition, they were married in 1943. There is a brief entry in her journal under 1943:

> "Got married today, Oct 2/43
>
> Grosvenor Hotel—Rm $3.50 per day
>
> Wedding Dress cost $29.00 Tracy's"

On October 3, 1943—the day after her wedding—she went to work with the rest of the family at the coffee shop, and the honeymoon was over.

As I leaf through the jumble of notes, lists, addresses, receipts and recipes, I imagine that she is talking to me—imparting information that she thought was important enough to write down. Under "1940" she wrote: "Accepted at Bank but Charlie Kent refused to let me go so I had to work at 2 jobs for a while till Xmas. Took music lessons, played (violin) in orchestra." Scattered throughout the journal in no particular order are lists of the different Chinese dynasties, American Presidents, all the members of families she knew, Christmas presents she had given to family members, instructions on how to craft a fish mobile out of tie-tie ribbons, and on how to buy a brassiere that fits, recipes for Chinese beef jerky, pesto sauce, tapioca pudding and mango ice cream, to name a few, and menus of banquets she had attended and dinners she had cooked for her friends.

Dec 12th, 1984
Tangerine Peel Duck Soup
Beef legaments & beef
& Lo hak
Curried Lamb
Chicken Wings & Salt Fish
Deep fried Quail
Vegetarian Dish
Cabbage tops
Tripe
Cold plate - jelly fish c̄ ginger
& cucumber -
Pomelo, Japanese Pear etc

Tong & Gerry, Fred & Lally
Lil & John
Aug 22, 1984
Soup - fish balls & pork balls
Chicken, Salmon, mushroom,
Beef & ligaments, beans
Squid & peas, roast
pork - prawns, steamed
duck eggs - Cold plate -
jelly fish, cukes, eggs & pickled
ginger - mustard greens
Pearl & Joe, Tong & Gerry
Fred & Lally, Alec & Bill
& Josephine -

One of Mum's journal entries.

That Mum deigned to write anything down was rare. She had a photographic memory and stored so much information there that it must have literally shorted out from being overloaded. In the last three years of her life, she suffered silent little strokes that destroyed her memory and impaired her ability to do even the simplest of things, like opening the oven door. But what she left behind, what had overflowed, I've tried to piece together, recreate, and adapt, in her spirit.

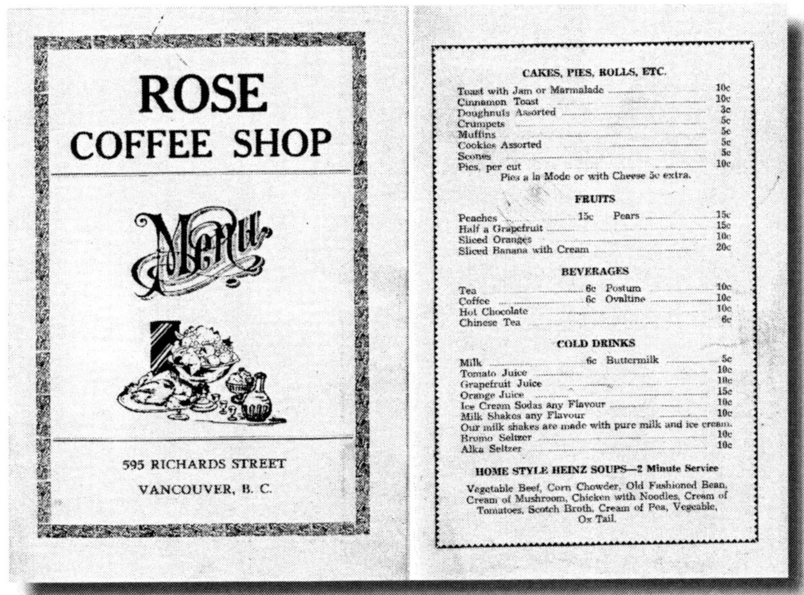

ROSE
COFFEE SHOP

Menu

595 RICHARDS STREET
VANCOUVER, B. C.

CAKES, PIES, ROLLS, ETC.

Toast with Jam or Marmalade 10c
Cinnamon Toast 10c
Doughnuts Assorted 3c
Crumpets 5c
Muffins 5c
Cookies Assorted 5c
Scones 5c
Pies, per cut 10c
Pies a la Mode or with Cheese 5c extra.

FRUITS

Peaches .... 15c Pears 15c
Half a Grapefruit 15c
Sliced Oranges 10c
Sliced Banana with Cream 20c

BEVERAGES

Tea .... 6c Postum 10c
Coffee .... 6c Ovaltine 10c
Hot Chocolate 10c
Chinese Tea 6c

COLD DRINKS

Milk .... 6c Buttermilk 5c
Tomato Juice 10c
Grapefruit Juice 10c
Orange Juice 15c
Ice Cream Sodas any Flavour 10c
Milk Shakes any Flavour 10c
Our milk shakes are made with pure milk and ice cream.
Bromo Seltzer 10c
Alka Seltzer 10c

HOME STYLE HEINZ SOUPS—2 Minute Service

Vegetable Beef, Corn Chowder, Old Fashioned Bean, Cream of Mushroom, Chicken with Noodles, Cream of Tomatoes, Scotch Broth, Cream of Pea, Vegeable, Ox Tail.

The menu for Rose Coffee Shop.

Author's Note

I signed up for this workshop with the idea of writing a tribute to my mother, Mary Lore Yip, who had a life-long obsession with food. She was unquestionably the best cook I have ever known. Although she grew up eating only Cantonese home cooking, she embraced every other kind of cuisine she ever tried and adapted it to her own taste. From her vast collection of cookbooks, television cooking shows, magazines, and friends of various ethnic backgrounds, she took the best and continually expanded her formidable repertoire. The globalization of her cooking mirrored the changes in our Pacific rim city and in the racial make-up of our families.

As a child my favourite fish was fresh (as opposed to smoked) black cod, available only in Chinatown. Today it is widely available in fish markets all over the city and on the menus of high-end eateries of every ethnic origin under the more sophisticated appellation, sablefish.

Over the years our palates have become more adventurous and more appreciative of diversity. Boundaries between different ethnic cuisines have been blurred. If movement toward a global cuisine can foster tolerance and an understanding of different cultures, then so much the better.

Some may decry the lack of a distinctly Canadian cuisine. I, for one, am glad that, in the spirit of eclecticism, we have taken the very best from every wave of immigration that has hit our Pacific shores and made it our own.

I am indebted to our editor, Brandy Liên Worrall, for her expert guidance, to my fellow workshop writers for their insightful comments, and to my *lo faan* husband and *hapa* children for their support and inspiration.

Candace Yip

Food Funnies: A Comedy of Flavours

Gail Yip

Chopsticks 101

Contrary to popular belief, Chinese aren't born knowing how to use chopsticks. In fact, using chopsticks is like driving a standard vehicle—you have to be coordinated. The fact that I never mastered the skill of driving a standard might tell you something about my chopstick skills.

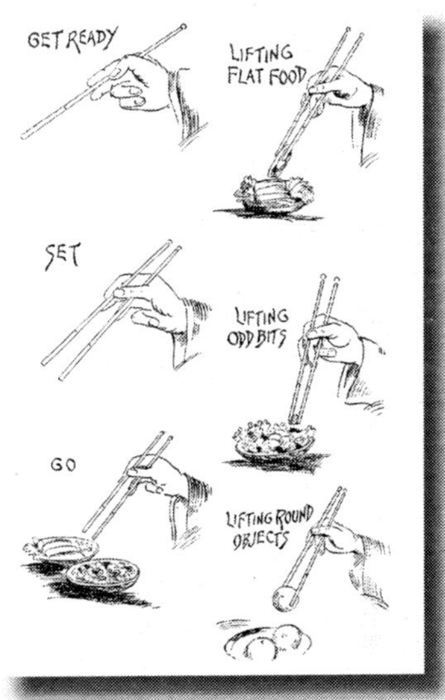

From *The Chinese Cook Book: Covering the Entire Field of Chinese Cookery in the Chinese Order of Serving, from Nuts to Soup*, ed. by Mr. M. Sing Au, 1936.

"You have to learn to use your right hand when you use chopsticks, or you can't sit with us at the dinner table," my mother said to me when I was five years old. The threat reverberated in my head. While other children were painfully separated from their blankies, I had to give up the comfort and security of my spoon. My days of adding gravy to white rice and mixing it all together—known as *loh faan*—were numbered. I would have to *pah faan*—bring the rice bowl up to my mouth; *yuung fay jee*—use chopsticks; and *gaap soong*—serve myself with chopsticks from the communal plates. One overwhelming obstacle was added to the newly required etiquette: I was left-handed, and Mom insisted on proper usage of chopsticks with the right hand.

At the time when Mom delivered her edict, I was too short to sit on a regular adult-sized chair. Instead, I sat on a "highchair," which was really a step stool. (I have since inherited that same step stool, which I currently use to reach the top shelf of my kitchen cupboards.)

Mom alternated between cooking *lo fan chan* (Canadian style) and *tong yun chan* (Chinese style) meals. Thus, I was only humiliated every other night as I mastered the craft of using chopsticks.

Depending on how the table was set, I knew what style of dining was to be anticipated. Forks, knives, spoons, dinner plates: *lo fan chan*. Chopsticks: *tong yun chan*.

During *tong yung chan* nights, proper protocol was required. Don't spread your elbows out too far; keep them by your sides. Make sure both chopsticks are even. Only take food that is directly in front of you—

Chopsticks and Bowls

THE Chinese use chopsticks because they consider the knife and fork barbaric. "We sit at table to eat, not to cut up carcasses," they say.

"Chopstick" is pidgin-English for small, tapering stick, which is commonly made of wood, bone, or ivory. The sticks are used in pairs. "Chop" is pidgin-English for "quick", the Chinese word for the sticks being fai-tze, which means "quick gentlemen".

Held between the thumb and fingers of the right hand, the chopsticks are used as tongs to take up portions of food, which is brought to table cut up into small, convenient pieces.

There are complex rules of etiquette concerning the chopsticks. They are even used as a code of signalling. For instance, to place the chopsticks across the top of the bowl and leave them so is a sign that the guest has completed his meal.

One is very particular not to drop a chopstick during mealtime. To drop a bowl or plate would be less embarrassing. Superstition runs high that dropping a chopstick is a sign of some forthcoming bad luck.

Spare chopsticks are never left on the table. If they are placed there for a guest who fails to appear, they are removed before dinner is srved.

According to an interesting reflection of Genevieve Wimsatt, the author of "A Griffin in China," the shape of serving dishes and implements of eating have had much to do with standardizing the food of China. It is somewhat difficult to carve a chop in a bowl shaped like a larger teacup; it is hard to manage a club sandwich with chopsticks; it is impossible to eat a charlotte russe from the fingers. Practically all Chinese food is so prepared that it can be served in deep bowls that retain the heat longer than a flat plate, and be readily managed by the expeditious help of the "nimble boys", as the Son of Han calls his chopsticks.

Imagine the amazement and disgust with which a delicate young lady might behold a native of Zululand gnawing a joint of half-roasted meat, and you will have some conception of the feelings of a high-class Chinese who sits down at a Western table, and sees beside his plate the terrifying array of knives, forks, and other implements that he will find necessary in dealing with his dinner.

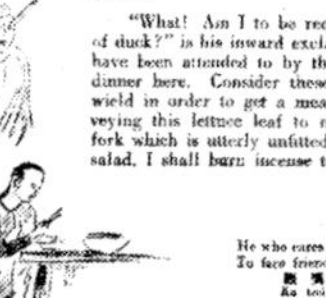

"What! Am I to be required, personally, to carve this leg of duck?" is his inward exclamation. "This is work that should have been attended to by the cook. Truly, one toils for one's dinner here. Consider these tools the foreign gentlemen must wield in order to get a meal. If I survive the ordeal of conveying this lettuce leaf to my mouth by means of this silver fork which is utterly unfitted for the business of disposing of a salad, I shall burn incense to the kitchen God!"

He who cares for his belly much more than his back,
To face friends in his rags is uncommonly slack.

From *The Chinese Cook Book: Covering the Entire Field of Chinese Cookery in the Chinese Order of Serving, from Nuts to Soup,* ed. by Mr. M. Sing Au, 1936.

don't cross over to the other side of the serving plate or bowl. Food is dropped into your rice bowl first—never directly into your mouth from the serving plate. Holding chopsticks two inches from the bottom tip is not permitted. Stabbing food is rude.

The dreaded evening arrived. The first night of Chopsticks 101. Sitting directly across from me, Mom instructed,"Hold your chopsticks like this."

With her left hand she picked up the first chopstick and placed the thickest part at the base of her thumb in her right hand. The narrower portion of the chopstick rested on the lower side of her middle finger. She brought her thumb forward to lock the chopstick in place. With her left hand, she picked up the other chopstick, placing it against the side of her index finger by the end of her thumb.

I absorbed all the intricate details. It didn't look too difficult. Except one minor detail: her actions were a mirror image of what mine should have been.

It was now my time to shine. I picked up the first chopstick with my right hand and automatically placed it in my left hand against my thumb.

"Oooopppps!" I blurted out, dropping the chopstick onto the food-laden table with a loud clatter. I was nervous and sweaty. My older sister Carol snickered and rolled her eyes.

Cautiously, I picked up the first chopstick again. Placed it in what I thought was the correct position. Locked the chopstick in position with my thumb. Then pain struck. My whole hand seized up. Fingers bent and curled, reminding me of a scary witch with gnarly fingers. Slowly, the pain subsided. I flapped my hand to relax my chubby fingers. I then repeated the entire procedure again. A bit more success. However, once both chopsticks were in place, I didn't have the dexterity to pivot the second one. Salty tears streamed down my face, stinging my cheeks.

I eyed the food on the table, my stomach growling with hunger pangs. All my favourite foods. *Jen sher joy* (pan-fried potatoes), *ham yer jing jer yook* (steamed salted fish with minced pork), *gai lan chow ngow yook* (stir-fried *gai lan* and beef). Much to my delight, I was eventually allowed to use my spoon that night.

Gradually, I honed my chopstick skills—but not without much trial and tribulation. I learned which foods were easiest to *gaap* (pick up with chopsticks). I was thrilled to discover that pieces of meat such as *cha shiu* (barbecued pork) and *bak jam guy* (white steamed chicken) did not break in half and fall away from the chopsticks. Stir-fried beans with black bean sauce, broccoli or *gai lan* with beef stayed together somewhat. Stir-fried spinach, *bok choy*, and *shui choy* with *jup* (sauce made of soy sauce, corn starch and water) were a bit trickier to *gaap*. They tended to slip through the chopsticks and plop onto the table. And holding chopsticks and shovelling rice into my mouth was weird. I often had more steamed rice on my lap than in my mouth.

After a few months of heartache, I mastered Chopsticks 101. I discovered that all foods did not require the same amount of pressure to hold. Messy meals became a thing of the past. No more food stains on my clothes. No more dropped food on the table in front me. On the table beside me. On me. On the floor. No more near misses of elbowing my sisters in the head.

Today, I am very adept at using chopsticks. I can retrieve that lonely pickle that floats and bobs around in the sweet vinegar at the bottom of the jar. I can also flip bacon in a wink of the eye.

And the reason I had to learn to use chopsticks with my right hand? To prevent bumping arms with my younger right-handed sister. Truth be told, I really think Mom and Dad thought I would accidentally impale my sister's eye. But there was always that possibility anyway—whether she sat on my left or my right.

Cha Shiu Treasure

As kids, my sister Wendy and I accompanied Mom on her weekly shopping trips to Chinatown in Vancouver. Being a carnivore with a deep-seated aversion to vegetables of any kind, I loved stopping at Kwong Hing on East Pender Street to buy *fwo yuk* and *cha shiu*. I thought *fwo yuk* was too fatty, but I always craved the sweet and salty flavours of *cha shiu*.

The meat guy at Kwong Hing on Pender Street gave me and my sister a *cha shiu* sample. He chopped the charred ends from the strip of *cha shiu*—the ends were the most flavourful parts. Then he placed the chunks into two waxed-lined sandwich bags and passed them to me and Wendy over the glass partition. I don't know if he gave us this small treat because Mom was a regular customer, or if it was because I stood there salivating, watching him with longing in my eyes while he sliced the meat into equal bite-sized pieces with his imported Chinese cleaver. Whatever the case, I was the luckiest girl in the entire world. This was pure gold!

With my treasure clutched in my left hand, we left Kwong Hing. On our walk back to our car, I gingerly opened the grease-stained bag and peered inside. Being ever so careful not to soil my left hand with grease, I extracted my precious nugget and nibbled on the charred tip. I savoured the blend of *see yow* (soy sauce), *hoisin jeung* and sugar, before biting off a small chunk. I sucked on the morsel with all my might, extracting all the flavours before swallowing. Heaven!

During the late 1970s and early 1980s Chinese cookbooks began making appearances in local bookstores. Mom found a *cha shiu* recipe that was almost as good as store-bought in Rhoda Yee's *Dim Sum Cookbook*. Mom made some changes and passed the recipe on to me. Since then, I have made my own minor modifications in order to suit my own taste and dietary requirements.

I usually double my recipe so there is some left for the family after my ample sampling. The beauty of this recipe is that unlike cooking a roast or a chicken, there are no telltale signs of sampling. But you must remember to eat an entire strip!

Cha Shiu, **Barbecued Pork**

3-3½ lbs boneless pork butt roast

¼ cup hoisin sauce

½ cup ketchup

½ cup sugar

2 Tbsp dark soy sauce

My (delicious) *cha siu*.

1.) Cut pork into 4 x 2 x 1 inch strips along the grain of meat.

2.) Mix together the remaining ingredients. Pour marinade over the meat. Marinate up to 24 hours in refrigerator.

3.) Preheat oven to 375 degrees.

4.) Line a pan with foil. Place a baking rack in pan and spray with non-stick spray. Place pork on the rack; pour in ¼ inch of water.

5.) Roast for 1 hour. Remove from oven and pour off the water.

6.) Turn meat, baste with leftover marinade. Add ¼ inch of water. Return to oven. Roast for 30 minutes, basting frequently.

7.) *Cha shiu* is done when it is tender and has a nice glaze.

Notes

1.) Choose a well-marbled roast. Fat adds flavour and prevents the pork from drying out.

2.) Marinade meat in a ZipLoc bag, making sure all sides absorb the marinade.

3.) Steaming prevents meat from drying out, while tenderizing it.

Chow Mein Delight

I am the champion of picky eaters. I hate all vegetables except carrots and frozen green peas. I remember the time Mom made me eat broccoli. I didn't like the way it felt all nubbly in my mouth. The taste of broccoli made me gag, and it seemed as though it took forever to chew before I could finally swallow it. The awful taste stayed in my mouth for a week.

But one thing I have loved since I was a kid is chow mein. I came by it honestly because Mom craved it while pregnant with me. There's nothing like the aroma of chow mein being cooked.

But first comes the prep work. As I slice and dice the onion, I have tears in my eyes. I remove the Chinese mushrooms caps from a bowl of water and squeeze out the excess water, the squishy feel reminding me of a sponge. Then being careful not to cut into my knuckles with the cleaver, I slice the mushroom caps as thinly as possible.

Now I prep the chicken. Deboning the partially frozen chicken breast freezes my fingertips. The chicken slips and slides around the cutting board, the fat getting lodged under my fingernails. I snap the breastbone; the chicken breast lies flat against the chopping block. Slicing the meat into bite-sized pieces is not difficult since the meat is still partially frozen and not yet contorting into weird, wobbly shapes. I add a dash of salt, pepper, sugar, soy sauce, and cornstarch to marinate and tenderize the sliced meat.

The most tedious job of this entire process is preparing the bean sprouts. It takes forever to wash and remove the green pods from the individual bean sprouts that were missed in the rinsing process at the factory.

With all five fingers intact, I begin cooking. A loud sizzling hiss—the moisture from the onions collides with the hot oil, splattering the sides of the pan. I stir-fry the onions as my eyes tear up again.

A loud pop—the bean sprouts hit the hot oil. Quickly stirring the sprouts, I add the seasonings: salt, pepper, a dash of sugar (Grandma Law's secret cooking tip: sugar enhances the flavour of cooking).

I cook the chicken last, resisting the temptation to sample. The succulent morsels of chicken are finally done, and I toss them onto the bed of Farkay noodles. With a little red vinegar splashed over my chow mein, I am ready to eat.

Mom used to buy chow mein from On Lock Yuen, an old Chinese restaurant located on Pender Street in Chinatown. One aspect about this restaurant that fascinated me was the entrance, which had swinging doors like an old Western saloon.

On Lock Yuen was known to be the "truck stop" for the farmers of the neighbouring communities. Perhaps this explained why the word *yuen* was used in the restaurant name—*yuen* being the Chinese word for "farm."

As we waited for our order, I sat upon a lopsided chrome chair and gazed around the restaurant. The chair was grease-stained. Plastic seat cover, torn. Foam cushion—exposed and crumbling, small bits chipped away.

Unlike most Chinese restaurants of the day, On Lock Yuen was not the cleanest of establishments. Used napkins littered the worn floor. Dried drops of soy sauce and other unidentified stains streaked the walls. Arborite tabletops cracked, embedded with bits of crud. Pesky black flies buzzed around the room, irritating customers. Tattered red crepe streamers hung from the ceiling fans, spinning round and round, making a *fleflefle* sound as they fluttered in the breeze.

Despite the questionable ambience, On Lock Yuen still produced the best chow mein in all of Chinatown. It was so good that I often wanted to eat the whole take-out order by myself.

Today, whenever my husband and I go to a mall with a food court, I must have my chow mein fix. I savour every bite. The flat noodles. The crunchy bean sprouts. The tender slices of chicken. The diced onion bits. The slivered Chinese mushrooms. Not quite like On Lock Yuen's, but it satisfies my craving.

Ah, but to be a kid again and have all those chow mein-eating years ahead of me!

Pork and Beans

It was a Sunday afternoon, and my sister Carol and I were preparing lunch for the rest of the family. The menu was bacon and eggs, Libby's Pork and Beans, and toast.

The bacon crackled and popped, tiny splatters of grease settling on the stovetop. Carol opened the can of beans using the electric can opener and scooped out the contents with a wooden spoon into the saucepan.

"Stir the beans, and make sure they don't burn," Carol said, as she used a pair of chopsticks to flip the crispy strips of maple-flavoured bacon.

On tiptoes I peered into the pot of pork and beans. The scene reminded me of a something out of a science fiction movie. Little volcanoes spewed threads of tomato sauce onto the sides of the non-stick pot. With the wooden spoon, I stirred the pork and beans gently first in one direction and then the other. I became mesmerized by the scene and the cacophony of sounds in the kitchen. Time stood still.

Blip blip blip of the cooking beans. *Pssssss* and crackle of the frying bacon and eggs. *Chz chzchz* of the toast being buttered.

Each stir of the beans became more vigorous, unlike the first gentle circles, one way and then the other. I was in a stirring frenzy, as though I was beating a cake mix by hand with 350 strokes.

Lunch was ready, and I got out a casserole dish to serve my contribution. I looked into the dish—what became of the pork? It disintegrated into the beans. What I served certainly didn't look anything like what was depicted on the Libby's label. Instead, I had my own creation: a reddish brown mushy blob with the consistency of mashed potatoes.

After this episode, I was banned from stirring the beans. But I must say, nothing stuck to the pot—Teflon-coated or not.

The Sticky Bun

"Hand me a sticky bun, Gail," Wendy said, as she reached backwards, her arm extended toward the back seat, palm up.

We were sailing down the highway somewhere in Alberta in August 1965. It was our first two-week family vacation. Dad had bought our 1964 Ford Falcon Station Wagon just for the occasion. It was pre-air-conditioning days, and it was stifling. There were six of us crammed into the vehicle with all our luggage and little room to spare.

Wendy was seated between Mom and Dad in the front. In the back I sat between Lori and Carolyn. Seat belts weren't mandatory back then, so without any problem, I was able to turn completely around and face the back.

Crouched on the backseat, I located the round Tupperware container with the freshly baked sticky pecan

Photograph courtesy of author.

1958—me, Carol, and Wendy

buns Mom purchased at the bakery close to our motel. As I struggled to remove the lid, the sweet scent of cinnamon permeated the air.

I peered inside. I examined each bun carefully. I chose the stickiest one. Trying not to disturb the others, I extracted the bun with three fingers. I placed the bun into my sister's waiting hand. I crammed it into her palm and twisted it back and forth about three times. With each spin, the bun became flatter, and the white gooey glaze oozed further outward onto her palm.

Wendy failed to see the humour in my shenanigans. I can still hear my sister screaming, "Muuuuum!" and Mom yelling, "Gaaaail, get the wet towel, it's not funny!"

Photograph courtesy of author.

My family in 1963. In the back—Dad, Mom, my sister Lori on Mom's lap, Grandma Chu; in the front—Carol, Wendy, and me.

Fried Chicken and a Secret Ingredient

"Hey, Gail, throw me the eraser," Carol called to me as she studiously did her homework at the dining room table.

"Okay!" I said, picking up my well used Pink Pearl eraser. I was also doing my homework, but at the kitchen table instead. With an overhand throw, I tossed the eraser to her, through the ten-foot galley kitchen, past the stove and fridge, through the door and into the dining room.

All the while, Mom was cooking everybody's favourite meal: fried chicken and French fries. The pot of oil sizzled and hissed as Mom prepared each piece of chicken, first dusting it with a mixture of flour and spices, then coating it with homemade breadcrumbs.

A few minutes passed. I yelled out, "I need the eraser!" The eraser whizzed through the galley in the reverse direction, past the fridge, stove and into my awaiting hands. After many dizzying trips being hurled back and forth, tragedy struck. The poor eraser landed in the pot of bubbling oil, beside a chicken drumstick, with a thud. It immediately became a pink melted blob, easily distinguishable from the rest of the pot's contents. I suppose we became careless with our tosses, or perhaps the eraser became lighter each time it erased our mistakes and went off course.

I know we didn't have fried chicken that night. I can't recall what meat Mom substituted the chicken with either, but I imagine her saying, "Would you like fries with that?"

Devilled Eggs

"It'll be too hot to cook, so let's have a barbecue tonight," Mom called out from the breakfast table. "I'll hard-boil some eggs, and you can make some devilled eggs, okay, Gail?"

"Yes, Mom," I answered from the living room. "Should we invite Yee Mah and cousin Ken as well?"

"Go ahead and tell them dinner will be around six o'clock," Mom hollered above the whir of the fan.

It was a sultry day—a real cooker. Mom usually did the prep work for our evening meals early in the day, before the kitchen became too stuffy. Hot summer days usually meant barbecues. What better accompaniments for succulent pieces of mouth-watering barbecued chicken and creamy potato salad than devilled eggs!

In the heat of the early afternoon, I prepared the devilled eggs. I stuck my left hand into the pot of frigid water where the eggs had been soaking since breakfast. I counted the eggs.

"Twenty-four halves—plenty for everyone," I muttered to myself.

After I scooped a hard-boiled egg from the chilly water, I gently tapped it on the counter to crack it. I peeled back the rough eggshell and the membrane.

"Divet, divet—whoops! Not another divet?" I exclaimed as I accidentally dug my thumbnail into the cool flesh of the egg white. Luckily, the dent was on the bottom and wasn't very noticeable.

I finished shelling the eggs and laid them on the glass cutting board. The slippery little devils slipped and slid all over the board as I tried to hold them down in order to slice them in half. After slicing an egg into two somewhat equal pieces, I scooped the sulphur-smelling yolks into a small mixing bowl. With a dinner fork I mashed the yolks into a paste and added seasoning salt, pepper, minced chives and bacon bits, then two huge scoops of Kraft Miracle Whip. Then I mixed it vigorously until well blended. I laid the cooked egg whites, cavity side up, onto a melmac serving tray and filled each cavity. I sprinkled a smattering of paprika over each half and placed the tray into the fridge until dinner.

At serving time I carried my tray of eggs downstairs, through the basement and then outside. But one obstacle stood in my way: I had to get through the locked aluminium screen door. As I juggled the tray with my right hand, I unlatched the door with my left. Unfortunately, I did not realize that the tray was tipping.

As though choreographed, each one of my masterpieces performed a graceful swan dive off the tray. They did somersaults in the air, landing on the ground and peppering themselves with the fine grains of sand that Dad used to fill the cracks between the patio stones. After I got the presence of mind to right the tray, only one lonely devilled egg remained planted, unscathed.

"Devilled egg, anyone?" I asked sheepishly. I wanted so badly to eat the tasty morsel—the only survivor that I had created so painstakingly only hours before.

Mom's scream still echoes in my mind: "Gaaaaaiiillll!!!!!"

Sa Tum Yow: **Not Just a Fruit**

"Me first! Me first!" cried Wendy, as she elbowed her way past me to stand beside Dad.

"No! You got to wear it first last year!" I hollered at the top of my lungs, trying to squeeze in beside Dad and her. "It's my turn to wear it!!"

The odd memory of this struggle between me and my younger sister is always conjured up by the sight of a pomelo. But not just any pomelo—definitely not the oversized grapefruit-looking type readily available today. The pomelos of yesteryear were the cone-shaped ones. Until recently, I did not realize that wearing the *sa tum yow* hat was a unique tradition created by my father.

With paring knife in hand, poised as if he were a skilled surgeon, Dad made the first incision on the yellow nubbly skin on the stem end of the *sa tum yow*. His cut released the citrus essence into the air.

Wendy and I fidgeted, hopping from one leg to another, as though we had ants in our pants. Sighing with impatience, we watched Dad remove the crown of the *sa tum yow*. He dropped the top onto the red Arborite tabletop with a small thud. This piece was fruit-free (a flawless record, Dad!).

Dad mentally divided the cone-shaped sphere into eight equal parts. He scored the peel from the crownless top. He was exceptionally careful not to puncture the flesh of the fruit. Down the curved sides of the fruit toward the flat bottom. . . . small droplets of moisture emerged from the surface of the peel from the pressure of the knife. Dad withdrew the point of the paring knife from within an inch of the blossom end. He repeated this procedure seven more times.

At last, Dad finally finished. Wendy and I hopped up and down, vying for his attention. Who was going to be the lucky one who got to wear the hat first?

Without gouging his thumb into the sticky flesh, Dad peeled back the skin of the *sa tum yow*.

"Careful, Dad, don't rip it!" I screeched, hands extended, grabbing at the pomelo.

"III'mmmm first!" whined Wendy, trying to crowd me out. "You're always firrrrst!"

In his usual manner Dad quietly said, "Pipe down, you two, or neither of you can have it."

In the palm of his hand, Dad displayed the fruit of his labour: a small bowling ball-sized sphere, still encased in its white sheath.

But the fruit wasn't the jewel that Wendy and I were seeking. The treasure was the yellow pomelo peel that Dad so meticulously and artfully preserved for us.

As big sister, I relented and said to Wendy, "Okay, you can go first."

Using the tiny indentation where the flower once blossomed as a marker, Dad placed the *sa tum yow* peel, skin side up, upon Wendy's head, midway between the top of her forehead and the nape of her neck. Correct placement was crucial. Because the peel was cut into eight somewhat equal sections, it draped her head like a pixie hat.

We took turns parading around the house, donning our *sa tum yow* pixie hat, as if it were a crown.

By morning, our hat was a sad reminder that Chinese New Year was over for another year. The yellow peel was no longer shiny and smooth; it turned black and dull. The spongy underside was in the throes of dehydration and looked like a shrunken head of an apple doll. Our hat was relegated to the compost heap.

Not knowing that the pomelo hat was not celebrated in every Chinese household, I had a rude awakening during my first year of marriage. At the time I was living with my husband, Ken, at his mother's house. They peeled the pomelo in the same manner as my Dad, but did not take the same care. I was in the process of reaching for the pixie hat but wasn't quite quick enough! Much to my chagrin, my brother-in-law Ray snatched it up and chucked it into the kitchen closet. It wasn't until years later that I discovered that my mother-in-law used it in her cooking!

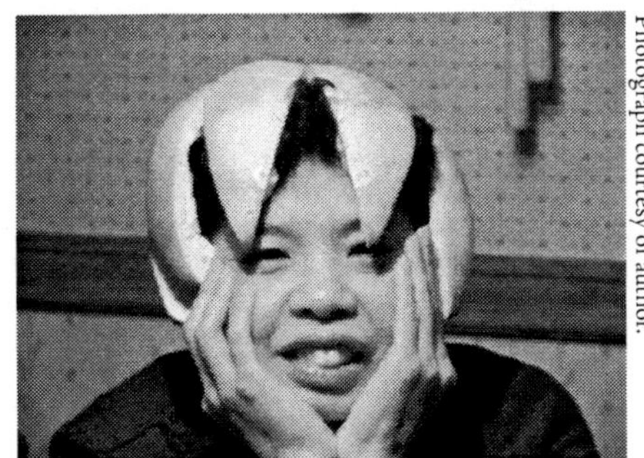

Photograph courtesy of author.

A *sa tum yow hat* fit for a grown-up!

Today, I still like to wear a *sa tum yow* hat, but it is more difficult to find the cone-shaped pomelos. Especially one that fits an adult-sized head!

Author's Note

March 2007

Hi Judy,

I have just completed another six-week writing workshop. It was somewhat labour-intensive—but I thoroughly enjoyed the experience. This go-around, the workshop was entitled "Food and Family," and Brandy Liên Worrall was once again our instructress. There were twelve students in the class—three men and nine women—and we bonded from the word go. We had so much to share with one another, and oftentimes Brandy had to reel us in when we went off on a tangent. Their stories were incredible and were often a history lesson for me.

We all had one thing in common: Food! It was kinda neat to hear the names of the same dish pronounced slightly differently, depending on the dialects. Oh... and the memories. The comfort foods of my childhood—eaten with spoon, then later with chopsticks.

In reminiscing with my classmates, one of our fondest memories was how scrumptious the apple tarts from the Hong Kong Café were. (Are we that old?)

Digging into the recipe "archives" wasn't my main purpose for taking this workshop. My main goal was to document my "fun time" experiences with food as a kid.

I did manage though to sort through and organize forty years of recipes—old family favourites that Mom once cooked, newspaper and magazine clippings, recipes from library books, friends and the internet. I realize now that I became a foodie sometime during Grade 8 Home Ec., as I still have recipes from back then.

What this workshop has prompted me to do is ask Uncle Kee (my dad's brother) for recipes that his mother—my grandmother—cooked. These are recipes that my grandmother brought with her from China in 1913, the year she immigrated to New Westminster with my grandfather and her two oldest sons.

It's getting late, and I must go. Is it time for a midnight snack?

TTFN,
Gail

P.S. Did I tell you Brandy is a fantastic instructress/editor? I just can't thank her enough for all her advice and encouragement.

A Chinese Canadian Cooking Opera in Four Acts

Ken Yip

Prelude

My mother was from southern China's Guangdong province, while my father was a second-generation Chinese Canadian born in Cranbrook, BC. Mom was the source of the family's Chinese traditions, superstitions, and culture, as they were passed onto her by her mother and grandmother.

Mom came from a peasant farming family, and being female, she did not learn to read or write Chinese. Instead, she learned how to be a skillful cook with a huge repertoire of delectable dishes ranging from entrées to desserts. Her style was peasant or village home cooking—nothing fancy but so flavourful. She understood the yin and yang of various ingredients and how to balance them for healthy living. She was also an herbalist whenever one of us was ill, bruised, or scraped. Her concoctions and potions ranged from liniments to poultices to soups—all reeked something awful and tasted even worse, but we did seem to recover faster.

It was the hope and expectation of all Chinese families to have many fat and healthy children. Mom was a very accomplished cook as evidenced by the many pictures of my little brother and me as we were growing up, in which we were both rotund, not just plump with baby fat. I had a weight problem until mid-high school.

Mom unceremoniously yet confidently went about providing for her family the best way she knew—through food. I've realized how I had totally undervalued her contribution to the family.

Act 1—*Ma Fa*

My wife, Gail, was trying to document some of her mother's recipes and techniques, and a weekend cooking event was planned to try and make *ma fa*. When I was growing up, this was a favourite snack that Mom made abundantly and frequently. She'd fry up enough to fill two or three one-gallon pickle jars. *Ma fa* is a crispy, deep-fried braided Chinese bread stick. It is extremely versatile, as it can be crumbled and sprinkled on top of congee or used as a seasoning for whole steamed fish. It had that combination of crunchy, buttery, saltiness like potato chips—and you just can't eat one. Unfortunately, I haven't had any in over twenty years.

My mother-in-law gathered together the ingredients and utensils, all the while trying to remember the original method. I spoke to her one evening as she was phoning to discuss the recipe with Gail. She was concerned that they wouldn't turn out. She said the last time she made them was with my mother over twenty-five years ago. The weekend arrived, and we pick her up along with a cardboard box full of ingredients, a jug of oil, and a wok.

My mother-in-law set about to prepare the dough. Everything appeared to be going to plan when suddenly she realized she had forgotten to add the butter. A quick adjustment was made, and the dough was ready to be worked. I watched my mother-in-law demonstrate her technique for making *ma fa*.

I remember helping Mom when I was little, sitting at our green Arborite and chrome kitchen table. I would pinch off a small piece of dough and hand-roll it into a thin strand about a foot long. The strand was then doubled over and twisted together, with one end looped around the other and tucked under to secure it like a knot. I always marveled at how quickly my mother could make one. It seemed that she could roll the piece of dough out to the right length in one motion, and she had this move, like a kung fu master, where she'd flick the doubled-over strand, and it would twist together all by itself. She could easily make ten to my one.

Gail and her sister Wendy were both trying their hand at making *ma fa*, following their mother's lead with lots of giggling and laughing. It was harder than it looked. Gail's mother used a double-braid technique. I couldn't resist anymore—I had to try to make one.

I took a piece of dough and tried rolling it out. It felt soft yet springy, almost elastic. I had difficulty in maintaining a consistent diameter for the strand, and stretching it only made it worse. I decided to scrunch it up into a ball and try again, at which point Gail's mother said that I've worked the dough too much and would have to discard it and start over with a new piece. Finally, I got a strand that I thought I could twist together. I didn't know what I was doing wrong, but my *ma fa* kept wanting to unravel. I made mine with a single twist like Mom showed me. I managed to make four keepers and one reject before the dough was used up. My proficiency hadn't improved at all.

My mother-in-law heated oil in her wok and began frying. The aroma of *ma fa* filled the kitchen, and I couldn't wait to try one. When the *ma fa* reached golden-brownness, my mother-in-law fished them out of the wok and stacked them onto paper towels to drain and cool.

As soon as they were cool enough, I snuck out one of mine, half-expecting to get my knuckles wrapped with chopsticks, just like when I was young. The taste was unmistakable—crunchy, savoury, melt in your mouth. Although on the one I made, where the strand was thicker, the center was a little chewy.

We sat down to enjoy the fruits of our labour and plan the next cooking session, discussing changes in the technique to make them easier to roll. While they were busily talking, I managed to sample all the ones I made, even the reject piece, which my sister-in-law had re-formed into a pretzel shape.

This occasion brought back not only a familiar taste from my past but also issues about Mom that I had not yet resolved for myself. As I was growing up, I didn't feel like we developed a strong bond. Nothing I accomplished seemed to please her. I bonded with my father a lot more, and my younger brother was her favourite. However, decades later, I realize now that Mom was just expecting more from me and was trying to help me be successful. This *ma fa* cooking lesson gave me the chance to reflect on all that Mom had ever cooked up.

Act 2—Pig Intestine Rolls

One of the most complicated dishes that Mom made was something she called *gee cheong fun* or "pig intestine rolls." It is a steamed rice flour crepe topped with a mixture of chopped preserved turnips, dried shrimp, Chinese mushrooms, water chestnuts, fresh green onions, and then rolled up. Sounds simple, but I remember being mesmerized watching Mom do all the intricate steps in making this delicacy. My job was to stack the finished product onto a tray in the oven to keep them warm.

My earliest recollections of Mom making this dish began with manually grinding the rice flour using a millstone. That millstone would find use again many years later in preparing snails, but that's another story. As soon as we could afford it, she used packaged ground rice flour from Chinese grocery stores, which cut out a tremendous amount of preparation time.

The next step was to prepare the ingredients for the filling or topping (*hum*). She placed dried shrimp in a rice bowl into which she poured boiling water to soften them. Soon a very strong fishy smell permeated the air. She did the same for dried Chinese mushrooms, releasing their characteristic pungent earthy aroma. While they were soaking, she peeled, sliced and diced fresh water chestnuts. Sometimes I would help peel. Now and then she would hand me a slice to taste—crisp, slightly sweet, and juicy with hint of earthiness. She'd then dice preserved turnips that had a foul rotten vegetable odor.

Next, she chopped green onions—it was hard to keep the little green ringlets from bouncing all over. By this time, the shrimp and mushrooms were softened enough, so she drained, chopped, and diced them.

Finally, she stir-fried all the ingredients, except for the onions, in a wok for a few minutes to blend the flavours together. Mom set aside the mixture. The final preparation step was to mix the batter, which was composed of several fine white powders as well as the rice flour, water, and a few tablespoons of Chinese oil. The pure white batter had a consistency like that of cream.

All the while, Mom, who was a huge Chinese opera fan, would hum the tune to one of her favourite operas. Now and then, she'd break into the chorus and sing a few refrains. With the overture done the opening act was about to begin. The stage was set, and the cooking musical took off.

Mom filled a two-decker metal steamer with water and placed it on top of the stove to boil. She used two large twelve-inch tin pie pans as the moulds for making the rice flour crepes. She peeled a root vegetable—sometimes a large carrot or a Chinese radish—and cut it flat so that it could stand in a small dish of oil. She used this as a brush to oil the pie pans. With the deftness of a Chinese opera singer wielding a pheasant feather duster, she'd start in the center, and with a few quick circles she'd sweep out to the edge of the pie pan.

Mom would scoop a ladleful of rice flour batter out of the bowl with a ceremonial ceramic ding as she struck the ladle to clear any excess. She poured the batter into the pan and quickly tipped the pan in a single circular motion like an opera singer flipping the huge hanging sleeves of her costume. This was to achieve an even coating on the bottom of the pie pan. She quickly placed it into the steamer, with the lid going back on with a discordant clang as only aluminum can.

After a few minutes, she prepared the other pie pan so it was ready to replace the steamed crepe in the steamer. She sprinkled a spoonful of filling and onions onto the finished rice flour crepe. With the spoon she broke the seal at the edge of the pan and tipped the pan up. The crepe crept down the pan, forming a perfect roll. It had a mouth-watering, earthy aroma. She oiled and battered the pan to start the process over again.

With the twangy strains of Chinese opera, accompanied by the discordant dings and clangs, the roar of boiling water, and clouds of billowing steam, Mom juggled these two pie pans so that they seemed to be floating in air—the skillful handling of the oil "brush," batter ladle, tongs, and spoon all kept them spinning. To a young boy who got dragged against his will to one too many Chinese operas, it was like Mom was performing a scene. And I always got something good to eat to make up for it. I would eat so many *gee cheong fun* until I just couldn't eat anymore. My favourite condiment was hot chili sauce or mustard. These rolls made great leftovers when pan-fried, for a final encore.

Act 3—Meatloaf

It is 7:30 a.m. Sleepy-eyed Grade 9 band students are filing into the music room for an early morning practice. As I find my third clarinet section, I sit and begin warming up with some scales, as is every other student with their instruments. The cacophony is defeaning and punctuated by clanging cymbals and trumpet solos. A sharp tapping of the teacher's baton on the music stand begins to quiet the class.

The teacher starts with an announcement—we're going on a trip to Portland, Oregon for a springtime Logger's Festival. But there's an unexpected catch: our band is not only going to play an evening concert, we're going to be marching in a parade as well. This is fine, except for the fact that we are a concert band and by no means a marching band.

The teacher tells us not to worry. Over the next two months, we practice a marching drill led by two members of the Royal Canadian Legion Pipe Band. We finally become coordinated enough to march and play our instruments, not just in a straight line but we're also able to turn corners!

The departure day arrives, and we pack our instruments and luggage into two busses and head to Portland. After an exhausting ride we find ourselves at a school gymnasium. The next morning, our hosts tell us that they have a treat in store for us, which includes lunch.

The other industry in Portland, besides logging, is meat-packing. We are going to tour the largest meat-packing plant in the Pacific Northwest. We boys think it'll be really neat, but the girls are less than thrilled. We board the busses and head off after a lecture from our music teacher and chaperones about behaving and paying attention. The tour will take about an hour; afterwards we'll be having lunch in the plant cafeteria.

We assemble single-file on the loading dock and enter by the back door. We are given white smocks and hard hats to wear. After the teacher and chaperones regain control after all the giggling and shoving, we're led into the main processing area. I don't think anything could have prepared us for the assault on all our senses.

The plant is the size of a football field. We parade by rows of hanging carcasses of skinned beef. The smell is stifling. The sounds of machinery and saws punctuate the general din of the plant floor. Several of the students gag, and most are covering their noses.

The next station is where the carcasses are cut in half by men in smocks, goggles, rubber boots and gloves, and hard hats, using electric chain saws. Each cut spatters blood all over their smocks. The carcass halves move along an overhead conveyor to the butchering tables for further rendering by huge band saws.

At the next section the sight of plastic bins full of cow skulls, tongues, eyeballs, brains, ears, and blood coursing in the concrete floor is enough to horrify most, if not all, of the girls, as well as several of the boys, who are led out a side door by one of the plant supervisors. By this time only half the band is still on the tour.

Accompanying my parents shopping in Chinatown has prepared me somewhat for the sight and smells of slaughter. This is not too different from watching the butchers at the meat stores on Pender Street. There, sides of fresh meat hang from ceiling hooks, along with all the delectable pieces of barbecued pork, duck, and chicken hanging from racks. Although the smells are all mingled, you learn to pick out the good ones from the bad. I remember watching Mom point to an unlucky chicken, which the butcher reached in and grabbed, with great squawking and flapping of wings. The butcher skillfully slit the chicken's throat and hung it from its feet for a few minutes to drain the blood. Then he put the still twitching chicken into a de-feathering machine. Soon the butcher pulled out a clean, glistening chicken, ready for cooking. Unfortunately, I stood too close to the butcher block and got splattered with stray bits when his cleaver hit bone.

We wrap up the tour with a demonstration of how the various cuts of meat are carved from the carcass. We follow the plant supervisors upstairs to the cafeteria and meet up with the rest of the group already seated at long tables. Many have their heads down on the table, and several are looking kind of green. Not everyone wants to eat, but I'm feeling hungry.

A large white plate is placed in front of me with something resembling a thick slice of brown bread smothered in a brown sauce. Beside it is a big mound of mashed potatoes, with green peas and carrots. More brown sauce tops potatoes, forming a small lake on top, with rivulets running down the sides. Small wisps of steam curl up from the plate, and the fatty aroma is unlike anything I've ever smelled before.

I lean over to my classmate and ask, "What is this?"

"Meatloaf," he mumbles.

I eagerly pick up my fork, cut off a small portion, coat it in the sauce, and place it in my mouth. A new taste sensation explodes—"Hey, this is good!"

It has a pungent spice and a smooth, almost velvety, texture that I have never tasted before. My classmate wrinkles his brow, tilts his head, and looks at me a little weirdly, "Never had meatloaf before?"

"Nope." But I know it won't be my last time.

When I get home, I describe to Mom this new wondrous dish I sampled earlier. To my surprise, a few days later, she prepares her version of meatloaf for dinner. She uses pork instead of beef and steams it like *hamh yue yook be-ang*—salted fish and pork. The texture is coarse, and the spices are missing, along with the sauce. I'm disappointed and try not to show it, but Mom can tell. She never makes it again.

Act 4—Almond Cookies (Ken's Mom's)

As I was growing up, I loved watching Mom cook and even assisted in preparing some of the ingredients, but I never developed a desire to learn any of her techniques or recipes. I was always amazed how she was able to create everything from memory. Regrettably, none of her knowledge was ever passed on. Or so I thought. Fortunately, my wife captured one of Mom's recipes—*hup tow soo* or almond cookies.

For decades, a small 3" x 5" plain white recipe card titled "Almond Cookies (Ken's Mom's)" had been stuck to a page with three other cookie and muffin recipes clipped from papers and magazines. This recipe card has been quietly waiting for over thirty years to recreate a memory and a connection.

With the discovery of this recipe, I was looking forward to reconnecting with Mom, at least through that wonderful aroma of toasted almonds that would fill the whole house. You can taste the bitterness of the almonds in the back of your throat just from the pungency hanging in the air. The thought of it brought me back to when I was young, showing me that I did have a bond with her after all.

Not knowing how to bake, my first attempt was an abortive one, even before I got to form the dough. The recipe card does not include any method instructions, so I began to carefully measure all the ingredients as listed on the card and pour them into a mixing bowl.

Gail came into the kitchen and immediately shouted, "What are you doing?!"

"I'm making cookies!"

"No, you're not! You're making a mess!" Gail's Lesson Number 1: "You have to start by creaming the shortening with the sugar, then gradually adding in the wet ingredients, and then the rest of the dry ingredients."

"Oh."

"Didn't you take home ec?" she asks rhetorically.

"So what do I do with this now?"

"Throw it out and start over."

After re-measuring all the ingredients and following her instructions explicitly, I finally got a nice gooey, sticky ball of cookie dough that smelled wonderfully of toasted almonds. I pinched off a small piece of dough and rolled it between my palms and placed the dough-ball on a cookie sheet. As I lined them up in rows, I noticed that the balls weren't uniform.

Gail's Lesson Number 2: "If you make them too big, they will join up during baking and form one big cookie."

I pinched off a little bit of dough from the larger balls to even them out. I remembered that Mom used a Chinese soup spoon to measure the dough. I finally worked through the dough and ended up with three dozen reasonably uniform balls.

I flattened each ball slightly and using my thumb, made a small impression into which I placed a toasted almond slice. I then beat an egg and brushed the top of each ball. I placed the two trays in the oven set at 300 degrees, eagerly awaiting the results of my labour. I peered into the tinted oven door window and saw that a few of the larger balls had merged into one big cookie, but most were spread just enough.

Gail's Lesson Number 3: "Don't keep opening the oven door! The baking temperature will not be even."

"But how can you tell when they are golden brown?"

I noticed that the kitchen was not totally filled with that wondrous aroma of toasted almonds that I remembered. I wondered if it was because the range hood fan was extracting that aroma and sending it out all over the neighbourhood.

Photograph courtesy of author.

Me and my mother, 1950.

Finally, the cookies turned golden brown enough, and I took them out to cool. I was thoroughly impressed with my handiwork. Except for the "big" cookies, most of them looked really good—golden brown and glistening!

It was the moment I'd been waiting for. I took a cookie and allowed the scent of toasted almonds to waft over me. I closed my eyes and took a bite. After the initial crunch, the cookie instantly melted in my mouth—sweet blending with a slight bitterness. I inhaled the rest of the cookie and said a silent, "Thanks, Mom."

Almond Cookies (Ken's Mom's)—Modified

1 lb shortening

1 lb sugar

2 eggs

1 lb flour

2 tsp baking soda

Crushed almonds

1.) Preheat the oven to 300 degrees.

2.) Cream the shortening and sugar in a bowl, mixing them together with a mixer or by hand, for a few minutes until light and fluffy.

3.) Mix in one egg.

4.) Mix in flour and baking soda, and finally, the almonds, saving some of the almonds to top the cookies. Mix until a dough forms.

5.) Using a large spoon (such as a Chinese soup spoon), scoop out some dough and form a ball.

6.) Line up the balls on a greased cookie sheet, making sure they are spread out enough. Flatten each ball and using your thumb, make a little impression into each cookie. Place an almond sliver into the impression.

7.) Beat the other egg, and brush it on top of each cookie.

8.) Bake until golden brown, approximately ten minutes.

Almond Cookies (Ken's)

Author's Note

At the beginning of the workshop, I couldn't have predicted the outcome of my stories. My original intent for writing was always to chronicle the histories of my father and grandfather. The workshop made me realize that I had totally ignored the contributions of my mother and the significance of her caring for our family through feeding us.

The exercises and feedback were the catalyst that led me to realize that my mother did play an important role in our family and deserved to be remembered for culinary skills and her love of Chinese opera. It dawned on me during the workshop that in a way, her two pleasures often combined into one, as she cooked and sang, keeping up with the Chinese traditions with which she was raised while also attempting to experiment with new ones.

This particular story chronicles my trying to reconnect to my mother with the help of other important women in my life—my wife Gail and my mother-in-law. Through their cooking lessons and "food archives," I have learned some of my mother's techniques, which she never directly taught me. But in trying to recreate her recipes, I realized that by watching her and spending time with her in the kitchen, I did learn bits and pieces—and memories—that have stayed with me throughout the years, long after she passed away.

Ken Yip

Just Dropping By

The following stories and essays in this section were contributed by people who took part in the workshops as guest speakers and hosts during our six weeks. Just like people dropping by a family gathering or even during any old evening at dinnertime, these contributors have added more dimensions to the stories and food we've shared.

Photograph by Brandy Liên Worrall.

Special guests and regulars at our first workshop potluck, held at Vancouver Museum. Seated from left to right—author Harley Wylie; special family guest, Steve Hopkins (husband of author Shirley Chan); and special guest speaker, Imogene Lim. Standing are one of Professor Henry Yu's INSTRCC students documenting the occasion, and author Ken Yip.

Imogene Lim, professor of Anthropology at Malaspina University-College, attended our special workshop potluck, at which she presented a collection of menus from her family's personal collection. Lim's father and uncle were well known restaurateurs in Vancouver's Chinatown. Lim also talked about having tea in Tanzania, and the quirkiness of food customs crossing cultures.

Lisa Moore is the co-owner of Rhizome Café, where our Wednesday evening workshop sessions were held. Lisa and her partner Vinetta have created a unique meeting space within their café, where community organizations can meet for events and activities. I think the Wednesday workshop participants would agree that Rhizome was a wonderful, welcoming place to exchange our stories and hammer out the details, while we were also being enticed by the rich smells of Rhizomé's culinary offerings. You can visit Rhizomé's website at **http://www.rhizomecafe.ca**.

Janice Wong, the award-winning author of *Chow: From China to Canada: Memories of Food and Family*, was gracious enough to give us guest lectures during our workshop, at which she discussed many of the behind-the-scenes details of writing, publishing, and publicizing her book. She offered the workshop participants tips and encouragement for writing their own food memoirs, and answered their questions regarding "writing recipes"—in all senses of the phrase.

Brandy Liên Worrall (*c'est moi*) was the organizer of the workshop and everything else that's gone into this book (and this sentence) that you're reading at this moment. The story included here in this section may or may not be part of her memoir when it finally gets written and published, but at least it's here!

Photograph by Brandy Liên Worrall.

Help yourself!

Henry Yu, a professor of History at the University of British Columbia, is a foodie who gave guest lectures during our six weeks. Professor Yu has created the Initiative for Student Teaching and Research in Chinese Canadian Studies (INSTRCC) at the University of British Columbia (**http://www.instrcc.ubc.ca**), and several of the students from his program video-documented the workshop, capturing intimate moments in the kitchens of some of the participants as they created dishes for our potluck.

Thanks to all those who took part in making our workshop a memorable and special food journey!

Notes from the Chow Mein Sandwich Chick

Imogene Lim

As with many individuals of Asian ancestry, I am frequently asked, "Where are you from?" The person inquiring either thinks I am foreign-born or is attempting to establish my ethnicity. My response is always: "Canada." With further prodding, I will say I am "Canadian of Chinese descent" and perhaps add "third-generation." I might "hyphenate" myself as "Chinese-Canadian," but I never attempt to pass or identify myself as "Chinese." Having been raised and educated in Canada (as well as in the United States), I am more at ease in Canadian culture than I am in Chinese. For myself, Chinese-ness is not a matter of my physical appearance. Rather, I identify with Chinese-ness through food.

W.K. Gardens pagoda menu.

Image courtesty of author.

Why food? My father operated a Chinese restaurant in Vancouver's Chinatown for most of his adult life. Dining out with my family was more than breaking bread or satisfying hunger. Led by my father, we were checking out the competition, scrutinizing the menu, critiquing a dish (too salty, too oily), determining the ingredients of a particularly agreeable dish or the manner of its preparation and presentation. This was a pastime to be shared. My father, known as "the boss man of W.K." by the chefs he investigated, was also remembered as a mentor by the chefs whom he taught. The preparation of and appreciation for Chinese food was my father's gift to me—my inheritance. Chinese cuisine remains my comfort food and the way through which I revel in my ethnicity and in which it is revealed.

Because of my personal connection to food, I have been motivated to study Chinese cuisine in the smaller urban areas of southeastern New England. As affectionately dubbed by friends who were induced (coerced) to join me in this food adventure, I became the "chow mein sandwich chick." For a segment of the population in New England, the chow mein sandwich was identifiably Chinese and a favourite item at local Chinese restaurants. Was this real Chinese food? It was for more than one town in Massachusetts, as both Fall River and Salem claim to be the originator of the chow mein sandwich.[1]

1. See my article, "The Chow Mein Sandwich: American as Apple Pie," *Radcliffe Culinary Times* III/2 (1993): 4-5.

Image courtesy of author.

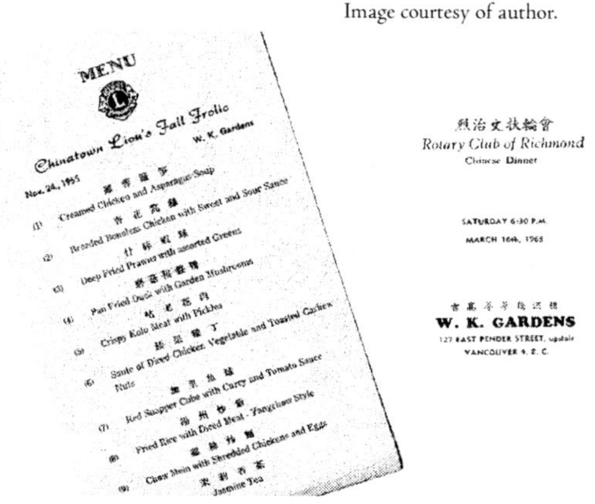
MENU

Chinatown Lion's Fall Frolic

W. K. Gardens

Nov. 24, 1955

(1) Creamed Chicken and Asparagus Soup

(2) Breaded Boneless Chicken with Sweet and Sour Sauce

(3) Deep Fried Prawns with assorted Greens

(4) Pan Fried Duck with Garden Mushrooms

(5) Crispy Kolo Meat with Pickles

(6) Saute of Diced Chicken, Vegetable and Toasted Cashew Nuts

(7) Red Snapper Cube with Curry and Tomato Sauce

(8) Fried Rice with Diced Meat - Yangchow Style

(9) Chow Mein with Shredded Chickens and Eggs

Jasmine Tea

Rotary Club of Richmond

Chinese Dinner

SATURDAY 6:30 P.M.

MARCH 16th, 1968

W. K. GARDENS

127 EAST PENDER STREET, upstair

VANCOUVER 4, B. C.

Chinatown Lion's Fall Frolic menu, 1955 (left) and Rotary Club of Richmond menu, 1968 (right).

As part of my study on Chinese restaurants and the chow mein sandwich, I browsed through several early English-language Chinese cookbooks. I was appalled when I read a recipe for "Chinese roast pork," which included boiling and frying. My immediate reaction was to critique the 1914 author as knowing little about preparing Chinese food. I deemed this an inauthentic recipe. But thanks to my father, I learned that this method of preparation was accurate for its time. This discovery served as a reminder that culture constantly changes.

The chow mein sandwich was the metonym nonpareil for the Chinese restaurant as found in southeastern New England. A close examination of Chinese cuisine in the North American context becomes a statement of immigration policy, adaptation, entrepreneurship, family, identity, and survival.

When Chinese pioneers first arrived in North America, they sought opportunity however they could. From the labours of gold mining and contract work, many eventually became entrepreneurs. The cafés and restaurants dotting the landscape were and are a testimony to this. Restaurateurs created a cuisine that was adapted to the foodstuffs and tastes of the locale—think of the ubiquity of chow mein and chop suey as menu items served in these establishments. The creation of the chow mein sandwich, therefore, was also a part of this history.

The evolution of Chinese cuisine continues not only in North America but also in Hong Kong, Taiwan, China, and other places with a sizable Chinese ethnic population. The fortune cookie created in San Francisco is found today in Hong Kong and China, and marketed as "Genuine American Fortune Cookies." Mayonnaise, the proverbial condiment of North American salads and sandwiches, now accompanies Chinese dishes prepared by Chinese chefs in Chinese restaurants; it is a Hong Kong-style sauce! Borrowings and changes from around the world—historic intersections—are a part of real Chinese cuisine.

The definition of "real" or "authentic" is a matter of a dialogue between restaurateur and consumer. Popular items continue to be marketed, no matter how good or useful the product is; the same is true for the dishes offered by a restaurant. Many Chinese menus in southeastern New England no longer offer the chow mein sandwich, but the die-hards still know where to find one. The heyday of this sandwich was in the 1940s and

1950s, yet in some local Chinese restaurants, it has remained a bestseller. As one restaurateur commented, "over two million sold!"

Who does not like Chinese food? Even for folks with conservative food tastes and preferences, Chinese cuisine offers something for everyone—especially from the local establishment. I have had individuals enthusiastically relate their introduction to egg foo yung (and other similar dishes). They mention their favourite Chinese dishes of chow mein (with hard crunchy noodles), sweet and sour pork, and chop suey. These are not the kinds of dishes selected by the reputed gourmet from a "real" or "authentic" Chinese restaurant. In contrast, folks in smaller communities insist that an establishment is something not worthy of being patronized if chow mein is missing from the menu.

Authenticity is a matter of acknowledging differences within a cultural setting. I remember reading in *The Daily News* in Tanzania the outrage of a letter writer. In a Chinese restaurant he had ordered genuine Chinese tea to impress his companion. His complaint was about the watery liquid of twigs received rather than proper tea with appropriate quantities of milk and sugar (the norm for well prepared tea in Tanzania—courtesy of British influence)!

I know what I like when the item in question is food. Having sampled many chow mein sandwiches, I have criteria to judge a good one. (The sauce and properly prepared noodles are a must!) It is not to be compared with other foods, but accepted for what it is. I am not alone when I say there are folks who find a chow mein sandwich thoroughly satisfying. The chow mein sandwich, as food or statement, is as unique as the circumstances that created it.

Food is very much a part of my identity—from daughter of a restaurateur to the chow mein sandwich chick. My enjoyment of chow mein sandwiches does not make me less Chinese. This particular food has an identity itself. For folks growing up on chow mein sandwiches, this was real Chinese food served in real Chinese restaurants. The chow mein sandwich, or chow mein, identified home and place. In the past, former Fall Riverites in the Los Angeles area would hold an annual reunion day. How would you have identified a Fall River reunion? By its food, which meant the inclusion of chow mein!

Canadian. Canadian of Chinese descent. Chinese-Canadian. Chinese. Authentic. Real. A list of words, descriptors. Their use or juxtaposition with others is deliberate because the matter of identity and the authenticity of that identity are questioned by others. Each of us has several identities based on our unique histories. For me, I am the granddaughter of a railway worker (coal miner, tofu maker), the daughter of a restaurateur, and a scholar in my own right.

Chow Mein Sandwich (à la Fall River)

1 (8 oz) pkg Original Hoo-Mee Chow Mein Mix (see ordering information below)

Hamburger buns or white bread

Brown gravy, optional

1.) Prepare chow mein according to directions.

2.) Place a hearty scoop of the chow mein mixture between a hamburger bun or between slices of white bread (preferably, square loaf).

3.) If using white bread, prepare a brown gravy mix and ladle gravy generously over the sandwich as if for a hot turkey sandwich.

Notes

1.) "Original Hoo-Mee Chow Mein Mix" is available in southeastern New England supermarkets, or can be ordered directly through:

Oriental Chow Mein Company
42 Eighth Street
Fall River, MA 02720
USA

2.) If you prepare your own chow mein mix, the key to its authenticity is in the noodles. They should be flat *deep-fried* noodles. The sauce (equal parts chopped onion and sliced celery cooked in stock, with—if desired—the addition of pork, beef, or chicken) is poured over the noodles immediately before serving. There should be some crunch to the textural mix.

Imogene Lim *is Chair of the Department of Anthropology at Malaspina University-College (Nanaimo, BC), and a founding Board Member of the Chinese Canadian Historical Society of BC. Her interest in food is gastronomic as it is academic. Some know her as the Chow Mein Sandwich Chick, while others know her for her desserts, specifically, ginger cheesecake and fresh fruit tarts. The subject of food is also one that she teaches: "Food and Culture" and "Food and Globalization." She was a guest speaker at the CCHSBC Food and Family Workshop potluck, at which she shared a story about Chinese tea in Tanzania, as well as showed a selection of Chinese restaurant menus from a collection begun by her uncle and father when they operated the WK Gardens in Vancouver's Chinatown.*

Chilaquiles

Lisa Moore

When I travel to Mexico and to the corners of its diaspora, I search for *chilaquiles*—crispy strips of corn tortillas and thinly sliced onions bathed in sauces, sprinkled with dry fragrant cheese and topped with eggs, sunny side up placed on top or scrambled together with the tortillas, with pureed black beans inside a halo of red sauce, swirled with soft *crema*. There's something about that combination of sauces and spices, the crunch of the tortillas, and the smoothness of the places where the sauce has softened them that conjures up in me the feeling of being deeply loved. There's something about the simple earthiness of corn and chilies and black beans that connects me to rebellion in distant misty mountains, and to the rhythmic thump of sneakers on urban asphalt, the thrill of thousands of voices raised in protest chant. There's something about *chilaquiles* and *salsa verde* that reminds me of furtive conversations among women, plotting and planning and loving a better world into being.

When I left San Francisco, I left behind my chosen community and family: a Latina immigrant women's group called Mujeres Unidas y Activas, organizers for immigrant rights and justice, and for the rights of women to live free from violence. It was from the members of Mujeres that I learned tactics and strategy—and that potent balance of anger and love that can enable human beings to overcome numerous attacks on all levels personal and political. I learned humour and grace, and I gained a quick tongue for raunchy Spanish jokes and for the welcoming chatter that can draw strangers into a room and make them feel instantly at home. It was also at Mujeres that my life as a vegetarian came to an abrupt end. Organizing for immigrant rights in the heart of a Latino community means sharing bowls of steaming pork *pozole* after a protest march, luxuriating in the complex flavours of chicken in thick, dark *mole* at a fundraiser, accepting with exclamations of joy a plate of juicy beef *carne asada* from a neighbourhood grill, and basking in the slippery cool of flaky white fish *ceviche*, dripping with the juice of backyard limes, made especially for me. It was also at Mujeres, that I—a white girl from the East coast—learned to eat chilies and make *salsa* and love *chilaquiles*.

Photograph by Henry Yu.

Rhizome's chilaquiles.

Socorro and I share a love for hot mugs of steaming Mexican *chocolate* and for *chilaquiles*—that breakfast dish known for its ability to revive stale tortillas and transform them into something delicious and new. She and I would rush out of a campaign strategy meeting or peer counseling training or community forum, and go to eat at a little restaurant on Mission Street. We'd talk about the events of the day and then, when the food arrived, we'd eat and drink and enjoy, mostly in silence. The last vestiges of sauce sopped up with crusty white rolls, we'd lean back to finish our *chocolate*.

Socorro would tell me elaborate tales about her childhood in Mexico, stories of imagination and creative tenacity that enabled her to survive a persistent, chronic hunger. We'd also talk about her kids—about the challenges they face to retain culture and language in a new land, and of her pain that her children will never fully appreciate what she had suffered to bring them to the U.S. Tradeoffs and forced choices, sacrifice and strength, resilience and humour, new beginnings and old traditions. Socorro and *chilaquiles* represent all of those things for me.

Raquel taught me to make *salsa verde*. When I first met her, I sat in her small kitchen and ate chicken *enchiladas verdes* she had made on her tiny stove with one functional burner. Raquel and I formed an instant friendship in those early days. We were both young; we liked to dance in the Mujeres office; we'd take her daughter to the park and talk for hours. But Raquel's life was complicated, and she was afraid. Afraid of the *migra*, far from her family, living with a husband who was unpredictable: often violent, often loving, jumping from gentleness to anger with little notice.

It would be years before Raquel actually showed me how to make the *salsa*. In that time since our early meetings, things would change again and again. Her husband brutally beat her and was jailed. She asked me to write out her testimony in English for her lawyer. In the laundry room of a secret apartment refuge far out in the fog, I recorded page after page of horrifying detail in shaky ballpoint pen. She struggled to raise her daughter alone and then decided to return to her husband, recently released, claiming to have changed. Years had gone by, and she cut off ties with those of us who had known her. And then, one day I ran into her on the street, and she invited me for dinner.

When I knocked on the door, I wasn't sure what I would find. There had been so many twists and turns along the way: Raquel's life had always been marked by choices of lesser evils: lesser danger, lesser degrees of living alone and hidden. Her husband answered the door and promptly went out into the street after offering me a perfunctory welcome, knowing that no measure of charm could melt through my icy hatred of him.

While Raquel pulled apart the chicken, fresh from the pot, wrapped it in warm tortillas, and lined the *enchiladas* up in a pan, she told me about the decisions she had made and her hopes that this time things would be different. That night she taught me to handle *tomatillos*: seedy, tangy fruit encased in sticky husks. She showed me how to roast them perfectly with jalapeño peppers until all are blackened, the *tomatillos* surrounded by their own thick juices. Then she blended them with onions, fresh cilantro, and just the right amount of salt and sugar. She taught me to heat the sauce gently on the stove until it changes from the bright green of raw cilantro to a deep olive. The *salsa verde* is thick and pungent, tangy and spicy and perfect.

When I first came to Vancouver, the city felt cold and alien, misty and moldy, staid and grey. I had left behind my vibrant, loving, angry community. I had given up a sense of belonging and meaning as part of a movement, and I was left feeling empty. It was *chilaquiles* and black beans and homemade *salsa verde* that I craved most.

When Vinetta and I discovered a Salvadoran restaurant on Commercial Drive, I cried into my *sopa de tortilla*, my *pupusas*, and my *chilaquiles* with spicy salsa. The crackly *ranchera* music and the food felt like home: like the California I had left behind—land of loud splashes of colour, boisterous bustle, history of struggle and resistance, Mexico and El Salvador and Guatemala, removed and displaced and reconstituted again.

We opened Rhizome Café in the hopes of creating a new home for ourselves and for others—a place where we could create a heartbeat of community and recover the pulse of life that we and so many others had left behind. When we were getting ready to open, I located the piece of paper where I had written down Raquel's *salsa verde* recipe long ago. I called Socorro and asked her for her own *chilaquiles* recipe, which she gave me over the phone amid promises that we would make them together next time I was in San Francisco.

These days, I make *chilaquiles* with Ranee, a Filipina immigrant in her mid-fifties. Together we cook brunch at Rhizome, and together we conjure up Raquel and Socorro's recipes to prepare dozens of *chilaquiles* orders each Saturday and Sunday morning. In the early morning before we open, we drink coffee and chat together as we chop onions and mix biscuit batter. Sometimes, Ranee reminds me of the Mujeres members. She is quick-tongued, loves to tell stories that make me laugh, and performs the work of the kitchen much as they do—with seemingly effortless dexterity and skill. Like the Mujeres, Ranee has lived many lives, raised children, crossed among worlds and cultures, and likes to work hard with love and with laughter.

Photograph by Henry Yu.

Ranee prepares the *chilaquiles*.

Once the café is open and the order slips begin to pile up, we ease into silence and quick, measured motion. She tosses the sliced tortillas into the oiled pan, waits for them to turn a golden brown, adds strips of red peppers and onions, then the scrambled eggs. In the salamander the eggs cook, and the tortilla edges get crispier. The red sauce is poured around the edges, it cooks again, and then the whole thing is transferred to the plate. This is my domain: the finishing touches. I spoon the steaming black beans onto the plate, hoping to achieve the all-important halo of red sauce around the edges, sprinkle the cheese, and add a dollop of golden-green *salsa verde*, flecked with the blackened bits of roasted chilies. As I garnish with fruit and with a flower Ranee has brought in from her garden, I pay silent homage to her and to Raquel and Socorro and all the other fighters who have nurtured me along the way. As I raise the plate to the service window, we both exclaim how beautiful the food is. And with a ring of the bell, the order is up.

Photograph by Henry Yu.

Ranee and me serving up the *chilaquiles*.

Lisa Moore *is a community organizer, popular educator, radio producer, and cook. In 2004, she moved to Vancouver from California, after working for ten years with Mujeres Unidas y Activas and other social justice groups. She has trained numerous women to be community organizers, has designed campaigns around immigrants' and workers' rights, and has experienced the joy of collective action to achieve seemingly impossible goals. Currently, she and her partner coordinate Rhizome, a café, arts venue, and community meeting space in Vancouver's Mount Pleasant neighbourhood.*

*This essay was inspired by and expanded from a posting on the food blog, "Recipes for Trouble" (***http://recipesfortrouble.com/2007/01/chilaquiles-recipes-for-life/***).*

One of the two CCHSBC writing workshop groups was held at Rhizome—the site where the stories of Lilly Chow, George Jung, Roy Mah, Gordy Mark, Dan Seto, Bob Sung, Hayne Wai, Evelyn Wong, Larry Wong, Todd Wong, and May Yan-Mountain were hammered out and fine-tuned.

Making *Chow*

Janice Wong

> Do not dismiss the dish saying that it is just, simply food. The blessed thing is an entire civilization in itself.
> —Abdülhak Sinasi Hisar

It seemed like a simple enough recipe; the basic ingredients included a strapping new computer, a resourceful page layout program, a few latent design skills, and a small collection of my dad's handwritten recipes. But key to the mix were memories of my dad, Dennis Edward Wong, who passed away in 1999, after a long life entwined in the business of feeding people.

I selected my favourite photographs—Dad as a baby, as a bright-eyed teenager, as Mom's handsome young beau—and I acquired a few more recipes from my siblings' collections. We had so few records of our family favourites—the food Dad prepared in our small, steamy kitchen, the dishes we loved and took for granted. How was it going to come together, how would I format what I'd begun referring to as "Dad's book?" I set aside the material. Projects with real deadlines intervened, and a year slipped by.

In July 2003 I travelled to my childhood home—my annual summer sojourn to Saskatchewan. Tucked in my suitcase were copies of the manuscript I'd titled *Chow*. I had finally formatted the photographs and the recipes. I'd made a still life photograph—a bowl, a pair of chopsticks and a fortune cookie, perfect for the cover. Dad's handwritten recipes and my meager collection of his letters—each one bearing a reference to food—had been photocopied onto frosty vellum. And I'd written an introduction, a brief narrative by which my nieces and nephews might comprehend the span of their Gung-Gung's life. The manuscript that eventually grew into my published book, *Chow: From China to Canada: Memories of Food and Family*, began as a gift to my family.

My friend, Sara, was also visiting her family in Saskatchewan that summer. Sara's a writer, and when she saw the manuscript, she understood something I hadn't yet grasped. She understood that the intimacy of a family story—a memoir woven with food stories and cultural anecdotes—would be welcomed beyond the family, even beyond the connected culture. She suggested that I consider sending out my manuscript for publication.

However, nearly another year slipped by before I acted on her suggestion. On the anniversary of Dad's birthday (as good a time as any, but maybe, just maybe, a little bit lucky) I sent *Chow* to three publishers. Within a month there were meetings and contract negotiations. The editors enjoyed the introductory material, but the narrative left them wanting more. A contract was signed that summer with a request for additional material and a completed manuscript within three months.

Not knowing what to anticipate, I kept to a tight schedule, beginning with historical research, visits to archives, and interviews with family and friends. I compiled two large binders of material and a tally of related websites—historical material on China, Canada, British Columbia and Saskatchewan; research related to Chinese Canadian immigration; Chinese culinary history; food science; and cultural and food-related anecdotes. And there was my chubby box of photographs.

Next came the task of dovetailing the daunting mound of material with the reminiscences that conjured my parents and their siblings, parents, and grandparents. I started with what I understood intrinsically: I began with a visual cue, a photograph that piqued my curiosity. In my hands I held a grainy image of my mom and Aunt Bea standing on an old boardwalk, Nanaimo, 1937. I began with a description of Nanaimo's Chinatown.

I wanted to have a relevant balance of the rich historical material—just enough to send the curious reader in search of more. At the same time, I was becoming increasingly attached to my family's stories. But the original introduction had evolved into a long succession of anecdotes and historical facts, and my editor and I were concerned—with the bulk of the manuscript at the front of the book, would readers engage from cover to cover? Would *Chow* seem split down the middle, half memoir, half cookbook? As a solution, we envisioned a book threaded with stories that placed Chinese village food in the context of Chinese Canadians and their history. The somewhat awkward manuscript was parceled into stories that were tucked between recipes; a hint of this, a hint of that.

Beginning with the family version of the book, there were a number of fortuitous incidents. Individuals I had met in unrelated circumstances, folks I hadn't seen in decades, were suddenly in a position to help with some aspect or other of research or publicity. And I kept crossing paths with people and discovering they were somehow connected to my family's stories.

One day I woke, thinking about a lamp that had been in the family for as long as I could remember. Later that morning, I spoke with my mom, eager to tell her about a photograph I'd found. She had assured me there weren't any photographic records of her old friend Ngui Suk, but I was certain I'd found one. Happy to know of the photograph's existence, she proceeded to tell the story of his return to China. Ngui Suk had been a Gold Mountain Sojourner, one of thousands of men who had left their ancestral villages and supported their families in China through decades of labour in Canada. He'd befriended my parents who were similar in age to his own children. The boat that carried Ngui Suk and his life's fortune caught fire and was lost at sea. Mom ended the story with a reference to the old lamp, his wedding gift to her.

Chance and opportune, the incidents continued, and I welcomed each one as a token of encouragement.

Next came the arduous task of editing recipes and creating an index. Procedures common to Chinese cooking—methods I'd always taken for granted—needed to be described in a safe, "foolproof" manner. My editor wondered why the chicken in *Bak Juhm Gai* would be left to bob around in its poaching liquid. How would someone grind the smoky *dow see* if they didn't have a mortar and pestle? Why would you use peanut oil? Arrowroot starch? I wrote a glossary and annotated the procedures of various cooking techniques. I even enjoyed the process of indexing, as it appealed to an innate fondness for cataloguing, organizing, and referencing.

Each day I sent portions of the manuscript to my friend, Marlene. Each night she would reply with her thoughts and impressions. This became a part of my process, a daily deadline I could focus on when the overall task seemed overwhelming. I was immeasurably assured by this exchange and by Marlene's steadying nature and wise advice.

As an artist, I looked forward to observing the book design process and creating additional still life photographs. Page size constraints necessitated the cropping of many of the old family photographs, and there were significant details—clues to the provenance of the images—that needed to be retained and carefully considered. I was very fortunate to be working with a designer who welcomed my concerns and suggestions. It was engaging work, and I didn't stop to think of how the book would be received. I was simply concerned with the process of meeting deadlines and trying to do something as well as I could.

Images courtesy of author.

Left: The cover of "Chow," the book for my family.
Right: The cover of *Chow*, the published version of our family's food memoir.

Slowly, I came to understand that *Chow* was also a gift to myself. It was evident in the generosity with which friends, relatives, and acquaintances shared their stories and assisted with the many aspects involved in creating and publicizing a book. And it was evident in the faces of strangers who attended the various events associated with the book. Folks lined up to tell me their stories. *Chow* created a connection and gave me a sense of community. At times I was surrounded by people who had known me and my parents at every stage of our lives.

"Your story is my story," a stranger told me at the airport in Toronto. "Your family story reminds me of my Grandmother's," this from a woman of Ukrainian descent. "My father took me to your restaurant every Saturday," a middle-aged man said at the Saskatchewan book launch. "Every Saturday" was a phrase I heard often. Many of the people in my hometown had made a point of stopping in to see Dad—often driving in from farms in the surrounding communities—to share a joke, a cup of coffee, an ice cream sundae, a bowl of won ton soup. And a repeated sentiment was the regret at losing a treasured family recipe when the person who knew how to make it passed on.

I also gained a deeper connection to my "Chineseness." I'd grown up in Saskatchewan in the 1960s, one of two Chinese kids in my grade school—the other one was my brother. Mixing in and speaking only English were priorities for my parents. Aside from the distinctions I chose to contrive, I didn't want to be different from my Caucasian friends. Through historical and familial research and recollections of my parents' generation, I discovered a lineage—a link to a history shared by all of the descendents of the first Chinese Canadians.

Restaurant life can be onerous, and the hours are long and demanding. When I was very young, Dad worked until midnight. By the time I was in school, he ended his workday at eight in the evening and what he needed after a fourteen-hour day was peace and quiet. Children don't easily comprehend or question the past, and busy parents seldom have time to reflect on it. What I didn't know about my dad I was to learn—through the book, through the generosity of shared stories and memories.

Should you decide to write your family's food memoir, generosity and fortuitous incidents will be there for you too. You need only to begin with what you understand—the food, a treasured photograph; a handful of memories that fire the senses.

Janice Wong *studied Fine Art at the University of Saskatchewan and received her BFA with Distinction from the Alberta College of Art and Design. Her work is exhibited and collected in Canada, Britain, Europe, Asia and the United States. Born in Saskatchewan, she has resided in Vancouver since 1986. Janice's first book,* Chow: From China to Canada: Memories of Food and Family, *was published in 2005. In 2006, it received Cuisine Canada's Gold Award for a culinary book in the category of Canadian Food Culture (celebrating culture and heritage).* Chow *also provided the inspiration for* Back to the Lotus, *a CBC documentary by Costa Maragos. For more information on Janice's work, visit* **http://www.janicewongstudio.com** *and* **http://c-h-o-w.blogspot.com**.

Janice was a guest speaker at the CCHSBC Food and Family writing workshops.

Chay Yaw

Brandy Liên Worrall

"You can't bring those smelly things to school—nobody's gonna wanna eat them," my best friend, Pisey, who was Cambodian, said.

"Yeah, they will—why not? Doncha think my mom's eggrolls are good?"

"Yeah, I do, but they're not gonna be good enough for everyone else. White people don't like that stuff."

"I don't believe you, Pisey. They'll love them! They never had anything like them before."

"Alright, you'll see," she said, turning away from me.

"What are you bringing?"

"Fried rice. It's normal enough."

Why didn't I think of fried rice? Mom's fried rice was also pretty good, and Pisey might have been right. Pisey was always right—always thinking of something a little bit faster than me. But they would eat the eggrolls, too, wouldn't they?

Pisey tapped me on the shoulder and said, "Just don't bring that fish sauce. They won't eat that for sure."

"How do you eat eggrolls without fish sauce?"

"Trust me—don't bring the fish sauce."

All day, I thought about Mrs. Johnson declaring Friday "World Food Day," when everyone in my Grade 4 class would bring in a dish to represent a different part of the world. We were supposed to give a report about our dish, talking about the part of the world it came from and anything else interesting about it. Afterward, we would all try everyone's dishes. I was quite certain that no one in my class ever ate any Vietnamese food, as the only Vietnamese food made anywhere near our small town in Pennsylvania was cooked in my house. And none of them knew anything about Vietnam at all, except for the war. I was sure they'd all love my mom's cooking more than anything else—Pisey didn't know what she was talking about. They'd get to see how great it is that I'm Vietnamese, that I get to eat this food whenever I want.

"Mom, can you make some *chay yaw*,[1] please?"

"Why you want that for?"

"I want to take them to school."

"Why you want to take those to school?"

"My teacher wants us to bring in food for the class—it's for a grade, Mom. We're suppose to bring in food and talk about where it came from."

"How many you want?"

"There are twenty-two people in my class, and the teacher."

"I'll make two dozen, okay?" I saw something in Mom that I rarely saw—excitement. She was thrilled that she could help me with my schoolwork, something that she never did before.

Photograph courtesy of author.

Mom at a Buddhist temple in Vietnam, in the 1960s.

While she started soaking the rice papers, I brought out my notebook and pencil, and asked her questions for my report.

"Mom, when did you learn how to make *chay yaw*?"

"My mother teach me when I was little—I start help her when I was five year old!"

"What did she teach you?"

"She teach me do this—" Mom showed me how she dipped the rice papers in the big bowl of water, then place them gently on a plate. "I no make them break." Looked easy enough.

"Can I try?"

She handed me a round, brittle sheet, and I sank it into the bowl. But when I brought it back up, it was all bunched and crinkled.

"No, you make it break! Give to me. . ." Mom took the smooshed ball by the forefinger and thumb of each hand and gave it a couple shakes. The ball unraveled, and she swept the delicate sheath onto the plate.

1. This was how I—and everyone else in my Pennsylvania Dutch family—pronounced the Vietnamese word for deep-fried eggrolls, but this is not how it's actually spelled (or pronounced for that matter). The correct spelling is *chả giò* .

"Can I try again?"

"No, too much trouble. You no know how—make break."

"How am I suppose to learn if you don't show me and let me try?"

"Here." She handed me another sheet. This time, I didn't make it crinkle together, but instead, when I tried to lay it on the plate, the middle of the sheet caught on the edge of the plate and tore a big hole in it.

"What you do? You waste too much—no more."

Photograph courtesy of author.

My dad, in the middle, with his parents, whom I call Pappy and Mammy, in February 1968, before Dad left for the Vietnam War.

Frustrated, I stuck to asking questions. Mom finished soaking the sheets and began mixing together the ground beef, cabbage and carrots (already shredded and stored in the refrigerator in big Ziploc bags), garlic, onions, MSG, salt, pepper, oil, and fish sauce.

"Uh, Mom, can you not put so much *nook mom*[2] in there?"

"Why?—then no taste no good."

"Okay."

She pushed her sleeves up to her armpits and thrust both fists into the mixture, squeezing meat and cabbage between her fingers, balling it up then breaking it apart. The garlic and fish sauce were blanketing the kitchen, and Dad called out from the living room, "Lien, you making *chay yaw?*"

"Yeah! You no can eat! For Brandy school!"

They shouted their conversation between rooms.

"What?!"

"Not for supper! You eat T.V. dinner!"

"Okay!"

2. Vietnamese fermented fish sauce. Again, that's not actually how it's pronounced or spelled, but that's what we in Pennsylvania knew it as. The correct word is *nước mắm*.

After she finished assaulting the meat and cabbage, she washed her hands, toweled them off, and returned to the rice papers.

"Mom, when did you learn how to roll *chay yaw?*"

"My mother no trust me—I make them too fat, make them break open. We never eat much—too much money to make. We eat them for New Year. I know how make them when I was, I don't know, maybe eight year old. I make them for your grandma—oh, she so happy I make them. She really love it."

"How did you know how to roll them eventually?"

"Oh, I practice with her. Sometime, she get so mad at me—I break them, and then she have to use two wrapper to fix it. She beat me, yell at me—tell me I no good. But I do better, and then she like it."

Photograph courtesy of author.

Mom and Dad in Vietnam in 1969, before coming back to Pennsylvania.

Better to leave out the beating part from my report. That might not go over well.

"So you only ate these for special occasions?"

"Yeah, you lucky, you know? Mommy can make for you anytime now, but when I was kid, we no eat like this—too poor. We eat lot of rice, then little bit of fat. That's it. You spoiled, eat what you want, waste food." She looked and pointed a meat-covered finger at me, and said, "You no waste food. When you no eat your food and throw away, you eat it when you die, with worms."

(She has uttered this afterlife curse to me so many times, that the shock of it has worn off, though to this day, I can't get out of my mind the image of a large pile of uneaten food covered in worms waiting to greet me in hell—because surely they don't serve up that kind of grub in heaven.)

In no time, twenty-four perfectly rolled *chay yaw* were neatly stacked in a baking dish. Mom heated up the deep fryer and poured in half the gallon bottle of vegetable oil. Eager to switch the conversation back to Vietnam so I could write up my report, I asked, "So how many *chay yaw* would you cook for New Year?"

"Oh, my, we cook lots! Hundreds, I don't know. We have to cook for all people who die too. We put food in front of altar, so they could taste too."

As the wet rice skins sizzled loudly in the fryer, I imagined hungry spirits coming down from the sky to get full on eggrolls, sweets, and rice wine. They had to eat enough to last them one full year, to keep them satisfied and hopeful for the year to come. And there was always enough to go around because Mom was a good cook, eager to please.

"Okay, done. I put away, and we put in oven in morning, heat up. When you eat these?"

"Um, I don't know, like I think two-thirty?"

"What? They get cold, no good!"

"They'll still be good."

"Okay, you want Mommy make you *nuoc mam*?"

I thought about what Pisey said and remembered the way the fish sauce smelled an awful lot like rotting garbage, despite its smooth, salty taste that I loved so much.

"Um, that's okay. I think that it would be too messy to take it."

"Okay. Now what? You ask Mommy more questions?" She looked hopeful, wanting to continue helping me with my homework. I, however, wasn't in the mood for any more lectures that happened to be told along the way.

"No, that's it. Thanks, Mom."

"Okay, I tired, work all day, never get done. If you no want no more, I go bed. Wake up early."

When I woke the next morning, the eggrolls were already heated up, wrapped tightly in several layers of tin foil, and waiting for me on the table. I put my hand on top of the foil, and it was still too hot to touch.

When I boarded the bus and sat down, I heard several kids say, "Ew, what's that smell?" Jason looked at what I was holding and asked, "What do you have in there—it stinks!"

"They're eggrolls—they're really good."

"You couldn't pay me to eat that."

Unbeknownst to me, the cooked cabbage, garlic, and onions were not an odor that people in Mifflintown, Pennsylvania were accustomed to. But I thought of Pennsylvania Dutch sauerkraut, which to me, didn't seem like a far cry from the eggrolls. I really started to doubt my selection for this class project, but I had to believe that all would be good in the end, as I sat through the thirty-five-minute bus ride, trying to ignore all the stares my covered tray was getting from kids around me.

Finally, it was time for Mrs. Johnson's English class, and all the students filed into the room, carrying trays and plates and dishes, all covered with foil, plastic wrap, and mystery about what the contents were. One by one, each student stood up and gave a brief two-minute report about their food selections, which were for the most part boring, predictable, and deemed as coming from the Pennsylvania Dutch: potato salad, pumpkin pie, pork and dumplings, and some even had the nerve to pass off cookies and brownies. Before my presentation, the two most interesting things to the class were Pisey's fried rice and Brooke's kiwis, which she claimed were from Mexico. Pisey reported on her Cambodian fried rice (what exactly made it Cambodian, I wondered, other than that she cooked it?), and everyone was impressed about how she ate it every day, rather than eating potatoes with her meat. She talked about how she cooked it with oil, peas, and bits of meat, about how in Cambodia, everyone eats rice every day with every meal (no kidding!). They thought it was so great, and they couldn't wait to eat the rice. Wait until they saw my eggrolls. . .

When I stood up and uncovered my dish, the students gasped and some even gagged at the smell rushing out of the pan. Some condensation flew off the inside of the foil, landing on those unfortunate enough to be sitting in the front row. The students were waving their hands in front of their faces, grimacing and glaring at me. Mrs. Johnson had to quiet the class, and she motioned for me to begin my report.

"I, um, brought these eggrolls that my mom made. In Vietnamese they're called *chay yaw*. They're made with meat, cabbage, and spices wrapped in rice paper and fried. I like them a lot; they taste really good, even though they might not smell so good." I smiled awkwardly and continued, "So, um, in Vietnam, you eat these for special occasions because usually you're too poor to eat them every day. Vietnamese people make a lot of them for Vietnamese New Year, which is a special occasion when you think about people in your family who died. You make them and set it out for them to eat too." The kids were all staring at me like I was a lunatic, then several of them snickered. "Okay, um, my mom learned to make these when she was eight years old. It's actually really hard to make them because the rice paper is really fragile and breaks easily. So she practiced a lot, and she got really good at it and made them for her mother." Mrs. Johnson gestured that maybe I should put the foil back on the dish. I fumbled with the foil, which was still in the shape of the top layer of eggrolls and the pan. I decided that I should wrap it up. "So, yeah, my mom made enough for everyone, so you can eat one, and I hope you like them." I quickly took my seat. The last person was next, but I didn't hear a word she said, as I ran over and over in my mind how I just offended everyone in the room.

When the reports were over, Mrs. Johnson passed out paper plates, plastic utensils, and napkins. We set all our dishes on five desks pulled together in the back of the room, and everyone lined up to get the food. I was fifth in line, and by the time I got to Pisey's fried rice, I could see that a sizable chunk had already been taken out of the bowl. My pan of eggrolls was still full, but I took two from the top, a bit soggy from sitting in the pan all day but still delicious, and sat down.

Everyone settled down to dig in, and I didn't have to look around to know that no one was eating my eggrolls. Mrs. Johnson took one to be polite, and she stopped by my desk and said, "Brandy, these eggrolls are so good. I never had anything like them before." And she took a bite in front of me to show me she was telling the truth. I smiled and thanked her for the compliment.

"How do you eat those things?" Matt watched me take a bite.

"They're good, and you're all stupid for not trying them!" I blurted out. I was sure that Mrs. Johnson heard me, but if she did, she didn't say anything.

"Your food stinks. Vietnam must stink too, if they eat stuff like that."

"Shut up. You don't know anything. You're an idiot." Matt snickered at me and moved away.

The bell rang, and everyone scrambled to pack up their food and catch the bus since it was the end of the day. I shuffled over to the desk where my pan of eggrolls sat, only four of them missing from the lot. I knew that Pisey ate one because she felt bad for being right.

Photographs courtesy of author.

What goes in—and outside—a *chay yaw*? Eggroll wrappers and Maggi seasoning!

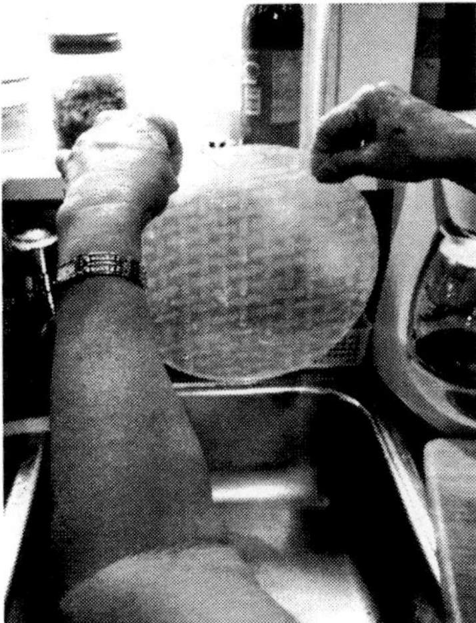
Mom wetting the wrappers…

…and counting the fruits of her labour!

I sat on the bus thinking about how I was going to explain to my mother why no one ate her eggrolls—the ones that she worked so hard to make at the last minute, the ones that she was proud of because she could help me get a good grade. I didn't even care that they smelled funny; in fact, I was hoping that they would stink up the whole damn bus.

I unlocked the door and put the pan on the table. All I felt like doing was sitting there in the quiet kitchen and staring at the pan, with my chin resting on top of the table. I heard Mom pull up in her cherry red Chevy Nova. The screen door opened, then the wooden door.

"Hey, they like eggroll today?"

"Um, we didn't have time to eat them. Sorry, Mom, so, I just ate a couple on the bus."

"Oh, well, now I no have make dinner. You and your daddy eat them." I felt terrible—like I failed everyone—the Vietnamese people, the White people, my mom most of all. And I hated it when Pisey was right—like she knew more about White people than I did. But I guess she did somehow.

I looked at Mom, who was staring at the eggrolls, just as I had minutes earlier. "I thought I shoulda tell you, maybe you should take fried rice. Easier to eat. Oh, well."

The eggrolls sat there, wrinkled and ready for supper.

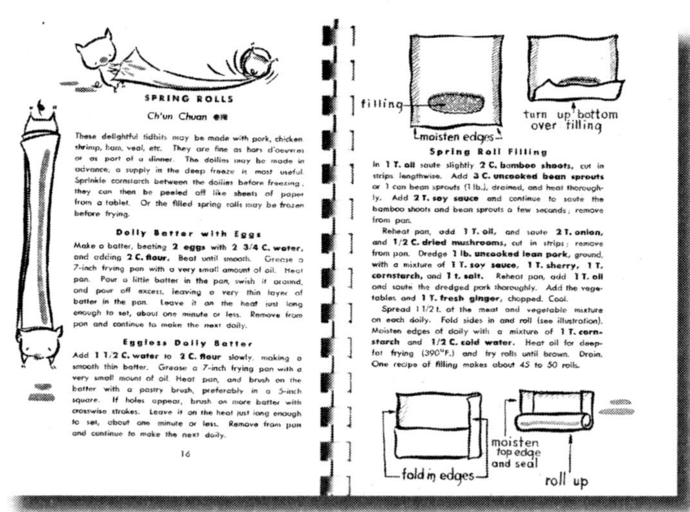

SPRING ROLLS

Ch'un Chuan

These delightful tidbits may be made with pork, chicken shrimp, ham, veal, etc. They are fine as hors d'oeuvres or as part of a dinner. The doilies may be made in advance; a supply in the deep freeze is most useful. Sprinkle cornstarch between the doilies before freezing; they can then be peeled off like sheets of paper from a tablet. Or the filled spring rolls may be frozen before frying.

Doily Batter with Eggs

Make a batter, beating **2 eggs** with **2 3/4 C. water,** and adding **2 C. flour.** Beat until smooth. Grease a 7-inch frying pan with a very small amount of oil. Heat pan. Pour a little batter in the pan, swish it around, and pour off excess, leaving a very thin layer of batter in the pan. Leave it on the heat just long enough to set, about one minute or less. Remove from pan and continue to make the next doily.

Eggless Doily Batter

Add **1 1/2 C. water** to **2 C. flour** slowly, making a smooth thin batter. Grease a 7-inch frying pan with a very small mount of oil. Heat pan, and brush on the batter with a pastry brush, preferably in a 5-inch square. If holes appear, brush on more batter with crosswise strokes. Leave it on the heat just long enough to set, about one minute or less. Remove from pan and continue to make the next doily.

16

Spring Roll Filling

In **1 T. oil** saute slightly **2 C. bamboo shoots,** cut in strips lengthwise. Add **3 C. uncooked bean sprouts** or 1 can bean sprouts (1 lb.), drained, and heat thoroughly. Add **2 T. soy sauce** and continue to saute the bamboo shoots and bean sprouts a few seconds; remove from pan.

Reheat pan, add **1 T. oil,** and saute **2 T. onion,** and **1/2 C. dried mushrooms,** cut in strips; remove from pan. Dredge **1 lb. uncooked lean pork,** ground, with a mixture of **1 T. soy sauce, 1 T. sherry, 1 T. cornstarch,** and **1 t. salt.** Reheat pan, add **1 T. oil** and saute the dredged pork thoroughly. Add the vegetables and **1 T. fresh ginger,** chopped. Cool.

Spread 1 1/2 t. of the meat and vegetable mixture on each doily. Fold sides in and roll (see illustration). Moisten edges of doily with a mixture of **1 T. cornstarch** and **1/2 C. cold water.** Heat oil for deep-fat frying (390°F.) and fry rolls until brown. Drain. One recipe of filling makes about 45 to 50 rolls.

From *The Art of Chinese Cooking*, by the Benedictine Sisters of Peking, 1956.

Brandy Liên Worrall *is a writer, editor, book designer, and community arts events organizer. She is currently in the MFA in Creative Writing program at the University of British Columbia and was the associate editor of* Amerasia Journal, *the premier journal for Asian American Studies, published by UCLA. She is working on a series of memoirs about her Vietnamese and Pennsylvania Dutch families. She lives with her two children, Chloe and Mylo, and her husband Henry in Vancouver, British Columbia. Visit her press at* http://www.lulu.com/rabbitfool.

Offerings

Henry Yu

April showers bring May flowers. The road is wet and black as I drive to my grandfather's grave, a pot of yellow flowers sitting on the seat beside me. I don't know what they're called—I'd forgotten to ask. It bothers me that I don't know.

I've done this for almost three decades, sometimes from different places but always at the same time, back for this ritual. It's called *ching ming* in Cantonese (清明), when the gates of the underworld open, and it's possible to commune with the spirits of ancestors. Sweeping the gravesite and pulling weeds after a long winter is the practical component of this spring rite, but there is something deeper triggered by this annual pilgrimage to the cemetery. I'm going home.

My grandfather is buried in Vancouver. For several weeks the doors to his world will be open. It is important that I visit him. Gifts will be brought, paper money burnt as offerings. There are no stores in the underworld; every year the essentials of life must be symbolically burnt and transported for his use. No expense is spared to provide all the luxuries and comforts possible. In Hong Kong I've seen huge paper models of BMW's, complete down to the smallest detail, sent as offerings. We are not so rich, but a banquet of food is still prepared for my grandfather—boiled chicken, *gai bow* (steamed buns with chicken filling), three shots of Johnny Walker whiskey. In addition, special money for the underworld, with bills in outrageous amounts like $10,000, will be burnt for his use. My grandfather worked hard all his life just to earn a living. He can be a rich man in the underworld at least.

Photograph courtesy of author.

My grandfather, 1962.

It's drizzling with the grey mist that envelopes Vancouver for much of the winter. True Vancouverites would never carry an umbrella in this kind of weather. Only tourists and those who have come to the city later in life feel the need to be protected from a little rain. I spot the familiar tree that marks his headstone. I had stood beside it over twenty-five years ago as he was being lowered into the ground, and ever since it has been the beacon for my journey home.

I'm visiting alone today. Tomorrow I'll come again with the rest of my family, but today is special to me: he was special to me.

◈ ◈ ◈

I remember the times he would take me to Chinatown, a place of wonderful and exotic smells, full of noise and people. For lunch he would buy me fancy sweet rolls, smiling as I wolfed them down. Refilling the gas tank, he called it. And when I grew tired, he'd coax me on with sweets, bribing my sore feet to walk a little farther. But my feet would always betray him, and he'd end up carrying me home. At night he'd bounce me up and down on his knee, making me scream with fright. I remember climbing on him as he sat, tugging his ears for support. I'm sure it must have hurt. But he never complained.

I lived the first six years of my life with my grandparents. Whoever I am is partly their doing. My parents were both busy at work, struggling to make do in an alien world—my mother cleaned motel rooms after the guests had paid and gone; my father was a mining engineer, rarely sighted because he had to travel to faraway places digging for someone else's gold. For most of my early childhood, my parents were forced to leave me with my grandparents. They were happy to have me, particularly my grandfather, who had spent most of his life living alone without his wife and child. My grandmother barely knew him when she came over with my mother and father in 1965. They had not seen each other for almost three decades. The first time he saw my mother had been when she was twenty-seven years old. I became the child he never had, showing me off to his old-timer friends in Chinatown.

Photograph courtesy of author.

My older brother George and me with our grandfather and mother, 1970, in Queen Elizabeth Park in Vancouver.

He's buried on a hillside overlooking Burnaby, a short drive from East Vancouver where we used to live. It's a beautiful view, and I'm sure he'd enjoy it if he could. But who knows. For most of the past twenty years, there was an empty plot beside his grave. It's so much like his life had been, waiting for decades for his wife to join him. She had raised my mother alone during the worst of the war years in China, gathering twigs to sell as firewood so she could buy food for her child. As she grew older, I tried to see her as often as I could, coming back to a pot of her homemade wontons or heaping pyramids of steamed *gai bow*. She'd awaken before sunrise to chop meat and fold wontons, though as the years went by her eyes began to bother her in the failing light. When my grandfather was alive, he used to chop the meat for her. His cleaver would thud with a butcher's sure rhythm, waking me from my sleep and making me think of his long voyages on the sea.

◈ ◈ ◈

Years ago, I would ride the ferry between Vancouver and Victoria. It is popular with tourists, who love the ocean passage winding through rocky islands, but the residents of Victoria also use the ferry, sharing the decks with the hordes of sightseers. Growing up in Victoria, my friends and I disdained the visitors much as a farmer would a plague of locusts. When I was seven, my parents had moved to Victoria to open a corner store, leaving my grandparents in Vancouver. I began to regularly ride the ferry to visit my grandparents, quietly enduring the tourists and the ninety-minute voyage. There wasn't much to do except sit in the cafeteria and eat—slowly. I always ordered French fries with gravy and the clam chowder.

Photograph courtesy of author.

My family at Chrismas, 1970. Standing—my father and mother; seated—my grandmother, me, my great-grandmother, my brother, and my grandfather.

Family rumour passed down said that the clam chowder became so popular because in the early years a Chinese cook had realized that they could use the abundant giant mollusks called geoduck (pronounced *gooey duck*) to pack the chowder with meat. Geoduck is a local marvel that the Chinese had learned to eat from the First Nations peoples. It is quite possibly the ugliest animal alive—a huge misshapen lump of meat with a vestigial shell, as if the inside of a clam had mutated into a clubfoot large enough to wear a human shoe. It is ugly enough that for years no one except Natives and the Chinese (who will eat anything) touched it. But chopped up with a cleaver and put into chowder, it is indistinguishable from clam bits and considerably cheaper. By the 1980s, geoduck had become a specialty in the high-end Chinese seafood restaurants that began to proliferate, and very quickly was driven toward extinction. The rarer it became, the more expensive it got and the more the Chinese wanted it, further exacerbating its demise.

Sitting in the ferry cafeteria several years ago, I picked through my clam chowder and noticed how few pieces of clam there were. It seemed bland and lifeless. Poking at my fries, I could hear the cooks, all old men, chattering in Cantonese. They were haggard and worn, the weariness etched into their faces. If you ride the ferry nowadays, you won't hear their voices anymore—they're all gone, that generation of old-timers. My grandfather lived the same life as these old men once, working as a butcher on a cruise ship between Vancouver and Alaska. I looked into their faces, tried to read their weary lines. What dreams did you have, *Ah Gong?*

Photograph courtesy of author.

BC pioneers: Gong Gong and his older brothers, 1955.

Why did you slave all those years to die a broken man? What drove you when you were tired and worn? These men knew the answer.

My mother said that when they first started living with him, my grandfather had an unnatural quiet about him as if he didn't know what to say. She thought it was because he had been alone so long, his only company a constant fear of being deported. My grandmother said that he wasn't the same man that she had married so long ago, that he didn't like to laugh anymore. She liked to tell me that I was the only thing that made him smile, and that this was the real reason my mother left me with them.

This morning I ate a bowl of milk and cereal. Its cold texture reminded me of the lost warmth of earlier years. If my grandmother had still been alive I would have begun this day with her *jook* and steamed buns. She would have kept cooking and cleaning, leaving me to watch and listen to her as I ate at the kitchen table.

I remember the year she had worried because my grandfather had been buried without a belt. She told me how she had awakened at night thinking about my grandfather walking around in the underworld having to hold up his pants. That day, I made a belt out of cardboard so she could burn it and send it to him.

◈ ◈ ◈

I plant the flowers and clear the debris that has cluttered his plot. Some leaves and twigs, some weeds. The grass is well kept and healthy; the wild geese help keep it cropped. I kneel and *kow-tow* three times in respect.

I'm back.

The words on his gravestone read Yeung Sing Yew, a name I still find jarring. He had lived all of his life with the name of Low Jang Yit; all of his mail was addressed that way, his number in the phone book. At the age of thirteen, he had entered the country under someone else's name, and he had kept his own a secret for almost his entire life. It is strange to see it finally revealed in the letters marking his death.

Sometimes people ask me why I work so hard, why I hate to make mistakes. I shrug and smile. I'm not sure they'd understand.

◈ ◈ ◈

I remember his funeral. Everyone was crying—some wailing hysterically, some with silent tears. Everyone was mourning for him in their own way. Except me. I guess I hadn't fathomed what had happened yet. It seemed so unreal that he could die. I'd had relatives die before, but they were only occasional faces, nobody whose absence I really noticed. He wasn't like them. He was the person who was there when I woke every morning, there when I went to bed every night. He could never die.

Then I saw his face. It was the same face I'd known all my young life. The same frown which he'd given me when I'd done something wrong, the same ears I'd pulled. But the eyes were shut, and I knew then he wouldn't be there anymore. Wouldn't be there when I'd fallen down or when my feet were sore or when I needed his help. Wouldn't be there. I cried.

◈ ◈ ◈

Those old cooks on the ferry—what dreams could have driven them to work so hard? Why would they have made themselves such weary men? For their children.

Because if they sold their lives and souls doing a lifetime of backbreaking labour, maybe their children wouldn't have to. Maybe their children would be better off, have better lives, be what the men could only dream of. They traded their lives for it.

◈ ◈ ◈

Twenty-five years after he had died, I took an Alaskan cruise with my parents and my pregnant wife. The glaciers were startling, but much of the rest of the voyage winding along tree-lined fjords reminded me of the countless ferry rides of my youth. Eating at the obscene buffets that filled the days, I felt my Gong Gong's constant presence. My mother and I didn't talk about it, but we both knew that my grandfather would have found it fitting, that his three decades below working in the kitchen would somehow be honoured by our riding in leisure above deck.

Photograph courtesy of author.

My grandparents in Hawaii, 1973.

No matter where I am living, I come back every year, to show my grandparents I'm well, let them look me over, see how I'm doing. I think that's all he'd really ask of me, just to visit once in a while. But I'll do more. Because I owe it to them, and I owe it to my children.

Yeung Suey Fun's Wontons

5-6 large dried Chinese black mushrooms

1 lb ground pork (ground turkey or chicken can be substituted)

1 Tbsp Chinese roasted sesame oil

2 Tbsp soy sauce

¾ tsp black pepper

1 Tbsp tapioca starch

1 lb shelled shrimp (1½ lbs with shells)

1 pkg wonton skins

1.) Re-hydrate mushrooms by soaking them in warm water overnight.

2.) Dice mushrooms into small pieces. Set aside.

3.) Mince the pork until it becomes a gooey mass.

4.) Add sesame oil, soy sauce, pepper, mushrooms, starch, and shelled shrimp, incorporating it into the pork with further chopping. (The starch incorporates the filling's juices when the wontons cook).

5.) Using a teaspoon, fill a wonton skin with the meat mixture, sealing the skin by drawing a wet line on the skin with a fingertip dipped in a bowl of warm water, and pressing it closed as if you were sealing a licked envelope. Repeat for all the skins.

6.) The wontons should be cooked in gently boiling water until they float (about 6-7 minutes, but don't overcook!) and immediately removed and drained. They can then be served with any broth, along with noodles or vegetables.

Henry Yu *is an Associate Professor of History and Director of the Initiative for Student Teaching and Research on Chinese Canadians (INSTRCC) at the University of British Columbia. Professor Yu was a guest speaker during the workshop, discussing the meaning and importance of family history and offering tips on how to research it.*

Photograph by Ed Whitebone.

The *Princess Patricia* was a veteran Canadian Pacific Railway steamer built in 1948 by the Fairfield Company of Glasgow. She joined her sister ship, the *Princess Marguerite*, on the BC coast as part of CPR's service connecting Victoria, Vancouver, and Seattle. In 1963, the "Princess Pat" was refitted as a cruise ship running between Vancouver and Alaska. Her last runs were during Expo 86, after which she was broken up for scrap. Source: Vancouver Maritime Museum, http://www.vancouvermaritimemuseum.com/.

Images courtesy of Brandy Liên Worrall.

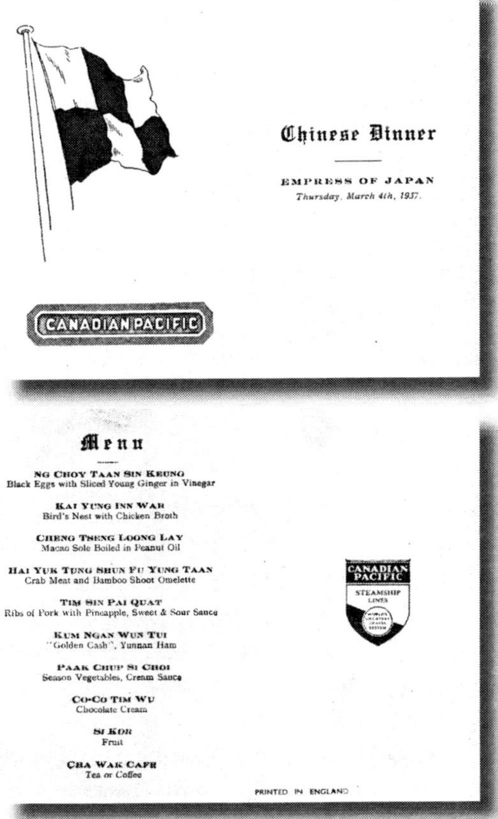

The two images above are from a Chinese dinner menu from the *Empress of Japan II*, in 1937. The original *Empress of Japan* was built in 1891 for the CPR. The ship was used on the Vancouver-Japan-Hong Kong mail service. The route was Vancouver, Victoria, Yokohama, Kobe, Nagasaki, Shanghai, and Hong Kong. She could accommodate 900 passengers—160 in first class, 40 in second class, and 700 in steerage, mainly Asian immigrants. During WWI, the ship was fitted out as an Armed Auxiliary Cruiser. When the war was over, she returned to company service in 1916, and made her final run in 1922. She was scrapped in 1928 and was replaced by the *Empress of Japan II*. Source: Vancouver Maritime Museum, http://www.vancouvermaritimemuseum.com/.

Two centuries ago Yuan Mei, popular writer of modern Chinese literature, said:

"There is a difference between dining and eating. Dining is an art.

"When you eat to get most out of your meal, to please the palate, just as well as to satiate the appetite, that, my friend, is dining."

From *The Chinese Cook Book: Covering the Entire Field of Chinese Cookery in the Chinese Order of Serving, from Nuts to Soup*, ed. by Mr. M. Sing Au, 1936.

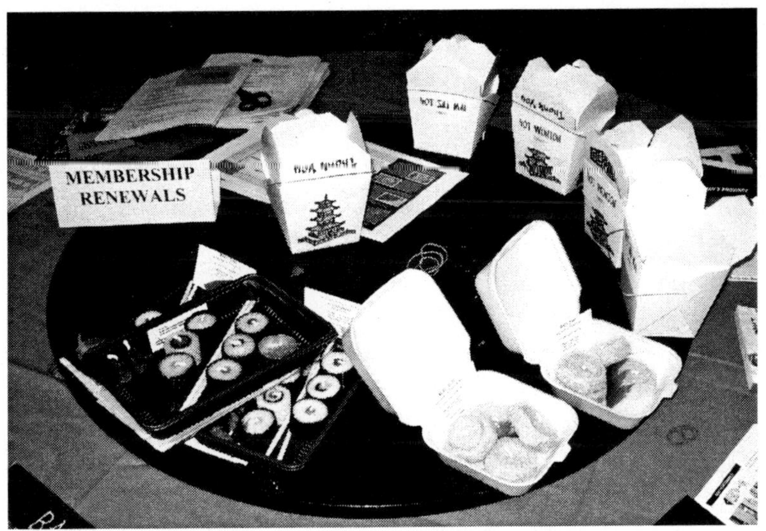

Dim sum, wonton and sushi candles, by Walter Quan, displayed at the Chinese Canadian Historical Society of BC's Annual General Meeting, March 10, 2007, at Foo's Ho Ho Restaurant in Chinatown, Vancouver. Photograph courtesy of Hayne Wai.

To become a member of the Chinese Canadian Historical Society of BC, please email **info@cchsbc.ca** or visit **http://www.cchsbc.ca**. To order additional copies of this book or our first publication, *Finding Memories, Tracing Routes: Chinese Canadian Family Stories*, visit our website. Educational, institutional, and retail bulk discounts are available.